Out of the Attic

A VOLUME IN THE SERIES

Public History in Historical Perspective
Edited by Marla R. Miller

Out of the Attic

Inventing Antiques in Twentieth-Century New England

Briann G. Greenfield

University of Massachusetts Press
Amherst & Boston

Copyright © 2009 by University of Massachusetts Press
All rights reserved
Printed in the United States of America

LC 2009017760
ISBN 978-1-55849-710-8 (paper); 709-2 (library cloth)

Designed by Sally Nichols
Set in Berkley Old Style and Bickhamm Script
Printed and bound by Thomson-Shore, Inc.

Library of Congress Cataloging-in-Publication Data

Greenfield, Briann (Briann G.), 1970–
Out of the attic : inventing antiques in twentieth-century New
England / Briann Greenfield.
p. cm. — (Public history in historical perspective)
Includes bibliographical references and index.
ISBN 978-1-55849-710-8 (pbk. : alk. paper) —
ISBN 978-1-55849-709-2 (library cloth : alk. paper)
1. Antiques business—New England—History—20th century.
2. New England—Antiquities—Collectors and collecting—History—20th century.
3. House furnishings—New England—Marketing—Case studies. I. Title.
II. Title: Inventing antiques in twentieth-century New England.
NK1133.28.G74 2009
745.10974—dc22
2009017760

British Library Cataloguing in Publication Data are available

For Morgan, with my love and thanks

Contents

Illustrations

Acknowledgments

While my own collection of antiques is sparse, writing this book has provided me with other kinds of treasures: the friendships, exchange of ideas, and fellowship of academic work. I would like to single out those who read and commented on parts of the manuscript in its many different forms and guises, including Tom Denenberg, Rob Emlen, Kathy Franz, Pam Henson, Steve Lubar, Patrick Malone, Susan Smulyan, and the late John Thomas. Each of you has made me a better thinker, writer, and scholar. Special thanks also go to Marla Miller, whose careful reading and thoughtful comments have made this a much better book. Those who commented on paper presentations and who informally shared their insights about museums, antiques, and collecting have helped me more than they know. I am grateful to Gretchen Buggeln, Richard Candee, Donald Friary, Charles Hummel, Brock Jobe, Sarah Johnson, Kathleen Kendrick, Gary Kulik, Sarah Leavitt, Susan McGowan, Shelley Nickles, Eileen Pollack, Michael Robinson, the late Rodris Roth, Jeanne Schinto, Ann Smith, Jeffry Task, Laurel Thatcher Ulrich, Shirley Wajda, Catherine Whalen, Aaron Wunsch, and Bill Yeingst. I am sure many of you have forgotten your comments, but I have not.

Several fellowships came key moments in this book's construction, each changing the character of the project in significant ways. I am happy to acknowledge the support of Brown University, the John Nicholas Brown Center, the Smithsonian Museum of American History, the Central Connecticut State University chapter of the American Association of University Professors, and the National Endowment of the Humanities and Winterthur Museum. I am indebted to the staffs of all of the above institutions as well as those of the Massachusetts Historical Society, Historic New England, Historic Deerfield Library, the Litchfield Historical Society, the Pocumtuck Valley Memorial Association, and Deerfield Academy Library. I am grateful to Rob Emlen for his discovery of George and Jessie Gardner's journals and for showing me what a rich resource they are for the history of antique collecting. Thank you also to those who were willing to share their personal stories and family papers with me, especially Albert Sack, Arthur Liverant, Peter Spang, Debby Hertz, and Edward Little.

As this project comes to a close, the work of those who helped bring the book to publication is foremost in my mind. Thank you, Gregg Mangan, for your careful and thoughtful help with editing and proofreading. I also thank Clark Dougan, my editor at the University of Massachusetts Press, who stewarded this project to publication, and Mary Bellino, whose wise copyediting and fact checking rescued me from many errors.

Finally, for support, friendship, and fun, I could not hope for better companions than my graduate student cohort in the Department of American Civilization at Brown University, my fellow fellows at the John Nicholas Brown Center and the Smithsonian Institution Fellowship Program, my housemates at Winterthur Museum, and my colleagues in the Department of History at Central Connecticut State University.

Out of the Attic

Introduction
Inventing Antiques

When the architect Charles F. McKim redesigned the White House in 1902, he outfitted it with a mixture of revival furniture, inspired by early American and French Empire styles. But in 1925 First Lady Grace Goodhue Coolidge challenged McKim's design. While McKim believed it was enough to reference the past with modern furniture manufactured in period styles, Grace Coolidge wanted to refurnish several rooms with actual early American pieces from the period of the mansion's construction. Congress had appropriated only $50,000 for White House projects, and most of that money was allocated for repairs to the elevator and other mechanical systems. Faced with these financial constraints, Grace Coolidge persuaded her husband to ask Congress to authorize the acceptance of gifts for the White House and to establish a temporary committee to advise on their acquisition.[1]

In the history of White House decoration, Grace Coolidge's project was a very modest one. So few donations came as a result of the 1925 congressional resolution that Coolidge and her advisory committee were able to redecorate only the Green Room, one of three state parlors on the mansion's first floor.[2] But the First Lady's interest in antiques was nevertheless important for what it suggested about changes in the public perception of early American furniture. While other First Ladies (including Edith Roosevelt, who slept in a bed purchased by Mary Todd Lincoln during her White House years), employed objects linked to past presidents, Coolidge did not limit her search to pieces with historical associations.[3] She was also not satisfied with the common revival furniture, which often embellished early furniture forms with profuse decoration and looked little like the originals from which they were derived. Instead, she valued early American furniture and believed such pieces to be of sufficient aesthetic caliber to furnish the nation's most prominent residence. Ironically, home-grown furnishings were rejected as too provincial for the president's home during the period of its construction. Early eighteenth-century White House occupants had almost always sought their furniture in France and England, the acknowledged centers of high-quality design. When critics of President James Monroe complained in 1817 that the White House was being outfitted with too many French furnishings, his staff replied that they were incorporating as many American-made pieces as possible, but that desirable objects simply could not be purchased in this country.[4] Coolidge's proposal was, therefore, a radical reinterpretation of the history of design, one that claimed a level of sophistication and accomplishment for early American craftsmen they had not enjoyed even in their own day.

What allowed for this reassessment of design that had transformed early American furniture into potential White House showpieces was nothing short of a new way of understanding the value of antiques, one in evidence at one of the largest museum projects of the decade, the American Wing, a new addition to New York's Metropolitan Museum of Art. Opened in 1924, the American Wing was a series of twenty period-room displays featuring early American household furnishings and adorned with antique woodwork taken from old houses. The museum had first turned its attention to American antiques in 1909, when it arranged a special loan exhibition of early American furniture and decorative objects as part of the citywide celebration commemorating the three hundredth anniversary of Henry Hudson's discovery of the Hudson River and the hundredth anniversary of Robert Fulton's steamboat. Only a year after this exhibition, a wealthy widow, Mrs. Russell

Sage, donated nearly nine hundred objects from the original exhibit, all of which she purchased from Eugene Bolles, a Boston collector. A favorite destination of Grace Goodhue Coolidge, the American Wing differed from many earlier exhibitions of early American antiques in the importance it placed on aesthetic display. As newspaper accounts reported, curators at the American Wing did not select objects based on their association with famous individuals or historic events. Instead, they made their judgments on artistic merit and concerned themselves with "beauty of line, proportion and decoration."[5] The result was a series of period rooms of such artistic beauty that they challenged traditional ideas about American design. "There is no trace in the work that came from native workshops of the 'inferiority complex,'" the *New York Times* concluded. "What Europe can do, we can do, and do better."[6]

The founders of the American Wing were not the first to display early American furnishings for their aesthetic qualities, nor would they be the last; in fact, the New York institution was following developments in New England. One of the first New England art museums to boast such a collection was the museum of the Rhode Island School of Design, which had been the recipient of Charles Pendleton's personal collection in 1904.[7] Eugene Bolles's cousin George Palmer sold some of his best eighteenth-century pieces to the Metropolitan Museum in 1918. After Bolles's collection took the national stage at the Met, other collectors across New England set their sights on museum making. Francis P. Garvan began a long relationship with Yale University in 1930, donating a large collection of American antiques and decorative arts (see chapter 3), while Maxim Karolik and his wife, the former Martha Codman, established themselves as Boston Museum of Fine Arts benefactors in the mid-1930s by building a collection of early American furniture, paintings, and silver to donate to the museum.[8]

Museum builders found early American furnishings attractive because they lent themselves to the construction of a specifically American style of art. Since their creation in eighteenth-century Europe, large universal survey museums have justified the nation state by transforming the luxuries of wealthy citizens and monarchal rulers into "art-historical objects, repositories of spiritual wealth, products of individual and national genius." Using the discipline of art history, itself an invention of the eighteenth century, the museum organized its aesthetic treasures chronologically and by national origin to construct a narrative of artistic growth. Such displays assumed a correlation between the development of art and the progress of civilization, allowing the nation to point to its artistic products as evidence of its spiritual and cultural might.[9] Many American museums imitated this European formula, first perfected in the Louvre, but lacked national art forms to place within the narrative. The household furnishings of wealthy early Americans filled this void and allowed for the production of a new national culture.

In this book I explore how Americans have come to value the household objects of elite early American families as *antiques*, not by explaining the points of rarity, age, ownership, origins, condition, and aesthetics that connoisseurs use to differentiate such pieces, but rather by examining the history of antique collecting and museum display in the first half of the twentieth century, a period that saw the invention of antiques as aesthetic objects and their enshrinement as museum artifacts. I use the word *invention* deliberately, in the sense that interpretations of history are *created*, not just by scholars paging through dusty tomes, but also by members of the public who construct, consume, and disseminate their own representations of history.[10] By recognizing that historical knowledge is invented, we also acknowledge that our understanding of the past has itself a history. As was demonstrated by the furor that erupted over the Columbus quincentenary in the 1990s, Americans today feel differently about the legacy of European colonization than they did at the beginning of the twentieth century.[11] Something similar is true of antiques. Most people did not care very much about American antiques in the mid-1800s; when more widespread interest in them began, toward the end of the century, they were valued primarily as mementos that symbolized important events and family ties, not as the accomplished art pieces and national resources we view them as today. Americans had to learn to value the decorative arts of their native soil, and specifically to value them as aesthetic treasures worthy of substantial sums of money and a prominent place in their most celebrated museums.

Grounded in recent scholarship on the social organization of tradition, or what is often called "public" or "collective" memory, my study takes as its starting point the idea that how people think about the past is important. Americans are frequently charged with not knowing their own history, but in fact the past is a dynamic part of their lives.[12] History supplies communities with the tools to define cultural values, build collective identities, challenge or maintain existing power structures, and manage cultural resources. From this perspective, decisions about which historic artifacts a museum should save and celebrate and which it should allow to decay and be forgotten are political ones, reflecting judgments about who and what matters most. Many individuals may not own or even appreciate antiques—indeed, antiquing has been largely limited to white Americans of the upper and middle classes—but the fact that the household goods of a certain age have been enshrined in museums, the nation's secular temples, demonstrates that they are deeply embedded in our society's cultural beliefs.

The road to valuing antiques has been a long one for American society. As Michael Kammen has argued, in the decades following the Revolution Americans defined their country by its newness. History was a yoke to be discarded, a force to overcome. In such an atmosphere, old furniture did not have much meaning, let alone value. By the nation's centennial in 1876, that attitude had begun to change. Faced with the uncertainties of a world marked by rapid urbanization, industrialization, and immigration, many sought refuge in the perceived simplicity of the colonial era, a movement often referred to as the Colonial Revival for its romantic investment in the past's symbolic value. Adherents formed genealogical societies and family associations, restored old houses, staged historical pageants, incorporated colonial motifs in new architectural construction, manufactured colonial-inspired furniture, and founded historical societies and historic house museums in great numbers.[13]

Antiquing and the appreciation for antiques grew slowly out of this new interest in history, as middle- and upper-class white Americans started to bring antiques into their homes to use as props in their decor. These early aficionados recognized the value of historic objects as a concrete connection to the past, a bridge across time. They tended to see them as important not for their physical qualities but as memory markers, tangible representations of the past valued for their association with famous individuals or local luminaries. The transformation of antiques from storied objects and family heirlooms to aesthetic objects in the first half of the twentieth century is at the heart of this study. Objects frequently take on new meanings even when their physical shape remains constant. A single table can be stylish, out-of-fashion (and later perhaps newly fashionable for its retro look), or simply functional over the course of its existence. In the case of antiques, forgotten pieces stowed in an attic or barn or relegated to functional use in a family's house were dusted off and pressed into new service as the priceless possessions of well-to-do collectors. At the same time, old furniture pieces, treasured as an expression of family history, came to be seen as embodiments of the American artistic spirit; they became what I call "aesthetic antiques" for the priority collectors placed on these objects' visual qualities and their proclivity to judge their quality based on stylistic elements.[14] As I will show, this transformation did not happen on its own. Rather, the process was fueled by a small army of antique collectors, curators, and dealers who did the work of locating old furniture, removing it from its former context, and restoring and displaying it to accentuate its visual qualities. For these dedicated antiquers, the aesthetic antique had cultural, political, social, and financial value.

The development of the aesthetic antique was connected to the emergence of the United States on the world stage, which created a demand for an American artistic culture. Following the Panic of 1893, the United States began to tie its future development to commercial exporting. While government policies and naval expansion provided the practical means for U.S. exports to compete on foreign soil, a cultural belief in the superiority of American civilization was also necessary. In the nineteenth century, this belief was promulgated largely by Christian missionaries, but as the United States forsook its isolationism and became a dominant world power, Americans increasingly sought to define a uniquely American culture, one that separated their country not only from less developed nations but also from the old powers of Europe. If the Colonial Revival was driven by a need to defend Anglo-American culture against the internal immigrant Other, the increasing nationalism of the twentieth century claimed a cultural sophistication to match the nation's burgeoning political, economic, and military might.[15]

The rise of the aesthetic antique was also fueled by the development of a consumer-based society that treated these newfound treasures as another category of retail goods.[16] Americans are often uneasy with the idea of antiques as commodities. On the one hand, we frequently describe antiques as "priceless" and remove them from the market to put them on display in museums. The museum as an institution is dedicated to this notion of an object so valuable that it defies market exchange. How else could a museum justify the expense of perpetual care if its collections' value were defined purely in economic terms? On the other hand, anyone who has ever watched the PBS or BBC versions of the program *Antiques Roadshow* knows how deeply price is ingrained in our understanding of these objects. The show's expert appraisers provide each object with a history, identifying its maker, area of origin, and period of production. These histories give the objects meaning and help establish their value. Still, the viewer knows that the most important part of any object's story is its market value, announced consistently at the end of each segment and clearly emblazoned across the bottom of the television screen. Price matters.

It is no accident that the very years that saw the transformation of antiques from family heirlooms into aesthetic objects also saw the proliferation of consumer goods, the construction of large department stores, and the dramatic expansion of the advertising industry. These structural changes were outward evidence of something even more fundamental, a new culture in which traditional Protestant values of sobriety and thrift were replaced by what William Leach has described as a "future-oriented culture of desire that confused the good life with goods."[17] Jackson Lears, who has traced the culture of consumption to its origins in the late Victorian era, places an antimodern ethic at the heart of this emerging worldview. To be sure, upper-class intellectuals who turned to the romance of Oriental culture, the Middle Ages, and in some cases the American past did so to escape an increasingly bureaucratic and materialistic world. But Lears argues that by extolling "authentic experience as an end in itself," these antimodernists "reinforced a shift from the Protestant ethic of salvation through self-denial to a therapeutic ideal of self-fulfillment through exuberant health and intense experience."[18] In other words, a fascination with the past was not only compatible with a contemporary consumer ethic, but often reinforced it. In this regard, buying and selling antiques worked to validate the new consumer culture by providing it with a historical dimension.

It is true that the consumer values promoted by antiquing were not exactly the same as those advanced by department stores, which championed endlessly changing styles and fashions in an effort to encourage consumers to purchase again and again. Antiquing denied fashion trends to embrace a belief in the timelessness of early American design.

Indeed, while the majority of dealers rejected restrictive definitions of what constituted "an antique" because it limited what they could sell, elite collectors such as Charles Messer Stow, editor of the antiques page that appeared weekly in the *New York Sun*, argued that true antiques were made before 1830, a year believed to mark "the end of an era of good design."[19] Those who joined Stow in restricting the category of antiques also implicitly protested the expansion of consumption. Electricity and automation lessened the demand for skilled workers and transformed industry, allowing it to focus on consumer markets with products affordable by a large population of Americans. Consumer society was built on this free flow of material goods, and many celebrated it as evidence of America's success in creating a democratic society.[20] In contrast, antiques promised the restoration of elite consumption and the clear demarcation of class lines. Even if middle-class buyers did become active antiquers, antiques, at least authentic ones, could never be mass-produced.

Still, antiquing cannot be seen as a reaction against consumption itself. The fact that department stores such as Wanamaker's, Lord and Taylor, B. Altman, Marshall Field, and Jordan Marsh established extensive antique departments, even though it meant making significant adjustments to their usual stocking procedures, demonstrates how compatible antiquing was with the new consumer culture (figure 1). If anything, the line between consumption and commemoration was an extremely thin one, and antiquing was often presented as a protracted shopping experience. Jordan Marsh's "Little Colonial House," opened in the 1920s to display the store's growing antique stock, closely resembled the new period rooms on display at the Metropolitan's American Wing.[21] By 1959, an antiquing manual was recommending antiquing to housewives because it offered the opportunity for more shopping. "Specific antique items are not always found at the first door, and may require some enjoyable searching for just the exact article you desire. . . . Women are known for their love of shopping, and this is one way to get in a lot of shopping with a little buying," author Leslie Gross reported.[22]

In this new world of consumerism, a retail structure developed specifically to facilitate the buying and selling of early American goods: the antique shop. From its inception, the antique market took advantage of existing New York fine-art auction houses such as American Art Association and Anderson Galleries.[23] But the antique business con-

Figure I. Jordan Marsh encouraged Christmas shoppers to buy antiques for their friends and families during the 1920s with advertisements like this one. *Antiques,* December 1922, 244.

structed its own venues, from high-end urban dealers to little country stores that traded as much in their rural charm as their actual wares. As Peter Buckley has noted, "antique stores" did not exist in the nineteenth century. Their closest approximation was the "Old Curiosity Shop," a lost category of retail that featured the old and the rare, but made no attempt to court fashion or sell goods aimed at home decor. In New York City, Buckley places the shift from curio shop to antique store around 1900.[24] New England boasted at least a few antique shops before the turn of the century, but it was not until after 1900 that antique stores appeared frequently in business directories.[25] By the 1920s there were so many antique shops that owners formed trade associations to promote business ethics and raise the standing of their profession.[26]

Perhaps the most important component of the antique market was the buyer. Collectors have always existed, but those interested in early American home furnishings were a rare group in the nineteenth century. Early collectors ran the gamut from powerful to peculiar; among New England's pioneers were Edward Lamson Henry, an artist who used antiques as props in his paintings; Benjamin Perley Poore, a Washington newspaper columnist, editor, and owner of a palatial estate called Indian Hill in West Newbury, Massachusetts; and Cummings Davis, a part-time newspaper delivery man who was committed to an insane asylum not long after the newly formed Concord Antiquarian Society declared him unfit to care for his own collection.[27] These early enthusiasts were soon to be joined by legions of new collectors. According to Steven Gelber, the number of Americans participating in hobbies of all kinds swelled during the first decades of the twentieth century. Hobbies ameliorated the bifurcation of work and home caused by industrialization and assuaged middle-class distrust of idleness by joining productive labor to leisure. But even more important for the history of antiquing, hobbies that focused on collecting reaffirmed the values of capitalism by offering the possibility of profit.[28] Regarded as both uplifting and lucrative, antiquing became respectable. The Walpole Society was formed in 1910 as an exclusive men's club dedicated to the appreciation of American decorative arts, including fine antiques. Several times a year, the group met to explore private collections, tour old houses, and visit museums, choosing a different location in the Northeast for each event.[29] In the 1930s the Walpole Society was joined by a plethora of collecting organizations specializing in specific classes of artifacts, including the Pewter Club, the China Students' Club, the Early American Industries Association, the Rushlight Club, the Wedgwood Club, and the National Early American Glass Club.[30] These new groups differed from their predecessor in important ways. They were dedicated to affordable items—small, sometimes mass-produced artifacts (such as glassware) that could be found in local antique shops, but that also gave collectors the opportunity to pursue rarer and rarer finds. The majority of the members were middle-class collectors with scholarly interests, but without the resources to compete for the most expensive categories of antiques. Only a small percentage of antique enthusiasts belonged to such groups, but they were evidence of a new era of middle-class collecting.

As I will argue, the transformation of antiques from family heirlooms to aesthetic objects and the simultaneous development of the antique market in the first half of the twentieth century profoundly disrupted the way Americans experienced the past. Gone were the traditional associational meanings that had linked historic objects to local heroes, honored ancestors, and respected statesmen. Twentieth-century antique owners were more concerned with classifying and naming their possessions' visual attributes. Terms such as Chippendale, Hepplewhite, and Sheraton, denoting specific design schools, now gave antiques new meaning and linked them to a past ordered by the development of stylistic traditions. At the same time, prices for antiques skyrocketed, making collectors keenly aware of their possessions' value in monetary terms. For many antiquers, buying and owning antiques became an experience in consumerism, as they learned to recognize differences in value, comparison shop, avoid deception, and make purchases that conformed to the new aesthetic standards. Because communities regularly use history to define cultural values and establish precedents for contemporary practices and beliefs, shifts in a community's relationship to the past, like the one described here, represent a much larger transformation in the way in which individuals understand themselves and their society. By adopting an aesthetic understanding of antiques and discarding more associational practices, Americans built a culture in which heritage, and the authority that it offered, could be bought and sold. They reinforced consumerism by celebrating their forefathers' affection for fashion and legitimized the power of elites by putting their material possessions on public display. At the same time, the focus on aesthetics and design minimized the importance of local storytelling traditions as a way to understand historic objects, eroding the value of local history and making way for a new nationally based, patriotic culture.

In exploring the invention of antiques as aesthetic objects and its impact on the way New Englanders experienced their pasts, I examine both the development of the antique market and the construction of museum displays of antiques. At first glance, the museum and the market might seem like strange bedfellows. It is certainly true that museums were the antithesis of the market in a very concrete way. Until relatively recently, when an object was placed in a museum the implication was that it would never be bought or sold again. Ownership was constant; speculation and trade were forbidden. In practice, museums deaccession objects in an effort to refine their institutional missions and limit expenses associated with collection care, and, of course they reap an economic benefit if an object is sold. But while deaccessioning is today considered a necessary part of responsible collections management, the open discussion of such practices is relatively new, dating back to the 1980s, and limited to the professional museum community. For most Americans, the museum represents a place in which objects are protected, not sold. Indeed, it was precisely the perception of the museum as free from commercial demands that made it so important to the collecting world. It was no accident that museums acquired so many American antiques during the market expansion of the mid-1920s. Markets and museums worked in tandem: one reinforced the object's value in economic terms, the other in cultural cachet. Both were essential parts of this meaning-making system; the museum's refusal to sell was a very real guarantee that there would be a space to define an antique's social significance and ensure that its value would add up to more than a number. At the same time, the antique market allowed those outside the professional world of collecting to interact with antique objects firsthand and become, in a sense, their own historians.

Much of the material of this book is presented through case studies, a medium that enables me to set the story of the development and impact of the aesthetic antique within the context of the concrete concerns that often faced antique collectors, dealers, and curators. While connoisseurs, curators, and other stewards of the past are influenced by their ideological beliefs, very often important collecting decisions are made for much more mundane reasons. The availability of objects and the money to pay for them, as well as the presence or absence of donors, all had a profound effect on the way individuals interacted with historic objects, displayed their finds, and constructed exhibitions.

In my choice of subject matter, I have focused primarily on blockbuster auctions, established collectors, and high-end dealers. These individuals and events helped create the new collecting canon that influenced many antiquers. My goal is to show how the new aesthetic antique was constructed, interpreted, and defined. I am also interested in antique aficionados who could not measure up, those who struggled to emulate prominent collectors and were thwarted by their lack of knowledge or funds, as well as those who deliberately rejected the new collecting standards. I acknowledge, however, that as powerful as the aesthetic antique was in shaping Americans' perception of the past, it was not absolute. Individuals could, and did, contest the popular approach to collecting that located Americans' cultural heritage in the possessions of elites. These collectors created alternative visions of the American past that favored the ordinary over the exceptional and work over aesthetic display.

Readers familiar with the history of antiquing will notice that some well-known collectors and museums are not included here. Henry Francis du Pont, for example, the millionaire collector who built the Winterthur Museum in Delaware, receives only brief mention. While my desire to include the stories of lesser known collectors and antique workers partly explains my subject selections, I have also chosen to make New England the center of this study. I wanted to examine the impact of antiquing on the region's identity formation, and to understand how selected museums, preservation initiatives, and collecting enterprises contributed to New England's evolving identity in the first half of the twentieth century. Building on the work of historians such as Edward Ayres, Dona Brown, Joseph Conforti, and Patricia Nelson Limerick, I had come to see regional identity as something that is actively imagined and constructed by an area's inhabitants and to see history as a way that people define themselves by creating stories about their origins.[31] What I found surprised me. While New England developed a burgeoning antique business, the market functioned with little regard to the region's sense of self. It is true that New England provided the hunting grounds for some of the earliest American decorative arts collectors, boasted some of the field's most important antique stores, and produced a rich collection of museum displays, but the market demanded that goods be mobile, free from the constraints of regional exclusivity, and ready for sale. By the 1920s, New England antiques mixed with those made in New York and Philadelphia in major art museum exhibitions. Several high-profile Boston dealers moved to New York City in order to expand their market, and collectors regularly praised the entire Northeast region for the aesthetic accomplishment of its eighteenth- and early nineteenth-century urban centers. Both the market and the goods in which it traded could not be limited to the New England region for very long.

My geographical focus, then, says less about the construction of New England's identity than about how the region's historic resources were employed in the construction of a larger national culture. Indeed, at just the same moment that antique dealers were developing a nationally based clientele, museum curators, both amateur and professional, were exhibiting the nation's cultural heritage using New England–made antiques as their subject matter. Contemporary scholars have strongly questioned New England's centrality in American culture, recognizing that while the Northeast has functioned as the nation's unmarked region, against which all others have been measured, it is hardly the birthplace of American literature, history, or culture.[32] Still, while many excellent studies have traced how New England's history and culture was constructed internally, few have unpacked how the perception that American history began in New England was cultivated.[33] By tracking the dissemination of New England's historic resources to a national public, both through museum exhibitions and through the antique market, this study suggests at least one avenue by which New England's heritage was transmitted to the nation.

In the chapters that follow I use a variety of sources and subjects to explore the history of twentieth-century antiquing in New England. In chapter 1 I examine the antique market itself, its origins in the early twentieth century, and the development of antiques as aesthetic objects. This focus on the object's physical attributes had far-reaching consequences, not only for how antiques were marketed and sold, but also for the way in which they were displayed, cared for, and valued. Chapter 2 looks behind the scenes to examine the role of dealers in promoting the development of antique collecting. Much attention has been paid to high-profile collectors, but very little has been written about the dealers who supported their efforts by locating and identifying the objects they celebrated with such enthusiasm. The fact that many of these dealers were recent Jewish immigrants who turned to antiques as a way to make a living demonstrates the degree to which the existence of a profitable retail market opened participation in the antiquing craze to those lacking the financial resources to become collectors. In chapter 3 I take the story of antiquing to an individual collector and would-be museum maker, Jessie Barker Gardner, a small-time collector from Providence, Rhode Island. Gardner had big ambitions, but she lacked the resources to realize them. Without the ability to spend freely, she managed her budget, dealt with fraud, and worried whether or not her collections and the house she displayed them in were up to par. Gardner represents an important class of collectors, serious about their hobby but constrained by the market. Chapter 4 offers the story of an individual town, Deerfield, Massachusetts. Deerfield, renowned for its long history of preserving and maintaining its past, has been the subject of much scholarship, in large part because of the extensive historical documentation available for the community. I take a different route to consider the ways in which the aestheticization of antiques eroded local and community histories and supported the development of a patriotic past. Finally, in chapter 5 I examine the backlash against the decorative arts market in the 1950s and 1960s. Not every collector could afford to participate in the existing market, and many opposed the aesthetification of historic artifacts. C. Malcolm Watkins, a Smithsonian curator, represents this alternative class of collectors. A native of New England and one of the Smithsonian's first professional curators to study social history themes through material culture, Watkins promoted a vision of collecting that celebrated the contributions of ordinary Americans and traditional craft processes.

Heralded by collectors and institutionalized in our nation's most prominent museums, the aesthetic antique provided Americans with an artistic tradition solidly rooted in their past. Many eagerly participated in this new way of understanding historic household furnishings. Some were drawn to antiques for the chance to make a profit, others hoped to emulate the new collecting standards for the cultural and social authority they offered, while still others rejected the practice of valuing historic objects for their artistic qualities altogether. Nevertheless, all who owned, collected, or studied early American furniture experienced the ways in which the new collecting practices placed issues of aesthetics over those of historical associations, favored the construction of national histories over local ones, and embedded the acquisition of historic household furnishings within the context of a consumer culture. By inventing antiques and the practice of antiquing, Americans invented a new way of experiencing the past.

Priceless and Price [1]
The Antiquing of New England

*I*n an archive in Delaware sit two inventory lists from a New Haven antique dealer named O. C. Hill. The first, dated 1902, is a handwritten list of each object in the shop and its estimated value. The descriptions are exceptionally brief. Entries such as "highboy," "tall clock," or "mahogany table" are the norm, but when Hill found it necessary to elaborate, the information he added took the form of specific associations. The most detailed of these goes to a "historical chair, one of the first six that the first minister that preached in Litchfield used." The list dated 1909, in contrast, is full of descriptive detail, focusing on the objects' physical attributes as opposed to the history of their ownership and use. Here, Hill uses the language of aesthetics to pinpoint specific decorative features and identify individual styles. "Rare Chippendale mirror in mahogany, carved shell in poor condition 39 by 18, an exceptional piece," one record reads. "A magnificent old sofa in mahogany, carved claw feet, carved S shaped ends, carved rim and back, brass line inlayed on back, the best I have ever owned or seen," claims another.[1]

In the seven years that elapsed between the two inventories, Hill also changed the nature of his stock. His earlier inventory included rifles, powder horns, books, warming pans, and bellows, objects that evoked the daily rituals of early American life but had little in the way of aesthetic pretense. By 1909 these were gone, replaced by Chippendale chairs, swell-front bureaus, and inlaid card tables. Unsurprisingly, the prices had gone up. The highest-priced item on Hill's 1902 inventory was a relic cabinet filled with Indian artifacts and coins, the entire collection valued at $250; the most expensive item on the 1909 list was a "set of ten old-carved ball and claw dining room or library chairs . . . pierced backs, elaborately carved, absolutely genuine old."[2] These Hill estimated at $1,100, a price greater than the value of his entire 1902 stock. Similar items also saw big jumps in value. While the first inventory listed an unembellished "mirror" for $1, the later included several more elaborately described ones with prices ranging from $10 to $15.

So what had happened? Why was Hill able to charge so much more for his wares in 1909 than he had 1902? What accounts for the marked difference in the way he cataloged his stock? As I will show, Hill was one of many antique dealers and collectors who transformed Americans' understanding of antiques in the first decades of the twentieth century by exploiting their visual qualities, effectively divorcing historic furnishings from their associations with noteworthy events or prominent individuals and recasting them as aesthetic objects. Redefining antiques as aesthetic objects not only drove the price of old furniture to previously unheard-of highs but also dramatically changed Americans' experiences with antiques. While earlier owners used antiques to tell stories about their families and communities, twentieth-century collectors focused on developing their aesthetic expertise, a skill set that included the ability to recognize specific styles, makers, and schools of construction and to make judgments about their quality.

This transformation from an associational object to an aesthetic one was also tied to the development of the antique as a commodity. To be sure, the aesthetic revolution did not initiate these objects' existence as commodities. Not only were associational antiques occasionally bought and sold, but the objects eventually labeled by collectors as "antiques" could also be put on the market as used furniture or, when they were first constructed, as household consumer goods. But the high prices brought on by the aesthetic revolution created a host of consumer issues. Those who wanted to bring antiques into their lives, whether they were serious collectors or ordinary homeowners, had to worry about the investment they were about to make. Were they correct in their aesthetic judgment? Would the antique hold its selling price? Was the article genuine or a fake manufactured to take advantage of escalating prices? Those who inherited family antiques faced similar questions as they worried about whether they should sell these now valuable items or hold on to the memories they represented. Antiques still functioned as a symbol of earlier times, of permanence and good taste. But in the new aesthetic era, antiques were increasingly associated with purchasing decisions, and with questions of fraud and monetary value. In this sense, the changes revealed in Hill's lists were not a simple shift in marketing strategies. Rather, they represented a profound transformation in the way Americans understood and experienced the past.

Old Things, New Meanings

Appreciating the change represented by Hill's two inventories requires understanding the meaning-making systems developed in the late nineteenth century that shaped Americans' relationship to the past and their appreciation for antiques. There is no better place to start than the Centennial International Exhibition of 1876, the first official world's fair in the United States, held in celebration of the hundredth anniversary of the signing of the Declaration of Independence. Scholars of memory have long pointed to that important anniversary as a turning point in America's appreciation of the past. Faced with this milestone of their nation's advancing age and concerned about what new technologies would bring, many Americans sought refuge in a time that was perceived as simpler. Held in the historic city of Philadelphia, the Centennial celebrated America's rush to progress, but its exhibits also provided many comparisons to the past. One such exhibit was the New England Farmer's Home and Modern Kitchen, an old-time kitchen in a log house juxtaposed with a modern restaurant (figure 2). Historical reenactments provided much of the entertainment in the log house. Costumed guides showed visitors through the cabin and demonstrated old-time craft practices. But

Figure 2. The New England Kitchen exhibit at the 1876 Centennial Exposition included many antiques. Peregrine White's cradle and John Alden's desk are both pictured toward the center rear. From Philip Sandhurst et al., *The Great Centennial Exhibition* (Philadelphia: P. W. Zeigler, 1876), 542.

important antiques also added to the display. There was a clock, said to be the first clock brought to Andover, Massachusetts, a chair made for the Massachusetts Bay Colony's first governor, and an ancient spinning wheel, reputedly brought on the Mayflower. Among the most prominent were a small cradle and desk with very specific claims. The cradle purportedly belonged to Peregrine White, the first child born to the Pilgrims in America.[3] As for the desk, tradition held that it belonged to John Alden, the Pilgrim settler made famous as Priscilla Mullins's suitor in Longfellow's popular poem *The Courtship of Miles Standish*. For both objects, associations were central to their meaning. Press accounts of the celebration said little about their appearance or physical attributes. It was the stories they embodied that received attention.[4]

The Centennial was one of the preeminent commemorative events of the late nineteenth century, but smaller celebrations, too, revealed a fascination with associations. In Providence, Rhode Island, the Gaspee Chapter of the Daughters of the American Revolution (DAR) held a "Loan Exhibition of Colonial and Revolutionary Relics" in 1892. Ostensibly organized to celebrate the one hundred sixteenth anniversary of the battles of Lexington and Concord and the seventieth anniversary of the founding of the Rhode Island Historical Society, the exhibition displayed historic artifacts associated with the families of DAR members. Anne Cooke Cushing loaned her great-aunt's slippers, worn "when she danced a minuet with Count Rochambeau." Mrs. Alfred Stone displayed a miniature depicting her grandfather, Nathaniel Appleton, and a silver plate used by General Washington at her great-grandfather's home. As Robert Emlen has argued, these items were chosen for their ability to enshrine the ancestral lines of Providence's old families, a need made all the more urgent by the large number of immigrants flooding Rhode Island's industrial cities.[5]

Associational antiques, like those displayed in Providence's DAR Loan Exhibition and at the Centennial, often drew their power from their connection to specific families and thus were rarely bought or sold; most often they were passed on through inheritance. But antique dealers, themselves members of a very new profession, understood the importance of associations and worked to capitalize on their value. Fred Bishop Tuck belonged to this pioneering generation of dealers. He entered the business in 1890, establishing his first shop in Exeter, New Hampshire. After a short stint in Andover, Massachusetts, he moved to Kennebunkport and dubbed his new Union Square store the "first antique shop in Maine." Tuck's shop was typical of many during those early years. He stocked a wide array of goods, from spinning wheels, warming pans, and old china to rough pine furniture, tall clocks, and mahogany sideboards. From Tuck's memoirs, it is evident that his business was a fairly successful one. He maintained a Maine location for most of his life and supplemented his income with winter stores in the South.[6]

Few objects in Tuck's shop could boast the distinguished pedigrees of the Peregrine cradle or the Alden desk, but associations were vital to his business. Tuck relates in his memoir his discovery of the story of Lord Timothy Dexter, who was supposedly tricked into shipping warming pans to the hot ports of West India but managed to turn a profit by transforming them into molasses dippers. Silly as it seems, the story created a salable commodity. Tuck reported that it allowed him to sell as many warming pans as he could find for $5 each. Less elaborate stories functioned just as well. A banister-backed chair's association with the first church in Danville, New Hampshire, ensured its value at $20, while a Staffordshire teapot's association with a Methodist minister's "donation party" secured $25.[7] When goods lacked their own stories, the experience of visiting in a rural antique shop could foster its own associations. Tuck deliberately cultivated an old-time atmosphere by installing a formal parlor and New England kitchen in his showroom. Such displays were prevalent at international expositions and regional museums, and Tuck's customers would have recognized these rooms as symbols of an idyllic preindustrial existence, transforming the experience of shopping into a direct encounter with a way of life long since past. For their part, Tuck's customers seemed to embrace such symbolism, adjusting their purchasing patterns to take advantage of the associative meanings his merchandise provided. Tuck described an incident in which a customer expressed interest in an extension dining table that dated to the 1820s. The customer, an urban vacationer, saw nothing unusual about the table; indeed, he claimed to have seen many similar examples in New York auction houses. But he bought it from Tuck, explaining that he would enjoy "using a table that was purchased at the first antique shop in Maine."[8]

Dealers like Tuck had a real impact on the public's understanding of antiques. With their assistance, fashionable homemakers decorated their parlors with spinning wheels, summer residents crafted atavistic rural retreats, and historical societies transformed old buildings into memory houses. In short, the stories they told gave old objects new life. But Tuck's generation could not claim responsibility for the astonishing prices that were soon to come. In order to achieve high prices, antiques had to function as more than storied objects; they had to become art.

The development of an antique art market was a slow process. Tuck noticed a change between 1912 and 1914, when he reported that original owners were beginning to demand such high prices for desirable furniture that many dealers were abandoning that end of the business altogether and specializing in old glass, china, and inexpensive prints.[9] But the roots of the process went back several decades earlier, to the emergence of a new breed of antique enthusiast: the collector. In the late nineteenth century, the majority of customers in New England's antique shops were women who purchased historic items as an extension of their role as stewards of the house and home. Believing in the ability of the home to instill spiritual and moral ideals, these women sought antiques both for their decorative quality and for their association with history and traditional values. But as early as the 1870s, these antique enthusiasts were joined by collectors, mostly male, whose goals went far beyond furnishing a room. Rather, they saw their collections as an end in themselves, a form of historical scholarship and a testament to the creative spirit. Many antiquarians themselves recognized the difference. Writing to Metropolitan Museum of Art administrator Henry Kent about early collectors, architect and antiquarian Norman Isham emphasized that true collectors were "distinct from the gatherers."[10]

In the early years, New England's antique collectors were centered on the cities of Hartford, Providence, and Boston. The Boston group included men such as Eugene Bolles, Charles Hitchcock Taylor, Dwight Blaney, Hollis French, and Francis Hill Bigelow. Three of the group, Bolles, French, and Taylor, placed their collections with major museums: the Metropolitan Museum of Art, the Cleveland Museum of Art, and Boston Museum of Fine Arts. But Francis Hill Bigelow appreciated the business of antiques as much as the objects themselves. A published scholar on the subject of American silver as well as an avid collector, Bigelow also purchased early New England silver from local church parishes and old families and resold it to other collectors. These activities Bigelow tried to keep secret, in part because his status as a dealer would damage his reputation with other collectors, and in part because the idea of treating a religious artifact as an ordinary commodity crossed a line, even within the collecting community.[11]

Hartford developed its own rich tradition of antiquing. Pioneering collectors included Dr. Irving Lyon, author of *The Colonial Furniture of New England* (discussed below), and Henry Wood Erving, a chairman of the Connecticut River Banking Company credited with discovering what he called "Hadley chests" (for the Massachusetts town near which many were found), a class of richly carved chests indigenous to the Connecticut River Valley. As William Hosley has argued, Hartford's antiquing community was not restricted to collectors, but included a support industry of furniture repairers, dealers, and reproduction specialists.[12]

Among the most colorful Providence collectors were Marsden Perry, an entrepreneur and public utilities mogul, and Richard Canfield and

Charles Pendleton, both professional gamblers.[13] Lacking the pedigree of an old New England family, and further hampered by their less-than-respectable professions, all three used American antiques to establish themselves as cultured connoisseurs. Canfield and Perry became early members of the Walpole Society, the exclusive men's group dedicated to collecting the colonial.[14] To ensure appreciation of his taste in perpetuity, in 1904 Pendleton donated his collection to the Rhode Island School of Design, which installed it in a fireproof facsimile of his own eighteenth-century house.

Until the founding of the Walpole Society in 1910, few of these early collectors maintained friendships or networks beyond their local environs. But even though they did not advance an organized or singular interpretation of antiques, their collections changed the way Americans would understand old things. Indeed, collecting in itself represented a kind of object-based scholarship. While variations in form and design were invisible to those who owned just a few odd items, the collector could observe stylistic differences, track regional variations, and compare similar pieces for quality and artistic achievement. In 1891 Irving Lyon published the first substantial study of seventeenth- and eighteenth-century domestic furniture. *The Colonial Furniture of New England* documented the new collecting with examples drawn from Lyon's own finds as well as those of several others.[15] A doctor in his professional life, he approached the study of antiques as a scientist, using probate inventories and wood evidence to formulate theories about the origins and functions of antiques found in New England homes. Lyon rarely commented on an object's aesthetic qualities. Rather, his most important contribution to the field was the then-stunning pronouncement that "much, perhaps the most, of the carved oaken furniture found in New England was made here" rather than imported from England.[16] But even though Lyon himself did not focus on aesthetics, his attention to individual objects, using detailed descriptions, construction information, and discussions of design, helped establish antiques as important in and of themselves, not dependent on tenuous associations for their significance.

As collectors began appreciating antiques for their intrinsic qualities, it was only a matter of time before they started making aesthetic judgments. In the first edition of his *Colonial Furniture in America*, published in 1901, Luke Vincent Lockwood peppered his text with words such as "handsome" and "fine."[17] But such pronouncements became much more numerous in an enlarged edition of the book published in 1913, and the addition of new examples encouraged him to speculate on standards of design. For example, by comparing several Hadley chests, Lockwood concluded that the clumsy repetition of surface design showed that the furniture maker was "experimenting," while a more regular pattern characterized a chest that was "better worked out."[18] Such comparisons and aesthetic judgments also reflected changes in the kinds of antiques that collectors were beginning to value. Most pioneering collectors pursued pieces from what antique collector and author Wallace Nutting dubbed "the Pilgrim century," but by the 1910s antique enthusiasts were beginning to value later pieces made in the Queen Anne, Chippendale, Hepplewhite, and Sheraton styles. One reason for this change was, of course, the passage of time. When Lyon started collecting, Hepplewhite furniture was little more than a generation old. His lack of appreciation for this relatively new antique is evidenced by the fact that he consistently misspelled "Hepplewhite" in his text as "Heppelwhite."[19] But as the nineteenth century faded into the twentieth, collectors began to expand their areas of interest. These "new" antiques were often more refined in style and more delicate in appearance. Seventeenth- and early eighteenth-century furniture often displayed heavy forms, complex carved surfaces, and bold geometric patterns, and in that way echoed Arts and Crafts furniture, a contemporary style popular during earliest years of the twentieth century. In contrast, later eighteenth- and early nineteenth-century furniture designs were marked by elegant lines, graceful curves, and fine inlays. Such furniture was easier for wealthy industrialists and modern businessmen to incorporate in their formal parlors. It was also easier for twentieth-century Americans, familiar with the clean lines of the emerging modernist design, to appreciate them along aesthetic lines.

Collectors were essential to the process of inventing new aesthetic values for antiques. It was through their success in assembling large collections that one could recognize individual patterns and decorative details. But the developing antique market also cultivated a preference for aesthetic values. The business of selling historic associations could be very difficult for the dealer. As one Boston antique dealer explained, "You can buy a lot of things sold with a story, but it doesn't mean anything. You can buy the story, but it doesn't get the item."[20] He was right. The fundamental problem with associations was that they were not physi-cally part of the object itself. No matter how much they embellished their wares, antique dealers were in the business of selling goods, not stories, and the distinction made associations weak in the marketplace. Antiques associated with a former president or famous poet might com-mand exorbitant prices, but the vast majority could not boast such con-nections. Most associations were like those adduced by antique owner Isabel Erskine Brewster when she described several vases as formerly owned by Miss Clara Louise Stinson, "a descendant of General and Mrs. Payson of Wiscasset, who were also among the original founders of the town."[21] In short, they were obscure and sometimes convoluted. Their significance mattered only to a limited, often local audience. But the mar-ketplace required objects to be geographically mobile. As antiques were bought, sold, and removed from their local context, the significance of their associations were frequently lost. For example, a chair once owned by a small-town minister would lose its relevancy when sold outside of the community. Similarly, a family heirloom could not function as an heirloom outside the family context.

A fictional story in the *Antiquarian*, a collecting magazine, made the problem clear. A young couple, proud of their developing collection, dis-cuss the value of antiques with their aging neighbor, the Major. The Major shares the couple's passion for antiques, which he views as "links" to "fine old traditions," but worries that the process of buying and selling dimin-ishes their value: "I meant that they lacked the intimate, the personal asso-ciations and sentiment that exists with the pieces which today are in the homes of the descendants of original owners. They lack *that* background which money cannot buy." The young couple is shocked to learn the con-sequences of their actions. "We had not stopped to think that with every single thing we had bought there was a severed thread of association."[22] Other collectors acknowledged the moral dilemmas that their hobby pro-duced. In an article published in the *Antiquarian*, the southern collector Carolyn Coleman Duke admitted that collecting could be bittersweet:

A collector must suffer many heartaches. Not because she missed the piece, but because she got it. If you ever buy a sideboard from a sweet, lovely little old lady, who is very anxious to sell it and even delighted with the nice check so much bigger than she anticipated, never stay to see the piece removed; for in her face there is revealed the sorrow of the Past. Each child stands by in silence and watches the last trace of their aristocracy lifted out of the house by a rough drayman. The mother gazes into space and remembers her childhood's happy days when it was resplendent with old silver, old wines and liquors and bowls of fruit. Then the memory of her wedding day, her mother and her grandmother; and then—then it is time to move away, for you feel your own tears beginning to flow and you wish you had never seen this sideboard.[23]

As Duke recognized, antiques came with a host of sentimental connections, and any antique buyer willing to knock on the doors of private homes had to be willing to break the ties that bound owner and object. But for dealers the problem was not just an ethical one, it was also financial. If antiques were seen as primarily sentimental in nature, the market would corrupt their value. In contrast, aesthetics provided dealers with the promise of permanency. Aesthetic qualities owed their existence to the object itself, the wood from which it was crafted, the intricacy of its carvings, and the gracefulness of its curves. They tied the object to the market in a concrete and solid way.

The new concern for aesthetics affected the perception of many different kinds of antiques. Collectors focused their sights not only on fine tilt-top tables, high chests, and Sheraton sideboards, but also on ceramics, glass, textiles, pewter, and silver. Like furniture, these decorative wares ran the gamut of rarity, aesthetic accomplishment, and price. In the mid-1920s collectors might pay a few dollars for a common green feather-edged plate or more than a thousand for a particularly desirable Stiegel-type diamond-daisy-patterned bottle.[24] Both provided budding collectors with a way to enter the market, but variations in price and desirability tended to reinforce market hierarchy. On one end of the spectrum were collectors willing to spend top dollar to secure the most beautiful antiques. They included people like Helen Temple Cooke, principal of Dana Hall, a girls' preparatory school in Wellesley, Massachusetts, who "wanted the very, very, very, best" pieces and was willing to pay the "very, very, very best prices."[25] Dealers too tended to specialize. Some, like Boston's Israel Sack and Philip Flayderman, positioned themselves on the high end of the market, relying on their extensive network of antique scouts to supply them with the best. On the other end of the spectrum were country shops like the Turkey Hills Antique Shop, owned by Sidney Francis and Frances Bell of Lunenberg, Massachusetts, who operated their business out of a small cottage embellished with black shutters and a picket fence to give the simple building a "colonial" air.[26] While collectors and dealers at both ends of the spectrum read collecting guides and antique journals, the divide was difficult to bridge. When Huldah Wellington Spaulding bought a hooked rug associated with the historic Wayside Inn in Sudbury, Massachusetts, for her small shop on Cape Cod, she at once recognized its value to the automobile manufacturer Henry Ford, who had recently purchased the building associated with Longfellow's popular collection of poems, *Tales of the Wayside Inn*. Spaulding promptly wrote to Ford, but was rebuffed by his secretary, and the rug remained unsold until Charles Woolsey Lyon, son of Irving Lyon and a well-known New York City dealer, arrived on his annual canvassing of Cape Cod shops. Like Spaulding, Lyon recognized the value of the rug's association with the Wayside Inn. But Lyon had connections that Spaulding lacked, and he successfully sold the rug to Ford.[27] Spaulding's tale is instructive for what it says about the market. Only a relatively small group of collectors could purchase the best. The rest read books, tracked auction prices, and dreamed of the day when their knowledge and taste would allow them to recognize an undervalued object and transform it into a "find." In this way, the aesthetic revolution affected more than the few who could buy. It influenced a whole spectrum of collectors who internalized its messages and made purchases at whatever level they could afford.

For a Price

By the late 1920s, antiques were selling for amounts that O. C. Hill and Fred Tuck would have found unimaginable. Newspapers such as the *New York Times* regularly published the results of auctions sales with headlines that must have appeared sensational. One of the most important of these early auctions was the Philip Flayderman sale. Flayderman was a high-end Boston dealer. After his death, his family liquidated his stock, selling some of his very best pieces at a New York auction in 1929. When the gavel closed the event, an individual tea table had sold for $29,000

Figure 3. This tea table, built in 1763 by Newport, Rhode Island, cabinetmaker John Goddard for Jabez Bowen, also of Newport, sold for $29,000 at the 1929 auction of Boston antique dealer Philip Flayderman. Photograph courtesy of the Henry Francis du Pont Winterthur Museum.

and a secretary for $30,000 (figure 3). A high chest brought $12,000, a table $8,000, and a sideboard $5,500. In all, the collection realized close to $430,000, with a per-item average of $840.[28] Such prices were nothing short of astonishing at a time when the average American income was just $1,405 a year.[29] But the Flayderman auction was hardly a singular event. Only a year earlier, at the Howard Reifsnyder sale, a high chest known as the Van Pelt Highboy sold for the record price of $44,000; a Philadelphia Chippendale armchair brought another $33,000. Before the stock-market crash reined in collectors and depressed prices, large auction houses, such as the American Art Association and Anderson Galleries, saw literally millions of dollars change hands.[30]

For antique collectors and dealers, high prices were to be celebrated as proof of the importance of American antiques. But while high prices do suggest the cultural value antiques had achieved by the late 1920s, examining how antique buyers and sellers priced individual objects can help us understand how antiques function as cultural objects. Indeed, most antiques sold for prices far below those achieved in New York auctions. Inventory lists from Whitlock's Book Store, an antiquarian shop and rare book seller in New Haven, Connecticut, are typical. One high chest lists for $112, another for $340. Secretaries and sideboards sold regularly for no more than a few hundred dollars.[31] In an aesthetic market, it may be obvious that what an object looked like would account for the differences in prices between the antiques at Whitlock's shop and those sold at the Flayderman auction. Certainly collectors looked to characteristics such as line, proportion, and the quality of an object's carving when determining its desirability and value. But, surprisingly, collectors rarely determined prices based on aesthetics alone. In fact, while collectors publicly upheld the value of aesthetics, a revised system of associations continued to influence purchasing patterns. An object's origin and the history of its ownership mattered and directly translated into differences in dollar value. The persistence of associations shows that even when valued for their aesthetics, antiques were not without historic and patriotic significance. Old associations were simply redrawn to accommodate the new aesthetic preferences.

On the surface, most collectors insisted that an antique's market value was directly tied to its visual characteristics. In February 1930, America's leading collecting periodical, *The Magazine Antiques* (founded in 1922 as *Antiques*),[32] ran a column recapping the Reifsnyder sale by the magazine's editor, Homer Eaton Keyes, writing under the pseudonym Bondome. Keyes wrote that relatively small differences in craftsmanship or design could have a big effect on price. To make his point, he cited the case of a maple butterfly table "whose turnings lacked the elegance demanded by particular connoisseurs." Even though Keyes described it as "really choice," the table brought a measly $460, compared to $1,500 for one that "more closely conformed to popular tastes." Other furniture items had similar stories. According to Keyes, an "unusual mahogany claw-and-ball chair from Rhode Island" would have brought much more than $150 if the top rail of its back "more perfectly composed with the rest of the piece," and a "late Sheraton serpentine card table with heavy, reeded legs" sold for less than half the price of "more delicately designed pieces of similar purpose."[33]

Valuing aesthetics in this way undermined the importance of two characteristics traditionally associated with antiques: rarity and age. In a 1939 article for *American Collector,* columnist Richard Huntley cautioned his readers that "age has far less to do with whether an antique is desirable than the strict meaning of the term would indicate."[34] Wallace Nutting, the antique authority, entrepreneur, and author of the popular reference guide *Furniture Treasury,* agreed. For Nutting, the idea that antiques were valuable "merely" because of their age was a fallacy that must be overcome.[35] Nutting and Huntley encouraged collectors to turn to "quality" as a more appropriate criterion. But while Nutting and Huntley used aesthetics to determine "quality," neither man suggested that such determinations were purely subjective. Indeed, by the 1920s antique collectors had adopted the approach of art historians and constructed a timeline identifying the stylistic development of the American decorative arts. Categorizing antiques according to specific schools of design, most often referred to at that time as Pilgrim, Chippendale, Sheraton, and Hepplewhite, filled a practical need by allowing collectors to at least roughly identify an object's age. But periodization also had an impact on the way collectors judged aesthetic quality. If antiques were to be understood as representational of a specific style, then their quality would be measured against the design traditions of that style. In this sense, a seventeenth-century William and Mary banister-backed chair could not be compared to its eighteenth-century Chippendale cousins. Each was seen as the embodiment of a coherent type, to be judged in terms of its own design tradition. In such a system, rarity could be considered a deficiency; the rationale was that a piece that varied too far from its type was constructed by a clumsy craftsman unfamiliar with the high-style conventions of his day. Once age was devalued, antiques were implicitly divorced from their traditional function as historical talismans whose value lay in their direct connection to the distant recesses of the human experience. By shunning rarity, collectors constructed a collecting culture that valued conformity and compliance over individuality and imagination. Such were the demands of the new aesthetic market.

Many factors influenced an antique's selling price, but one of the most difficult to understand is the issue of historical associations. On the surface, most antique enthusiasts vehemently denied the value of purely associative objects. When the rocking chair that President Lincoln was sitting in when he was assassinated sold for $2,400, Homer Eaton Keyes believed it a sham. "If an uglier piece of furniture was ever achieved by the imagination of man, I have yet to see it," he wrote in the guise of Bondome. "Surely one of many exactly similar chairs turned out from the same factory, it could be duplicated in a secondhand shop for an insignificant sum."[36] Keyes's criticism focused on the chair's appearance and the ease with which it could be replaced. But when it came to objects already praised for their aesthetic qualities, associations could actually add to their value. Indeed, for many years *Antiques* regularly ran a column on "pedigreed antiques," a term used to describe aesthetically significant objects whose ownership could also be traced to the family of an American statesman or member of the social elite.

The existence of a market for these historic objects shows that even if antique experts denied it, many collectors still valued associations and the patriotic and nostalgic sentiments they engendered. Henry Ford, one of the biggest antique buyers of the 1930s, loved pedigreed antiques. "If I got anything historical," Boston antique dealer Israel Sack recalled, "Mr. Ford bought it." He gave a few examples: "I bought the General Stark collection direct from his house . . . and Henry Ford bought it. Anything from John Hancock he bought."[37] Philip Flayderman was among the most successful in marketing associations. When Flayderman purchased a family heirloom, he asked the seller to provide him with a sworn statement of its history.[38] In most cases, the documentation provided at least adequate proof of the antique's history and translated into higher prices at the auction block. For example, the 1929 Flayderman auction included an anvil owned by Paul Revere. The piece bore no distinctive marks, but when coupled with the appropriate paperwork it drew $9,700.[39]

The auction held after Flayderman's death also contributed to a new kind of historic association. Although many objects in the Flayderman collection bore distinct histories, those commanding the highest prices were so-called labeled items, furniture and other objects that retained their maker's original label or signature. The labels represented a kind of documentary history, fixing the object in time and attaching it to an individual. But the individual in question was not a statesman, patriot, or founding father—nor even a president's wife or mother—but a craftsman, the person directly responsible for its appearance and design.

The cult of the craftsman, directly tied to collectors' new appreciation for aesthetics, became increasingly important during the 1920s. Antique journals regularly published new research identifying individual makers and attributing specific objects to them based on construction and style.[40] The first early American craftsman to achieve posthumous fame was Duncan Phyfe, a New York state cabinetmaker known for his Sheraton, Regency, French Directoire, and, later, Empire creations. Phyfe was a favorite of R. T. H. Halsey, the chairman of the Metropolitan Museum's committee on American decorative arts; Halsey's research and collecting helped establish Phyfe's twentieth-century reputation. Phyfe was also the star of the legendary New York Loan Exhibition of American Antiques sponsored by the Girl Scouts of America in 1929. The show featured forty-eight pieces of identified Phyfe furniture and dedicated an entire section of the catalog to his work. The importance of Phyfe's name in selling furniture was well known to exhibit organizers. As the collector Louis Guerineau Myers acknowledged in his entry in the Girl Scouts Loan catalog, Phyfe's name had become "the plaything of every auctioneer, every furniture dealer and every furniture buyer in the country. Every man's work during the first years of the nineteenth century is foisted on poor old Phyfe."[41] Phyfe's name stands out in surviving account books of the New York antique firm of Ginsburg & Levy for the years from 1911 to 1919. The books contain only the briefest descriptions of the company's wares, but regularly attribute specific pieces of furniture to Phyfe.[42]

Phyfe did not remain alone for long. The names of such cabinetmakers as Goddard, Townsend, Chapin, McIntire, and Savery soon appeared in dealers' advertisements and auction catalogs. For those who believed in the purity of aesthetics, linking price to maker was a gross deviation from valuing antiques for their inherent physical qualities. In *Antiques*, Homer Eaton Keyes, again writing as Bondome, reported that the antique industry was hurt when collectors went "scrambling for labels": "American collectors, too many of them, who believe that they are buying quality or interest or aesthetic charm, are really neglecting these attributes. . . . If the specimen is choice, what difference does it make who fabricated it?"[43] But such protests were few and far between. Collectors flocked to the labeled pieces, perhaps because they satisfied a number of problems. First, they helped make buying easier. For most collectors, making judgments based on aesthetics alone could be a pretty scary business. Who was to say that one person's "masterpiece" would hold up under the judgment of another? Antique manuals often counseled would-be collectors to develop a discriminating eye, visit museums, attend auctions, and study dealers' showrooms. But developing a sophisticated appreciation for aesthetics took time, and good taste was never a guarantee. In an atmosphere of such uncertainty, marked or labeled furniture offered reassurance while maintaining faith in the antique as an artistic expression.

At the same time, the existence of labeled pieces helped collectors construct an American artistic tradition. Since Irving Lyon's discovery in the 1890s that many American antiques were not English exports but were crafted in this country, collectors had seized on the idea of antiques as evidence of the nation's artistic accomplishment. While even the most brazen antique aficionados had a hard time comparing America's old furniture to the fine arts of sculpture and painting traditionally celebrated by the museums of Europe, with the opening of the American Wing at the Metropolitan Museum of Art in 1924, Americans began to see antiques as a specific form of art. Describing his own discovery of American antiques, Robert W. de Forest, president of the Met and the funder of the American Wing, spoke of how tentative was his early appreciation of their quality: "We began to ask ourselves whether American domestic art was not a chapter, or at least a paragraph, in the history of art."[44] The well-known art critic Royal Cortissoz wrote in *Scribner's Magazine* that the Met's display of American antiques provided proof that "the instinct for art was implanted and nourished in the genius of the American people."[45]

High-style furniture alone was not proof of an American artistic tradition, however. America needed not only art, but artists. As Carol Duncan has argued, since the development of national art museums in nineteenth-century Europe, the category of "Great Artist" has functioned as evidence of nations' spiritual wealth. Representing the citizenry, they act as proof of a population's collective accomplishment. But as Duncan also makes clear, the "Great Artist" was a category invented by the new discipline of art history, which rescued individual artists from obscurity and provided them with appropriate biographies.[46] By identifying individual craftsmen and researching their pasts, antique collectors were following in this tradition, transforming the makers of their furniture from obscure workers into named and celebrated artists.

Another kind of association was so fundamental to the antique market that few connoisseurs ever commented on it: the requirement that for an antique to be truly valuable it must be "American." Stock problems were inherent in the antique business, and many dealers included European, especially English, antiques among their wares. By the 1930s America was flooded with English antiques. An article in the *Antiquarian* reported that "a number of English dealers, both wholesale and retail, have established themselves in this country. . . . They import large quantities of English antiques and find a ready sale for them."[47] For many Americans who wanted to furnish their homes with elegant old things, English antiques could be preferable to American. Not only were they often more ornate, but they were also directly tied to a long tradition of European artistic accomplishment, a history no American suggested the young country could match. But while the market for English antiques remained steady, few sold for the high prices achieved in the Reifsnyder or Flayderman sales. English antiques simply did not have the kind of patriotic associations that American pieces did. They were valued as objects of elegance and style, but not as national treasures.

This enthusiasm for American furniture undermined connoisseurs' claims that the market was based on aesthetics and not associations. No contemporary writer exposed the market's contradictions with greater zeal than the novelist Kenneth L. Roberts. In his 1928 book *Antiquamania*, Roberts poked fun at those who tried to justify higher prices for American-made furniture in a satiric dialogue in which a seemingly clearheaded father tries to explain the difference between English and American Chippendale furniture to his son.

Rudolph: What is the difference, Father?

Father: Several hundred dollars a chair, my boy.

Rudolph: No, I mean what is there about an American Chippendale chair that makes it more valuable than an English Chippendale chair? I suppose it is because a well-known American sat in it.

Father: Do not, I beg of you, Rudolph, make the mistake of thinking that sentiment or association has a market value. Some people are foolish enough to buy a chair because George Washington sat in it, but you can take it from me that this fact doesn't add a cent to the value of a chair.

Rudolph: Then why is it, Father that American Chippendale is worth more than English Chippendale? . . . Was it because American chairs were more beautifully made than English chairs?

Father: No, my son. The English chairs were usually more elaborate and ornate . . .

Rudolph: How is it that one tells the difference between an American and an English Chippendale chair?

Father: Well, it's one of the things that one learns by experience. . . . Nobody can tell the difference by just looking at them.

Rudolph: Then an American Chippendale chair isn't more beautiful or better built than an English Chippendale chair, but is more valuable because it was made in America.

Father: That is it exactly, my child . . .

Rudolph: But you said that sentiment and association have no market value![48]

Roberts identified the key issues that made higher prices for American antiques so problematic—the lack of an aesthetic explanation, the denial of associative values, and the difficulty in distinguishing between English and American designs. Antique collectors knew that early American cabinetry was largely derivative, but Roberts's choice of Chippendale furniture was particularly apt since eighteenth-century pattern books allowed America's best cabinetmakers to nearly replicate English designs. Roberts's point was simple: those who valued American Chippendale over its English predecessor were simply embracing the patriotic associations of American-made goods.

The gulf in price between American and English antiques was evidence that patriotism was part of the appeal for collectors, who valued the fact that these were American-made goods, and dealers, who charged accordingly. But the preference for American antiques was also evidence of the persistence of associations and their importance in constructing value in an antique. Certainly associations had changed from the earlier practice of establishing an antique's American identity through patterns of use and ownership. The new associations made Americanness an act of construction and creation, a natural response to the idea of the antique as an aesthetic object. If what gave an antique its value was its appearance, then would not the buyer want to know more about the individual responsible for devising and executing its design? Twentieth-century connoisseurship has largely been a response to this focus on construction. Connoisseurs have used specialized knowledge to identify who made an object, when he or she did so, and where. Uncovering this fundamental information revolutionized the antique industry and allowed collectors to place objects in both space and time, but it also transformed the very nature of antiques as historic objects. No longer witnesses to the past, able to bridge time through their extended history of use, antiques became inextricably linked to a specific, and relatively short, moment in time: the moment of their creation.

The Trials of Being a Collector

As the editor of *Antiques*, Homer Eaton Keyes kept up with auction prices, studied connoisseurship, and followed important collecting trends. But when asked about the value of specific antiques, his response was purposely vague. "A good many questions as to the value of privately owned articles boasting a greater or less degree of age come to *Antiques*," he told his readers. "Unfortunately it is impossible to give, in such cases, any satisfactory answer. Few antiques possess what may be called intrinsic value. They're worth what they will bring."[49] Keyes went on to suggest that readers interested in finding out what their treasures were worth either put them up for sale or, if warranted, hire a qualified appraiser.

If it was hard for an expert like Keyes to make a commitment about price, it was even harder for the hobbyist to navigate the antique market. For those who were not familiar with what connoisseurs considered the perfect curve of a cabriole leg, dramatic price disparities, like the ones Keyes described in his February 1930 column in *Antiques*, made the market difficult to understand. How would the average customer know quality? Would his aesthetic choices expose ignorance or confirm taste? What could he do to become a true connoisseur? The new aesthetic antique, while profitable for the dealer, was in many ways hard on the buyer. Not only did it require collectors to educate themselves in the new aesthetic canons, but as prices climbed, every purchasing decision became one of serious financial risk. Collectors coped as best they could, placing themselves in the hands of reputable dealers, studying auction reports, and comparing prices. More intrepid collectors tried to circumvent dealers altogether and purchase directly from New England's old families. But collectors' attempts to steer their way through the market had a profound impact on the nature of antiquing itself. As many collectors focused their efforts on locating bargains and ensuring the value of their purchases, antiquing started to look less like an encounter with the past and more like a consumer experience.

For most antique collectors, navigating the marketplace required a significant amount of self-education. The Philadelphia collector Phoebe Phillips Prime assembled twenty-three scrapbooks of clippings of newspaper articles, antique dealers' advertisements, and exhibition catalogs in her effort to catalog eighteenth-century craftsmen in her region. Organized by object category, time period, and form, the results would have allowed her to compare similar objects, identify stylistic traits, and make aesthetic judgments.[50] For the typical collector, popular antique journals, auction catalogs, and collecting manuals were an important source of information. But, as many acknowledged, there was no substitute for the actual experience of seeing, examining, and appreciating the real thing. Obtaining such experience, however, could be quite difficult. Collectors could certainly frequent the many museums that were beginning to feature American decorative arts. Indeed, Charles Over Cornelius, a curator at the Metropolitan Museum of Art, believed that museums should explicitly serve collectors by exhibiting objects that would help them establish proper standards of judgment.[51] But museums were limited in the sense that they displayed only the most illustrious examples. For most antique collectors, the "museum piece" far exceeded anything they could ever hope to acquire. For this reason, shopping represented a kind of consumer research for novice collectors. Frequent trips to antique shops allowed them to compare wares, track prices, and apply discrimination. The practice was so widespread that dealers complained frequently of customers trying to take advantage of their expertise. "The knowledge of antiques cannot be absorbed through the pores," admonished dealer Wilton Lackaye in an article for *American Collector*. "Do not expect a dealer no matter how willing he may be, to tell you in fifteen minutes what it has taken him fifteen years to learn."[52] Israel

Sack seemed to agree. In a full-page advertisement in *Antiques* he set out several rules for collectors, among them "Never try to beat an antique dealer," and "Treat the dealer right and be treated right in return."[53]

Consumers found their end of the transaction even harder to bear. Indeed, antique buyers were placed in a difficult relationship with dealers, who had the advantage of handling a vast number of individual pieces, knowing where they came from, and inspecting them at leisure. The result was that dealers were in a position of power. Although large auction houses such as Sotheby's and Christie's dominate the market today, in the early twentieth century individual antique dealers were far more powerful. New York–based auctioneers, such as Anderson Galleries, hosted important sales and achieved record prices, but most antiques, even those of the rarest quality, were sold through individual dealers who cultivated potential buyers and set prices based on their experience of what the market would bear. In many ways, setting prices was a creative act. A high price tag could reinforce an object's rarity. For his part, Israel Sack prized the nickname "Crazy Sack" given to him by other Boston dealers for the high prices he paid and the even higher prices he charged.[54] High prices helped Sack set his goods apart and establish his reputation as a premier dealer. At the same time, a low price could damn an object, and collecting manuals often warned collectors to be wary of bargain prices, which might indicate inferior quality, poor construction, or worse yet, forgery. "Another thing to be studied is price," advised antique author Walter Dyer. "If this is too low, there is ground for suspicion. The dealer knows he can get a good sum for a genuine antique, and a low price is the opposite of a guarantee."[55] Dyer went on to say that while antique prices were far from fixed, a familiarity with market prices would allow the buyer to judge not only the deal, but also the article itself.

With the rising popularity of cars, some collectors tried to subvert the dealer by traveling to small rural shops and knocking on the doors of private residences (figures 4 and 5). Collecting manuals of the time sometimes encouraged such behavior, relating stories of wonderful treasures to be found on country roads. In his book *The Lure of the Antique*, Walter Dyer included a photograph of a typical colonial house with the caption "When you are on the hunt for old China or furniture in the country, be on the look-out for houses like this."[56] Caroline Woolsey Ferriday, whose antiques are preserved in the Bellamy-Ferriday House Museum in

Figure 4. Photographer Mary Harrod Northend (1850–1926) posed this scene of an intrepid antique collector about to purchase a silver teapot from a private home. Photograph courtesy of the Winterthur Library: Joseph Downs Collection of Manuscripts and Printed Ephemera.

Figure 5. Antique authorities Robert and Elizabeth Shackleton advised fellow collectors to search the porches of rural homes like this one for old chairs and other finds. From Robert and Elizabeth Shackleton, *The Quest of the Colonial* (Philadelphia: Penn Publishing, 1923).

Bethlehem, Connecticut, began her collecting career in this fashion. In an inventory of her collections she reported owning a "very handsome Spanish-foot roundabout" purchased off a rural porch "after much persuasion and the exchange of $15.00." On another occasion, she bought a bible box from a neighbor just "up the street."[57] Success could be elusive, however. As early as 1910, Dyer admitted that it was pretty hard to find things by going door-to-door, but maintained that the "casual drive through the country" was still "the pleasantest way to collect."[58]

Door-to-door collecting was not without its perils. As the reports of auction prices trickled down to rural communities, collectors sometimes found themselves facing belligerent owners. Fearful of urban pickers and confident of the inherent value of their possessions, these emboldened owners often demanded exorbitant prices, even if their "antiques" fell into the category that elite collectors labeled "old junk." At times, the situation was so bad that the prices advertised in swanky urban shops began to look like bargains. One rural New England collector said that she preferred to do business with urban antique dealers because their knowledge of the market meant that they would not confuse "old" with "expensive" or "rare":

> A city dealer is apt to have a fairer evaluation of his wares than many a farmer in the country, who often has the unshaken idea that every old thing is very valuable, and that "people of means"—a favorite expression hereabouts—are willing to pay any price. To twice tell the tale, there is my little old lady out on the hills, who still believes in her mistaken mine of wealth, that ancient, unpolished highboy. And once I hurried off without my lunch to see a treasure of an old desk, and found a rickety, jiggly soft-wood thing, painted a bright red, with one twisted willow-pull still on it, so broken that it was fit for nothing else than the wood pile, and all the modest owner wanted was $75.00!
>
> I could go on unendingly: the old "flow blue" [china] that a farmer declared was over 250 years old—had, in fact, "come over in the Mayflower"; that time in the unsuspecting days of my youth, when an honest husbandman sold me a quite modern Windsor chair for more than it had cost when it left its recent furniture-shop home; an uninteresting, scrolled, scrawled, late-empire sofa for which a country woman wanted, as I remember the price, something like its weight in gold.[59]

Whether these farmers and rural sellers knew what their things were worth or were indeed so ignorant of the market that they assumed impossibly high values, their willingness to demand good prices demonstrates that a profound transformation had taken place: antiques had become commodities. Collectors had colonized the countryside, and no place was safe from market transactions. Even those who did not frequent antique shops, auctions, or dealer shows could not ignore the knock on their door, the knock imploring them to enter the market.

The inescapability of the market had profound consequences for dealers and collectors alike. Part of the attraction of antiques was that they were seen as symbols of a purer time in America's past, a time before industrialization and urbanization had ushered in an era of corruption and greed. But as antiques became commodities and the countryside became a marketplace, nothing could remain pure. By the 1920s, collecting manuals regularly cautioned antique buyers to be wary of rural finds. Apocryphal stories about rural tricksters abounded. One such tale involved a collector who happened upon an old farm where a cat was drinking milk out of a china bowl, which the collector recognized as a piece of valuable Staffordshire. He knocked on the door and, hoping to acquire the bowl without alerting the farmer to its value, asked if he could purchase the cat. The farmer quickly agreed and the collector followed by saying that he should take the bowl as well, so that the cat would have something familiar. "If I give you that bowl, how will I sell my cats?" asked the crafty farmer as he collected his money and handed the duped collector his new cat.[60] In another story, a farmer placed newly crafted Windsor chairs on his porch. He never claimed to own antiques, but urban collectors, assuming that rural origins guaranteed authenticity, offered handsome sums for the chairs. A variation on this story recounted an elaborate scheme to sell reproduction china by planting it in the kitchen of farmers who lured unsuspecting collectors into their homes with the advertisement of fresh eggs for sale.[61] Whether or not such tales were true, their believability was rooted in real economic conditions. New England farmers had been in financial distress since the late 1880s, when competition from large-scale agricultural production in the west began to make New England's small, rocky farms almost unprofitable. If the countryside was in need of cash, it would be corruptible. But what made this corruption so ironic was the source. It was the search for antiques, symbols of purity and timeless values, that brought the countryside to moral ruin and created a new kind of stereotype: the rural confidence man.

Faked, Forged, and Spurious

Corruption also extended to the objects themselves, as the many stories of fakes and forgeries show. Huldah Wellington Spaulding told a typical story set in her small Cape Cod antique shop. On a December afternoon, two women pulled up to Spaulding's shop in their car. One of them explained that they were in "serious financial straits and compelled to part with some of their dearest possessions," and they offered Spaulding a maple low chest with duck feet and a Georgian mirror, both of which she gladly purchased for $250. Inspecting the pieces the next morning, Spaulding and her business associate discovered they were fakes. In the low chest she found modern nails concealed behind wooden pegs. The mirror contained old glass, but its entire frame was reproduced. "We were a couple of greenhorns," Spaulding admitted. "But it might have happened at any time to any dealer, as the woman had her story perfected in a big way, and we were thoroughly impressed by her evident sincerity and apparent earnestness."[62]

Perhaps the most publicized antique scandal in the early years of the market centered on the sale of Oriental Lowestoft china. Commonly confused with English ceramics manufactured in Lowestoft (hence the popular name), Oriental Lowestoft was manufactured in China during the eighteenth and nineteenth centuries. Painted with coats of arms, religious symbols, ships, and other designs, it was intended for British and American markets. By the 1920s, pieces painted with American designs had become highly desirable among collectors and large services nearly impossible to find. But in 1930 a Mrs. Clementine Briggs Doran of Holyoke, Massachusetts, and William J. Cooke of Philadelphia sold a 232-piece service painted with the New York State crest, and reputedly passed down in the Van Rensselaer family, to Edward F. Cloran, a Boston art and antique dealer. Cloran promptly sold the set to another Boston dealer, Clinton I. Nash, for $51,226, or about $220 a dish. According to popular accounts, the fraudulent china escaped detection until dealer and collector Edward Augustus Crowninshield got a look at it. "Running his fingers over the 'Van Rensselaer' plates he announced at once that they 'didn't feel right.'" Closer inspection proved that the service was plain porcelain, painted over the glaze and sanded to produce the appropriate texture. The case made the national press, resulted in criminal charges, and lead to the discovery of a man *Time* magazine characterized as "the traditional sinister oriental" of crime fiction—a Japanese porcelain repairer who produced the set in his Manhattan shop.[63]

For most antique buyers, affairs like the Van Rensselaer Lowestoft forgery reinforced what they already knew. Rising prices provided ample incentive for forgers to supply an expanding market. Indeed, the forgery trade was so widespread that counterfeiters' shops flourished in London,

Paris, Florence, Rome, and Dublin, some manufacturing specifically for the American market.[64] Forged antiques fell into three general categories. Wholesale copies, made out of either old or new wood, were the rarest. They were the most difficult to produce, requiring highly skilled craftsmen and a detailed knowledge of historic styles. More common were embellished originals, genuine antiques made more expensive by the addition of inlay or carvings. Walter A. Dyer cautioned his readers about many of the most common of these scams. Forgers, he said, would add hoods to flat-top high chests, carve sunburst patterns on a drawer, pierce the splats of plain chairs, and manufacture pie-crust tables out of simple tilt-top models by carving their edges.[65] Finally, there was the widespread practice of constructing whole antiques out of old parts. The collector C. R. Clifford suspected such a scam when he learned that a New York dealer had purchased a collection of what he described as "firewood, —chair backs, broken seats, table legs, some good examples of thirty-inch mahogany table tops . . . escutcheons, eighteenth-century brass handles and mounts" from a Vermont barn.[66] Because assemblages and embellished antiques contained real parts, many collectors referred to such creations as "spurious antiques," a label that recognized their historic origins, yet still condemned their manufacture.

For their part, forgers perfected a host of special skills. They learned how to create the appearance of aged wood by burying newly constructed pieces in backyard lime pits and manure piles, masking fresh cuts with potash, ammonia, and other chemical treatments, sanding down the backs of chair feet to simulate wear, and counterfeiting wormholes with specially crafted tools.[67] Many dealers and collectors professed to see through such tricks with ease. Charles Woolsey Lyon remembered discovering a clearly faked antique desk on display in a competitor's front window. "I stood there and I laughed until I guess everybody passing thought I was crazy. It had been gone over with a triangular stamp to fake worm-holes, and there they were—the neatest worm-holes you ever saw—and all in groups of three.[68]

Dealers did have an edge when it came to exposing fakes. Handling so many antiques gave them an eye for a historical ornament, improper woods, and modern finishes. Those with experience in cabinetry and woodworking had an even bigger advantage. They knew the way aged wood moved and they could recognize the marks of modern tools. But beginning antique buyers had no such protections. Collecting manuals and magazines could alert them to the existence of fakes or teach them about forgery techniques, but the kind of hands-on experience necessary to avoid deception would only come with experience and often costly mistakes. Surprisingly, popular antique writers showed little sympathy for those taken in by the forger. Since antique buying was seen as an expression of discernment and taste, those who purchased spurious pieces were often chastised for their lack of knowledge. "The worse faker is not the maker or the dealer in fakes," complained Wallace Nutting; "He is the person who has spurious furniture in his house and allows his friends to think it genuine." Illustrating his point with the story of a New York magnate who misrepresented his birch furniture as mahogany, Nutting concluded that the man deserved reproach whether or not the deception was intentional: "If he knew it nobody could respect his character. If he did not know it, nobody could respect his capacity."[69]

Nutting's comments are a testament to the twentieth century's contempt for spurious antiques and the individuals who owned them. But antique owners did not always feel that way. Before the development of the antique art market, the practice of altering historic objects was frequent and open. Dealers scraped and refinished furniture to meet market expectations, old house enthusiasts improved their homes by installing fanlights, columns, and other decorative features, and even serious collectors created new antiques out of old parts. One such collector was Walter Hosmer. Born in the 1830s, Hosmer lived most of his life in Hartford, Connecticut. By all accounts, he was a private man, variously labeled as "mysterious," "silent," or simply a "hermit." He was also an avid collector, known for his extensive inventory and cabinetry skills. Irving Lyon featured many of Hosmer's pieces in his *Colonial Furniture of New England.* Still, Hosmer, an upholsterer by trade, was never beyond manufacturing new antiques, many of which were assumed to be authentic. The Boston collector Eugene Bolles, who purchased antiques from Hosmer, is reported to have asked, "What's the damned cuss making now?"[70]

A 1915 account book of Ernest C. Molinder, a cabinetmaker who repaired antiques for Springfield, Massachusetts, antique dealer Edgar E. Mead and his customers, reveals that deliberatively manipulative practices extended into the twentieth century. The book shows that Molinder regularly altered and embellished antiques for his boss. A record dated

April 7 reads, "repairing and inlaying of 1 cherriton [Sheraton] 4 leged [legged] leaf table." Another describes "making a clock case into a medecin cobber [medicine cupboard]" As a dealer, Mead could have passed off Molinder's creations as the real thing. But Molinder did not reserve his skills for his employer; he also completed similarly invasive work at the direction of the shop's private customers. The records show that a Mrs. A. J. Perkins had Molinder lengthen the legs of a slat-back chair. Another customer's request was more complicated: she asked Molinder to remake a plain table into a tilt-top table. The job took eleven hours and included the construction of new wood turnings.[71]

Such deliberate work would not have lived up to the standards of the new antique collectors who valued authenticity of construction as integral to an object's aesthetic value, but nineteenth-century consumers were much more accepting. As Rodris Roth and Christopher Monkhouse have demonstrated, popular opinion invested even obviously engineered objects, such as chairs manufactured from old spinning wheel parts or modern furniture in the style of exaggerated period designs, with historic value.[72] Why did nineteenth-century antique owners tolerate such manipulation? Why did it later become such an anathema? The answer lies in the new aesthetic market, which tied an antique's value to the object's physical being. When early consumers displayed antiques for their historical associations, manipulation was easy to accept. An old high chest's ability to conjure up the charm and beauty of yesteryear was hardly affected by an individual's decision to add decorative finials. Nor would a broken chair lose its status as a family heirloom if its owner commissioned new legs. Indeed, such objects could be altered or "improved" and still maintain their associative functions. But when collectors began to value antiques primarily as aesthetic objects, toleration vanished. Because appearances mattered, they could no longer be manipulated. Alterations, additions, or improvements compromised the antique's integrity as a coherent artistic expression. They undermined the antique's physical structure, and with it, its primary value.

Ideas about aesthetic quality and physical integrity collided when it came to the question of how the consequences of an antique's age should be treated. Should a collector scrape and resurface worn finishes to reveal the antique's beauty, or should he maintain its physical integrity, leaving it, as the saying went, "in the rough?" The problem was a complicated one. On the one hand, blemishes, dents, and decaying finishes compromised the antique's aesthetic quality. When eighteenth- and nineteenth-century craftsmen produced their wares, they did not expect that an owner would kick the object and smudge it with dirt before placing it in his parlor. But a hundred years of use could produce just such a battered effect. For this reason, early twentieth-century collectors often "did over" their antiques. Indeed, when Fred Tuck met the young Israel Sack at a Boston auction around 1905, he asked the cabinetmaker and nascent dealer to scrape several corner cupboards and "put them in good repair."[73] According to Sack, Henry Ford and Henry Francis du Pont also refinished antiques early in their collecting careers.[74] For collectors interested in aesthetic quality, refinishing made a lot of sense. A good finish would show off the craftsman's design by directing the viewer's attention to the object's lines rather than its surface. But by the late 1920s collectors tended to shun the practice. "You see that hard wood with the patina," Israel Sack recalled chastising Ford. "That takes 150 years of natural wear. . . . If you take that and plane it . . . neither you nor your children, nor your grandchildren, can afford to wait 150 years for that patina to grow back again."[75] The decision to preserve original patina might seem like an aesthetic one, but it had important economic consequences as well. Not only was it harder to conceal spurious "improvements" on unrefinished furniture, but maintaining an original finish also protected the object's rarity, and thus its economic value.[76]

The idea of the antique as aesthetic object made such practices particularly important. If a piece of furniture was valued primarily for its appearance and not its age, would not a modern copy be just as good? Many collectors grappled with that very question. Certainly much of the furniture marketed as "traditional" bore very little resemblance to real antiques. Among the more extreme examples was the Erskine-Danforth corporation's "ladder-back bed," a design that whimsically transformed chair backs into headboards, but many other pieces of mass-marketed furniture simply did not stay true to form.[77] It was very difficult to adapt traditional designs to modern factories that used powerful machines, glues, and molded woods to craft their products.[78] Beginning in 1917, Wallace Nutting attempted to capitalize on the popularity of antiques by making reproduction furniture. But as Thomas Denenberg has argued, the profitability of the venture was undermined by Nutting's allegiance to Arts and Crafts principles, which made it difficult for him to cut corners, even though he necessarily adopted modern machinery and production methods right from the start.[79] *Antiques* made no apologies for including reproduction furniture makers among its advertisers, claiming that those who purchased faithful copies were cultivating a taste for the real thing.[80] Dependent on advertising revenues for survival, the magazine derived obvious economic benefit from finding beauty in newly constructed wares, but for antique dealers high-end, handcrafted reproductions could be ruinous. Why would collectors pay exorbitant sums in the name of rarity when a newly made piece could be just as aesthetically pleasing? Valuing patina was the solution to their problem. In one sweep, it maintained the importance of an antique's visual character over perceived historic associations while at the same time preserving its rarity and denying reproducibility. It was much more than an aesthetic preference. Simply put, it was economic.

Geographies of the Antique

The antique market had an important effect on the way people cared for and thought about antiques, but purchasing patterns and supply systems also affected the relationship between region and trade. During the early years, antiquing tended to reinforce the idea of New England as a distinctly historical place, especially as dealers mined the countryside for more examples of early American furniture to sell. But the antique trade also brought about the exporting of many of New England's historical resources to other regions, blurring the lines between New England's heritage and the nation's. New England residents began to cultivate their historic resources: antiquers scrounged dusty attics, investigated old barns, and knocked on farmhouse doors, all in an effort to bring more wares to market. But the process of making New England an antiques center did not stop at its borders. Indeed, New Englanders did not hesitate to augment their antique supply with southern imports. In 1892, Fred Tuck, the Maine dealer who conscientiously cultivated regional associations by recreating an old-time New England kitchen in his shop, made his first trip south. Realizing he could not satisfy the demand for mahogany sideboards by relying on local stock, he traveled south of the Mason-Dixon line to replenish his wares.[81] He reported the trip as a success and began making regular winter visits south to look for new stock. Tuck recognized regional differences in the materials he found in the South. He believed the furniture to be smaller, an asset for owners of modern homes. But Tuck did not specifically market his new finds as "Southern," nor do his diaries suggest that he deceitfully labeled them "New England." These unidentified southern imports simply became part of New England's antique supply, enhancing the region's reputation as a historic place.

New England's early success in branding itself as a region rich in history and antiques is particularly striking when considered against the South's failure to accomplish the same. While dealers such as Tuck consciously mined southern communities, a process that points to the availability of southern antiques, the region did not develop the reputation of an area with its own tradition of early American furniture construction. Typical was a 1925 article in *Antiques* describing a gateleg table as "rare" because of its southern origins.[82] Southern antique businesses did exist, especially in Charleston, South Carolina, which in 1931 had developed the country's first historic zoning ordinance and was consciously marketing its historic character to the tourist industry. Indeed, Charleston businesses had enough customers that dealers supplemented local wares by importing antiques from England, in the same manner as their northern competitors.[83] Even so, the Metropolitan Museum's American Wing did not represent Charleston's antiques and architecture in its period displays, a fact that angered many of the city's elite.[84] At the same time, avid antique collectors and scholars regularly denigrated the South's contributions to the decorative arts. As late as 1949, American Wing curator Joseph Downs claimed that "little of artistic merit was made south of Baltimore."[85] Downs made his comments at the first Williamsburg Antiques and Decorations Forum, a conference of antique collectors and curators sponsored by Colonial Williamsburg and *Antiques*. Downs's remarks made a stir, especially since the conference was held in Virginia, and they eventually led to the reconsideration of the South's contribution to early American furnishings, the showcasing of southern antiques at the 1952 Williamsburg Forum, and the opening of the Museum of Early Southern Decorative Arts in 1965.[86] Such displays of southern antiques were important to the region's ability to claim an artistic heritage, but what makes them particularly notable is just how late they were in coming. Collectors celebrated antiques produced

Having just received a large collection of New England antiques, we have marked everything at a low price for the holiday season to warrant a quantity business. Over 1,000 hooked rugs from which to make a selection.

We urge your attendance as early as possible while the greatest values are available.

THE NEW ENGLAND ATTIC

25 East 55th Street
NEW YORK CITY

Figure 6. As this advertisement shows, dealers marketed New England antiques to New York buyers. *The Magazine Antiques,* December 1929, 538.

in New England and the mid-Atlantic for half a century before considering their southern counterparts.

While New England boasted one of the first developed antique markets, dealers found the regional market restricting, especially as they looked to cultivate a larger customer base. National antique publications, especially *Antiques*, helped dealers overcome the limits of a New England market.[87] From its inception, *Antiques* recognized the ability of print media to nationalize the trade. Always close to the market, the magazine first set up shop in Boston, a natural choice given the city's prominence in the American antiques world, but from the beginning, editor Homer Eaton Keyes recognized the existence of a larger national market. For this reason, the first issue opened with an apology and a promise: "After such an array of brave words and fair promises, it may yet not be surprising if a brother rises from the rear row and remarks that he is pained to detect in this first number an unduly dominate aroma of cod fish—this being his not altogether subtle way of suggesting that early New England concerns occupy a rather disproportionate amount of space in these pages. Probably the brother is right. But *Antiques*, merely because it happens to be published in Boston, has no intention of sticking immovably to New England."[88]

Subsequent issues did engage a more diverse subject matter, but more important than the magazine's coverage was its ability to connect dealers to distant markets. In many ways, *Antiques* functioned as a proto-eBay. Shop owners used advertisements to publish lists of their wares, customers wrote in with their wants, and dealers responded with photographs or home deliveries. In a call for advertisers, *Antiques* made its power clear. The ad showed an outline of the nation blanketed by a copy of the magazine; the caption read, "In every large city and in every small town, from the Atlantic to the Pacific, from Gulf to Canadian border, those who buy antiques read *Antiques*."[89] The implications were clear. For the antique market to grow, dealers needed to break down geographical barriers and cultivate a national audience.

Antiques moved to new offices in New York City, on Fourth Avenue, in 1929. Prominent dealers also relocated to the city. Israel Sack established his first New York City store at 383 Madison Avenue in 1928, moving the very next year to a new location on East 57th Street between Fifth and Madison. Sack's move to New York corresponded with a change in his advertising practices. After leaving Boston, he began to use the phrase "specialist in American antiques" to describe his business; previously he had most often represented himself as an expert in "old New England furniture."[90] With the popularity of antiques expanding and New England caught in a recession, New York was a logical move. It gave dealers access to the fine art market and existing auction houses as well as to the city's wealthy residents and visitors (figure 6).

The shift in the market and the new focus on cultivating customers outside of the region also meant that New England began exporting its historic treasures. "There is something fascinating and at the same time bewildering about the movement of antiques," J. Herbert Smythe Jr., the editor of *Antiques Dealer*, wrote in 1951. "We recently saw a van load of antiques in a small cross-roads town in Georgia on its way south or west. The trailer truck carried Massachusetts license plates. We witnessed the unloading of another van load of antiques in the Pennsylvania Dutch country, and learned that these are items that had been purchased in Maine and Vermont, and that they would ultimately be bought by dealers in New York, Philadelphia, Washington and Richmond."[91]

Encouraging such movement, museums in the Midwest and West began establishing their own antique displays. Among public museums were the Art Institute of Chicago, the Detroit Institute of Arts, the Nelson-Atkins Museum in Kansas City, and the City Art Museum of St. Louis, as well as individually funded museums such as the one established by oil heiress Ima Hogg at her home, Bayou Bend, in Houston, Texas. These developing institutions purchased antiques not because they wanted to emulate an eastern phenomenon, but because they saw antiques as a cultural heritage that belonged to the nation as a whole.

If New Englanders protested the dispersion of their ancient furnishings, little record of it exists. More common were complaints about the removal of historic interiors for reconstruction in museum displays. When the Metropolitan Museum of Art established the American Wing, William Sumner Appleton, founder of the Society for the Preservation of New England Antiquities (now Historic New England), protested museum officials' decision to use an interior removed from a 1740 Georgian-style house built in Portsmouth, New Hampshire, for the Jaffrey family. The house was in serious disrepair and enjoyed little likelihood of being "saved," but Appleton saw its removal as a kind of cultural poaching, the historic treasures of New England being removed from their original contexts.[92] Appleton similarly protested when, in 1937, Israel Sack and Leon David, another Boston antique dealer, sold The Lindens, a Georgian-style house in Danvers, Massachusetts, built in 1754 for the Tory merchant Robert Hooper, to the Morris family of Washington, D.C. George Maurice Morris was a Washington lawyer, and his wife, Miriam, was an avid antique collector who made several donations to the Smithsonian's history displays. The Morrises had planned on building a replica of an early American mansion on their property on Kalorama Road in the city's Northwest Quadrant, but during the Great Depression historic originals became so inexpensive that the idea of dismantling and moving one such building from its New England home and reconstructing it in Washington suddenly became practical. David and Sack had already sold the interior woodwork from the house's parlor to the Nelson-Atkins Museum before selling the rest of the building to the Morrises for $12,500. In response to Appleton's charge that the Morrises were diminishing the building's historic value with the move (to their credit, the Morrises hired an expert—Colonial Williamsburg's resident architect, Walter Mayo Macomber—to supervise the process), the couple offered to sell the house for their purchase price to anyone who would restore it in situ. But the building was located in a rundown industrial neighborhood in Danvers, and there were no takers.[93] While collectors such as the Morrises might face criticism for relocating an early New England home, disapproval rarely surfaced in the case of antiques leaving the region. Antiquarians and preservationists who valued New England's historic resources had already come to see antiques as consumer objects, subject to the market's demand that they be geographical mobile.

Marketing History

The antique market was not the only way early twentieth-century New Englanders engaged the past. With the Colonial Revival still going strong, they joined patriotic and familial societies, restored historic houses, masterminded civic celebrations to honor important community anniversaries, wrote local histories, and researched old newspapers and legal records. Many also collected outside of the antique market, forsaking expensive carved chests for primitive lighting devices or obsolete tools. Even though creative individuals explored history according to their own passions and preferences, the development of the antiques art market transformed the way many Americans experienced the past. Artifacts once valued only for local or family associations had become aesthetic objects. The shape of a high chest's leg or the quality of its carvings suddenly made the difference between the piece being celebrated as a national treasure or left to obscurity in a family parlor. Learning to navigate this confusing world occupied many collectors as they trained themselves to distinguish what Albert Sack, the son of Israel Sack, would later call "good, better, best."[94]

At the same time antiques became aesthetic objects, their value as commodities exploded. Perceptions of artistic quality provided many collectors with the justification for spending tens of thousands of dollars on a single object. But the process of turning antiques into commodities was not a simple one. Antiques had to be discovered, severed from their local environment, and set loose in the market, a procedure that required a veritable army of pickers, dealers, and private collectors ready to make the case for their artistic accomplishment. In many ways, it was a radical procedure, divorcing artifacts from their historical context and releasing them to the nation. But it is a legacy that remains with us today. Who can live with the family china or grandmother's silver without at some point wondering, "What is it worth?"

2
The Jewish Dealer
Antiques, Acculturation, and Aesthetics

*I*srael Sack arrived at Ellis Island in 1903. He was barely twenty years old at the time, but his life was already marked by a willingness to reinvent tradition. Born to a fairly prosperous Jewish family in Kovno, Russia (now Kaunas, Lithuania), he studied the Bible and the Talmud and prepared to become a merchant like his father. But he also grew up under the oppressive rule of Russia's Czar Nicholas. Eager to break free and avoid the draft, he apprenticed himself to a cabinetmaker at age fourteen. The work compromised his family's social status, but Sack reasoned that tools were a universal language and would provide him with the skills to emigrate. He was right. At eighteen, he contracted with a local agent who specialized in smuggling Lithuanians into Germany. The trip was perilous. Russian officials nearly caught Sack as his party camped for the night in an abandoned barn, but he managed to tunnel his way out and escape into the night before Russian authorities broke down the door.[1]

Arriving in Boston after a year spent in London, Sack quickly found a job working in a cabinet shop on Charles Street. In Russia and London he had built new furniture, but on Charles Street he found a whole other industry at work—the antique industry. Fueled by the invention of the antique as an aesthetic object, Boston's antique business was on the rise. The 1904 Boston City Directory shows only three self-declared "antique" shops, but by 1918 the number had jumped to twenty-eight, and by 1924 to forty-seven.[2] These figures actually belie the extent of the industry's growth, since many antique retailers (Sack's new boss included) identified themselves as cabinetmakers, furniture dealers, and even junk men.

As a business, antiquing extended its reach beyond the middle- and upper-class collectors who participated as hobbyists to include ambitious immigrants with their own American dreams. Indeed, Sack was not alone as an immigrant Jewish dealer in the antique trade. Many New England antique dealers, especially in the early years, were also Jewish immigrants. Sack's Boston competitors included Leon David, an Austrian immigrant who started out in the furniture repair business; Joseph Epstein, a Russian immigrant who came to antiquing from the junk trade; Philip Flayderman, the dealer whose 1929 auction drew record prices and who himself was born in Russia; Flayderman's partner, Hyman Kaufman, also a Russian immigrant; Samuel Tishler, from Germany; Joseph Grossman, from Lithuania; and David Jacobs, who came to Boston from Russia's Polish territories in 1902.[3] New York City saw a similar concentration of Jewish dealers that included the legendary firm of Ginsburg & Levy, founded in 1901 by John Ginsburg and Isaac Levy, two junk dealers from Manhattan's Lower East Side.[4] While many histories of antiquing emphasize the important role of early collectors in locating and identifying aesthetically accomplished antiques, little has been said about Jewish dealers' contributions. In many ways, Jewish dealers are easy to dismiss. Already socially and economically far removed from the collecting public, they were further ostracized because of their status as dealers, workers who provided the day-to-day labor in the antique trade but could not claim permanent ownership of the objects they handled. Indeed, while many early collectors' names are enshrined in the museums they endowed, dealers are rarely recognized for finding rare pieces. But no history of antique collecting can afford to ignore Jewish dealers. Working at the very foundation of the market, they provided the trade's stock. Adaptable to the new language of aesthetics, they located many important pieces, separated commonplace examples from the extraordinary, and packaged and marketed them for sale. Finding, classifying, and distributing historic objects, Jewish dealers were important collaborators in the invention of the antique.

Becoming Americans

Why did Jewish immigrants choose to enter the antique trade? In a 1926 article in the *Antiquarian*, "Yankee" dealer Frank J. Lawton postulated the existence of a "subtle racial affinity" between Jews and early American craftsmanship, claiming that "nowhere in the world have the teachings of the Patriarchs been promulgated more literally and devotedly than on Pilgrim soil."[5] As romantic as Lawton's racially charged theory was, Jewish dealers' affinity for American antiques can more easily be explained by what the business could do for them. As scholars of American multiculturalism have noted, Jewish immigrants embraced American culture with ferocity. Unlike other eastern European migrants, Jews came to the United States with the intention of staying. According to Roger Daniels, only about 5 percent of eastern European Jewish emigrants returned to Europe, compared with return rates of 20 percent for Lithuanians as a whole, 36 percent for Slovaks, 66 percent for Romanians, and 87 percent for several Balkan groups.[6] This desire to make their American lives permanent meant that Jews sought not just economic stability, but status and acculturation. By manipulating middle-class standards of refinement, behavior, and dress, Jewish migrants achieved an important measure of assimilation, one that would separate them both from new arrivals and from other immigrant groups.[7]

The world of objects offered a natural avenue for Jews to obtain the status they sought. Eastern European migration coincided with a huge expansion in the material abundance of America. As Andrew Heinze has suggested, Jews embraced this culture of consumption. They used credit systems to furnish their homes and discarded traditional garments in favor of fashionable, ready-made attire. But Jewish immigrants did not simply consume goods. As peddlers, dry-goods merchants, garment manufacturers, and small shop owners, Jews became part of American retail culture. Arriving with commercial traditions cultivated by their experience in eastern Europe, many Jewish immigrants quickly took to the streets, selling clothing, shoes, kitchen utensils, hardware, food items, and a host of other products. The payoff was significant. A survey in 1906 found that New York City peddlers averaged between fifteen and eighteen dollars a week, a level of earning comparable to the wages associated with many other occupations. Yet Jews tended to treat peddling as a stepping stone; according to Heinze, Jewish peddlers often spent only five or six years on the street before investing their profits in a new business.[8]

For these market-savvy entrepreneurs, antiques were a natural retail medium. Tied to the junk trade, a favored occupation of Jewish entrepreneurs, the antique business was both open and accessible. An article in a 1936 issue of *American Collector* claimed that hundreds of American antique dealers went into the trade for one simple reason: "Do you know of any other business that can be started with practically no money, where a room or an old shed serves as a shop and your equipment consists of a cheap automobile and some dollar stationery with your name and the word, *antiques*?"[9] The author went on to enumerate the advantages: low overhead expenses, substantial sales volume, the ability to sell only for cash and thus eliminate credit problems, and, of course, the potential for great profits. Indeed, there were financial benefits for antique dealers at all points on the spectrum, from the knickknack salesman operating out of the trunk of his car to the high-end retailer specializing in museum-quality pieces.

Nathan Liverant's story is typical of many Jewish dealers who moved from the used goods business to the antique trade. Born in Odessa, Russia, in 1890, Liverant immigrated to New York City when he was still a boy and learned the craft of a furrier. While helping a friend with a delivery to a rural coat factory, he discovered the small Connecticut community of Colchester. Like many Connecticut country towns, Colchester was losing its Yankee population as its old families abandoned their rocky farms for more profitable ventures in nearby cities and western lands. With cheap land and a small manufacturing center, the town quickly became a destination for Jewish immigrants eager to escape the overcrowded conditions of the Lower East Side and willing to try their hand at farming. These resettlement activities were funded in part by the Baron de Hirsch Fund in Germany and its U.S. subsidiary, the Jewish

Agricultural Society, which offered future farmers low-interest loans and farm education programs to assist with the transition.[10] For Liverant, Colchester's rural countryside and established Jewish community made it an attractive alternative to his New York life. And so, in an era in which the American Jewish experience was closely associated with an urban existence, Nathan Liverant packed up his belongings and moved with his young wife and son to rural Connecticut.[11]

Liverant had no desire to become a farmer. Farming was hard, and starting an agricultural business without prior experience could only be classified as risky. So he set out performing odd jobs, transporting passengers to and from the Colchester railroad station, and selling used goods to his rural neighbors. According to family tradition, a small country auction held in the 1920s provided the catalyst for Liverant's entry into the antique business. At the auction, he won the bidding for what he considered just another old piece of furniture. But after the sale, another attendee approached him, offering to buy the article for several times what Liverant had just paid, his rationale being that it was an "antique."[12] Advertisements placed in local newspapers show that Liverant soon began offering antiques among his wares while maintaining a broad business in used household goods. Typical was a 1930 auction announcement in the *Hartford Courant* that included modern furnishings and appliances—a gas range, a water heater, rugs, parlor suites, and bric-a-brac—alongside an antique maple bed, a gold leaf mirror, and a pine secretary. The only indication that Liverant recognized the separate value of these two categories was the capital letters used to highlight the word ANTIQUES[13]

Liverant continued to operate much the same way throughout the 1930s, taking advantage of the fact that many financially strapped owners liquidated their estates during the Great Depression (figure 7). Using a flatbed truck with wooden sides, Liverant traveled to affluent Fairfield county, near the New York border, where he purchased the contents of wealthy homes. He then returned to Colchester and resold the contents to area farmers. By the mid-1950s he had opened a store in a former Baptist meeting house and began consistently advertising his wares as antiques. The push to abandon the used furniture and estate trade came from Nathan's son Zeke. Like his father decades before, Zeke learned the profitability of antiques from a specific incident. According to his son Arthur, Zeke was a boy of about twelve when he located his first "find"

Figure 7. Nathan Liverant promised a "Clean Sale" with everything sold for the "High Dollar" at this 1930 auction. Photograph courtesy of Nathan Liverant and Son.

among his father's stock. The piece was an eighteenth-century silver muff-ineer, or sugar shaker. Young Zeke recognized the piece as similar to one he had seen in his father's antique books and asked if he could hold it for a dealer who specialized in antique silver. When the dealer arrived, he recognized the muffineer's value to silver collectors and offered the boy a hundred dollars, a price far in excess of what his father's country customers would have paid and one that provided new shoes and clothes for everyone in the Liverant household. Zeke was hooked, and he began improving his family's stock to compete with high-end antique dealers.[14]

The Liverants' story is instructive in the ways in which antiques provided an avenue for entrepreneurship. While many Jewish immigrants worked independently to start their own businesses, antiques had the distinction of combining retail skill with a carefully honed education in design. Antique dealers did not trade simply on luck. Rather, the success of any sale depended on the dealer's ability to identify specific styles, recognize fakes, judge standards of craftsmanship, and separate the ordinary from the extraordinary. In this sense, antiquing was a knowledge trade, one that rewarded both hard work and careful study.

As antique dealers, Jewish immigrants became authorities on the American past. Because antique enthusiasts aimed to identify each object in their collections by its date of construction, place of origin, and stylistic type, dealers needed a broad understanding of stylistic developments, craft traditions, and regional geographies. For example, in order to identify where an individual piece of furniture originated, the experienced dealer might employ his knowledge of trade routes and their influence on the woods employed in specific regions. He might consider what role patterns of migration and immigration played in the transfer of aesthetic styles or how the development of local economies affected the growth of cabinetmaking shops and the supply of antiques from a given region. Not all dealers could command such knowledge, but as antique publications such as *Antiques* and the *Antiquarian* printed new research and disseminated information, dealers became increasingly savvy about the nature of their stock. For the Yankee customers who entered the dealer's showroom, these Jewish immigrants had become an important source of information about their own heritage.

Many collectors resented their dependence on Jewish dealers, who often found themselves the object of anti-Semitism within the antique community. Providence collector Jessie Barker Gardner was typical in ascribing forgeries to Jewish dealers. After blaming her experience with a fake William and Mary dressing table on a Boston Jew who eyed his customers "sharply," she deliberately prohibited Jewish experts from examining her Chippendale armchairs (see chapter 3).[15] Walter Dyer hit another common refrain when he insinuated that Jewish dealers corrupted the business with their greed, concluding that many a dealer's "birth and breeding" made it "impossible for him to appreciate a single thing he owns, except as it represents cash."[16] The fact that Jewish dealers were new Americans, far removed from the Yankee stock that antiques had come to symbolize, underscored their outsider status. It was easy to blame problems of the antique market on them, prohibit their membership in social clubs, and bar them from collectors' gatherings. Indeed, the high concentration of Jews among antique dealers most likely fueled prohibitions against dealers joining select collecting clubs, a policy not practiced by the Grolier Club, the exclusive society for bibliophiles.[17]

Still, antiques provided an entry point into American society that few other retail trades could match. No other ware could make its seller such an authority on American history, art, and culture. For Jewish dealers, antiques offered an opportunity to wrap themselves in American heritage. The value of American antiques as a path to acculturation is evident in the career of Israel Sack, the Jewish immigrant who became one of the country's most prominent dealers (figure 8). When he arrived in Boston, Sack found a position as a cabinetmaker in the shop of William Stephenson, himself an Irish immigrant. Stephenson's shop was located on Charles Street at the bottom of Beacon Hill, the Brahmin neighborhood where many antique collectors resided.[18] Recounting his early years in Stephenson's shop, Sack recalled his former employer as an antique counterfeiter, an individual with an "allergy for genuine things." Here Sack learned the tricks of the counterfeiter's trade: how to age new wood with ammonia fumes, add inlay to simple country stock, and manufacture new pieces out of old wood. But he also learned about the legitimate side of the antique business as well. He made contacts with the Boston collectors who frequented Stephenson's shop and brought their finds for repair. He also learned about period styles and aesthetic forms, even if it was only to construct forgeries.[19]

Sack stayed with Stephenson only two years before starting out on

Figure 8. Israel Sack posed for this photograph in 1953, commemorating his fifty years in the antique business. Photograph courtesy Albert Sack, from Albert Sack, comp., *Israel Sack: A Record of Service 1903–1953* (New York: Israel Sack, Inc., 1953).

his own. In 1906, he made his first appearance as a businessman in the Boston city directories. The listing places him at 50 Charles Street and also connects him to a partner, Samuel Tishler. A cabinetmaker like Sack, Tishler was a German Jew who immigrated to the United States in 1888.[20] It is difficult to know what role Tishler played in Sack's early career. Sack did not mention Tishler in an oral history conducted by the

Henry Ford Museum, and Sack's only living son has no knowledge of Tishler. But Tishler's presence is interesting for what it says about Sack's place within the larger Boston Jewish community. Like many East Coast cities, Boston experienced a wave of Jewish immigration beginning in the 1870s. Fleeing the economic and political oppression of Russian rule, Jewish immigrants arrived in large numbers. By the end of the 1890s, Boston counted approximately 40,000 Jews among its roughly 560,000 residents, an eightfold increase from two decades before. These numbers put a strain on the Boston Jewish community, which before the 1870s had been a fractured one, split between a small group of wealthy, accul-turated German Jews and a larger community of religiously conservative Polish Jews. Already divided, and already dealing with economic and religious differences, Boston's Jewish community did not experience the same level of social strife that marked the arrival of Russian Jews into the prosperous Jewish communities of many other cities. Here, Polish and German Jews worked quickly to assimilate and support the newcomers with the construction of local charities and benevolent societies.[21] In this context, Sack's partnership with Tishler, who had been in the country for almost two decades, might have provided him with a link to the larger Jewish community and its economic and social resources.

Sack connected with Boston's Jewish community in other ways as well. When he first arrived in the city, he was taken in by a distant rela-tive who provided him with a place to stay on credit.[22] By 1910, he had married and was living with his new in-laws, Russian Jews like himself. Sack's wife, the former Annie Goodwin, had immigrated as a young girl and grew up in the United States. Her brother Joseph worked as a col-lector in a credit house, and his father also found employment there.[23] But while Sack was forging links to Boston's Jewish community, he also embraced the culture of his new country. From the beginning, he under-stood the importance of cultural traditions and met them with a willing-ness to adapt. In his oral history, he described how he learned to work with ethnically diverse business associates by taking on their cultural traditions as if they were his own. Most important was the lunch ritual. Each day Sack would meet one of his antique collectors, dealers, or sup-pliers for lunch, and each day he would choose a restaurant reflecting his lunch partner's heritage. If his supplier was Armenian, Sack would find an Armenian restaurant. If it was Friday and his associate was Catholic, he would eat fish. As he later put it, "It's so much easier to be like the other fellow than have the other fellow be like you."[24]

Sack's readiness to take on new traditions prepared him well for the antique field, where he soon adopted an enthusiasm for American design as strong as if he were born to it. Throughout his career, he maintained that it was the beauty of American antiques that attracted him to the field and provided him with the drive to succeed as a dealer.[25] As a cabinetmaker, he was well positioned to appreciate these things for their craftsmanship and aesthetic beauty, but he also appreciated them because they were American. Sack's son Albert recalled that when his father was asked why he dealt only in American antiques and did not regularly include European imports among his wares, he replied, "When I came to this country, I went native."[26] The comment is telling for what it says about Sack's desire for acculturation. Here was no atavistic immigrant holding on to his Old World ways. Here was a new American deliberately embracing the heritage of his adopted home. Indeed, he used the tradition of the American craftsman to see himself as part of the American story. Writing to Henry Francis du Pont in 1950, Sack told the collector that early American furniture makers were individuals of "skill, courage, and initiative" who freed themselves from the "superstitions and traditions of Europe."[27] In constructing these craftsmen as immigrants, he drew a direct line from the furniture he loved to the choices he had made in his own life. If those who had fashioned the country's artistic heritage were true Americans, than so was the antique dealer who made them available to the collecting community.

Just as Congress passed the Immigration Act of 1924, restricting the number of southern and eastern Europeans permitted to enter the United States, Sack had risen to become one of the nation's most important brokers of Americana. His flagship shop was located at 85 Charles Street, in a brick building with an elegant fanlight topping its front door. At various times he also had a hand in retail outlets on Boston's Milk, Beacon, and Chestnut streets, in nearby Marblehead and Danvers, and in New London, Connecticut, as well as several New York City locations. Sack also developed a hardware business, I. Sack Fine Cabinet Hardware, which grew to include wrought iron, wood turnings, and reproduction lighting. But Sack's most important asset was his reputation. His customers included the foremost collectors of the day, individuals such as

Maxim Karolik, Ima Hogg, Henry Francis du Pont, and Henry Ford, as well as wealthy New York collector Mitchell Taradash. Museum curators, too, numbered among his clientele, and he helped secure significant pieces for many museums in the Midwest, including the City Art Museum of St. Louis, the Art Institute of Chicago, the Detroit Institute of Arts, and the William Rockhill Nelson Gallery in Kansas City. As Wisconsin collector Stanley Stone wrote on the occasion of Sack's fiftieth year in business, Sack's name had become "a byword all over the land" and his influence permeated "the homes and lives" of the many who had become his "eager students."[28]

Like other Jewish immigrants of his generation, Sack embraced American business culture as part of the transition to his new country. According to his son Albert, by the late 1920s Sack was doing one and a half million dollars' worth of business a year.[29] While no records exist to support this claim, he was clearly buying and selling an enormous number of goods. A single letter from Henry Francis du Pont to Sack, dated January 15, 1929, details du Pont's debt for "articles purchased before Christmas" at more than $70,000.[30] Another itemized bill from 1928 shows du Pont buying twenty-nine objects for $136,000.[31] Selling such large volumes was a testament to Sack's commercial drive. Unlike other businesses that need only expand their manufacturing plants to meet customer demand, antique dealers are limited by the rarity of their wares. Sack evaded supply problems by purchasing large groups of antiques from New England's early collectors. An article in *American Collector* reported that Sack began this practice in 1918 when he purchased the Wallace Nutting collection. Claiming that Sack had purchased *the* Nutting collection was probably a bit of a marketing boast, since Nutting sold the majority of his items to the Wadsworth Atheneum through a deal with J. P. Morgan in 1924.[32] Sack's son Harold remembered his father's first large purchase as the Arthur F. Kelley collection in 1927. Kelley was an early collector from Worcester, Massachusetts, and one of Sack's longtime customers. Purchasing the collection, which Kelley had diligently assembled over a number of years, took Sack's business to a new level. As his son Harold remembered it: "The ultimate success of that first deal gave my father a keen taste for doing things on a much bigger scale. The rapid disposition of an entire collection such as the Kelley pieces seemed to solve his ever-present supply problem. As a lone operator, no longer would he have to use his valuable time seeking out individual pieces, a time-consuming process for the dealer, who also thereafter had to make each and every sale to his customers personally."[33] Sack followed the Kelley collection with his biggest endeavor, the purchase of the George S. Palmer collection.

Born in Montville, Connecticut, in 1855, George S. Palmer was the youngest of five brothers who established the firm of Palmer Brothers, which specialized in the manufacture of bed linens and cotton goods.[34] An antique aficionado in an age in which there were few of his sort, he was encouraged to collect by his cousin Eugene Bolles, the Boston lawyer and avid collector whose finds became the foundation for the American Wing and an early customer of Israel Sack. Palmer and Bolles deliberately constructed complementary collections. Without the deep pockets of his cousin, Bolles focused on pieces of the early colonial period, while Palmer, the successful manufacturer, specialized in later mahogany pieces in the Chippendale, Queen Anne, Sheraton, and Hepplewhite styles.[35] Collecting in an era with few competitors, Palmer and Bolles were able to assemble sizable collections of impressive quality. The pair's largest purchase was the collection of Walter Hosmer, the Hartford upholsterer known for his private ways and his propensity for constructing spurious antiques. Hosmer rarely sold any of his belongings. But in a bold move, Palmer and Bolles knocked on Hosmer's door and demanded a price for the entire collection. The timing was right. Recently dissuaded from placing his collection with a historical society by a gentleman who complained that old furniture just got in the way of the books, Hosmer sold the cousins his life's passion. In this one transaction, Palmer acquired sixty of his best pieces.[36]

About 1908 Palmer built Westomere on the bank of the Thames River in New London, Connecticut. Designed by architect Charles Platt, the house imitated the lines of Westover, the ancestral home of the Byrd family of Virginia. Using Westomere as a showroom for his antiques, Palmer continually improved his collection, keeping only what he could use in his home and replacing pieces as better-quality ones became available.[37] In 1918 he donated many of his best pieces, sixty-five in all, to the Metropolitan Museum of Art, where they joined those donated by his cousin.[38] Palmer sold the remainder of his collection to Sack in 1928, along with Westomere and its collections of American and Dutch paintings, Chinese porcelains, and English salt-glazed ware. The resulting auction, held at New York's Anderson Galleries, was a huge success for Sack. Headliners included a Simon Willard banjo clock that sold for $2,000, two mahogany chests attributed to the Philadelphia cabinetmaker William Savery, which earned $8,000 and $7,200 respectively, and a bonnet-top, block-front chest-on-chest that brought $8,600.[39]

Sack's acquisition of the Palmer collection was an immense undertaking. Collector and dealer Edward Crowninshield reported that he had visited the New London house and was amazed by what Sack had done. "Besides this really beautiful house, he has this remarkable collection of furniture, as fine as anything I have ever seen. . . . It is, of course, a tremendous undertaking for any dealer. And what Lyons and I could not figure is how he would ever be able to swing it."[40] How Sack could finance such an immense purchase is an excellent question, but once he had done it, he took on the lifestyle of a wealthy American businessman. He moved his family into the mansion and resided there for over a year. To maintain a sense of lavish display, he kept Palmer's staff on the payroll: gardeners, maids, and all.[41] Westomere had become a dealer's showroom, but it also functioned to transfer some of its former owner's status to the immigrant from Lithuania. Newspaper reports referred to Westomere as an exhibition rather than a showroom and listed Sack as its owner without mentioning the fact that he was also a dealer.

Buying Westomere was not the first time Sack had success using real estate to elevate his business and his social standing. In 1924 he purchased the King Hooper House in Marblehead, Massachusetts. Built in 1745 by the merchant Robert Hooper, the three-story Federal-style mansion contained a banquet hall, a ballroom, and an elaborately carved staircase. Rather than simply filling the house with objects for sale, Sack transformed it into what he called a "place of demonstration." He restricted the furniture to his finest specimens and arranged them in functional settings, an effect clearly meant to mimic the emerging period rooms of prominent art museums. The result constructed Sack as both a wealthy New Englander and a public philanthropist, an effect made possible by the house's dual representation as an old family home and public museum. He reinforced the impression that the house was something more than a salesroom by encouraging browsers. "I know of no place where a student of fine American antique furniture can better undertake to establish his standards of quality, or where the home-maker can more satisfactorily visualize the ensemble of early furniture in its proper setting," he proclaimed.[42] But while Sack's business ventures provided him with the trappings of gracious living, reality was never far away. According to Harold Sack, his father would frequently invite customers and dealers to dinner. These were ostensibly social occasions, but they often ended up as sales. Every time Sack sold the family sideboard or traded away the dining room table, his wife was forced to empty her drawers and rearrange her furniture. Harold, who called his father's furnishings "vanishable antiques," recalled that "there were times when it was a bit like being an actor in a constantly changing stage set."[43]

Advertising provided Sack with another way to construct himself as an American connoisseur. Like the heritage market itself, advertising was a relatively new industry in the 1920s. Between 1919 and 1929 advertising profits more than doubled, and the ads themselves changed from discreet announcements placed by independent shopkeepers to major media campaigns masterminded by professional agents.[44] For the antique business, the advent of advertising depended on the emergence of new specialty publications. Both *Antiques* and the *Antiquarian* owed their continued existence to those who advertised in their pages. To assist dealers, *Antiques* published a thirty-two-page booklet titled *New Thoughts on Advertising Old Things*, which promised to teach dealers the fine art of advertising and help transform them into "progressive business men."[45] The magazine's advertising department provided examples of different kinds of ads, pointing out how space, images, and copy could be used to create an impression.

The first example was a large, full-page notice placed by Sack himself. Whether Sack designed his own ads or enlisted the aid of an agency is not certain, but his advertisements demonstrate fluency with modern advertising practices by presenting themselves as an educational resource that would help buyers navigate the confusing world of consumer society.[46] In general, he ran two distinct kinds of advertisements. The first type was text-based, often without any pictures at all, and presented Sack as a trustworthy elder statesman of the antique market revealing tricks of the trade to new collectors. Between 1922 and 1923 Sack ran a series of advertisements outlining the principles of collecting; among the eye-catching headlines were "Buy From Your Ancestors: Sell To

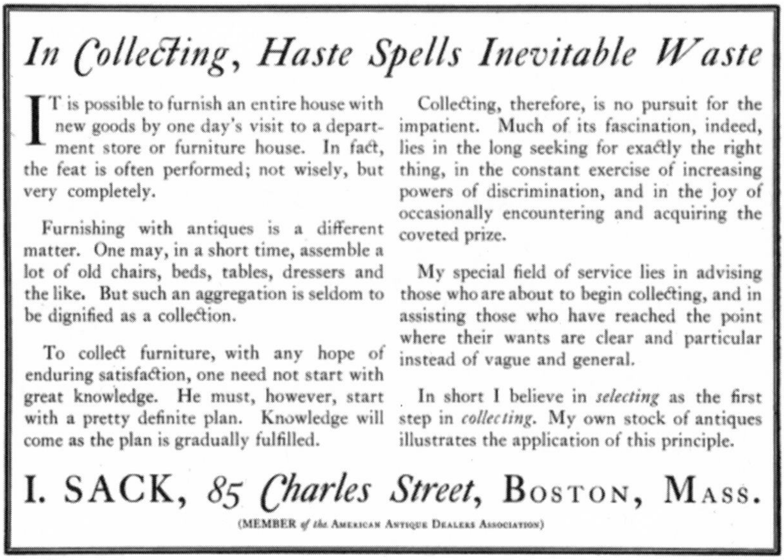

Figure 9. Sack dispensed collecting advice in text-based advertisements like this one. *Antiques*, October 1922, inside front cover.

Posterity," "Special Qualities Which Age Imparts," and "Where Honesty Alone Is Insufficient."[47] Each ad presented a kind of primer, instructing potential collectors on issues such as selecting antiques for the home, understanding historic finishes, and choosing a dealer (figure 9). One refrain remained central in Sack's advertising campaign: the promise of discrimination. "I have been in the antique business for now upwards of seventeen years, specializing in furniture. In that time, I have personally examined and passed on thousands of examples, good and bad. I can tell the fakes from the true, the choice from the commonplace, the scarce from the usual," he assured his readers.[48]

Of course, other dealers also promised customers good advice. But what made Sack's advertisements unique was the way in which they combined both sophisticated analysis of the market with moral stories and provocative maxims similar to the ones he would have known from his lifelong study of the Talmud. Typical was a 1925 advertisement titled "Better Learn by Success Than Seek Profit from Mistakes," in which Sack counsels potential customers to make their first purchases quality ones because "association with that which is good has a way of sharpening the critical facilities."[49] Another ad, from 1922, tells the story of a man who outfitted his new home with "stylish" furniture only to find that the things he had once been proud of looked "commonplace" once his " taste and knowledge improved."[50] By focusing on issues of taste and style, Sack attacked one of the biggest problems for new collectors: the need to show themselves to be cultured and refined. In that sense, selling antiques was only one of Sack's services. Often more important was his promise to sell discrimination as well.

The second kind of ad Sack routinely used was picture-based. Like the text ads, these could be seen as educational, teaching connoisseurship through representations of choice antiques. Typical was an advertisement that ran in the June 1928 issue of *Antiques*. A Chippendale-style chair faces directly forward. The background is blank, allowing the viewer to appreciate the chair's elaborately pierced splat (figure 10).[51] On its own, the image provided a visual lesson in connoisseurship, illustrating the stylistic and aesthetic qualities that gave the object value. Such pared-down visual messages were common for Sack. Often his ads showcased a small group of antiques or even an individual item—a mirror above a small table, or perhaps a single chair set against a white backdrop and turned slightly to emphasize its sculptural qualities. The editors of *Antiques* acknowledged that these kinds of ads would not bring quick sales. They believed that dealers looking to find immediate buyers would be better off showing the variety of their merchandise with multiple images and stock lists. But Sack's ad worked to establish his reputation as a top-of-the-line dealer; in their view it communicated his "good taste" and "standing in the field."[52]

Deals like the Kelley and Palmer purchases turned Sack into a successful American businessman. They not only connected him to some of the leading collectors of the day, but also made him one of the biggest dealers in the business. But these successes also tested his ability. In 1928, *Antiques* reported that Sack's October auction at the Anderson Galleries "seemed to start on the wrong foot and limped rather badly during the first hour," but "found its stride" and finished in "fine form."[53] When the stock-market crash and ensuing depression began to affect the antique business, Sack remained optimistic. He decided to take advantage of the business slowdown and buy out one of his biggest competitors, Benjamin

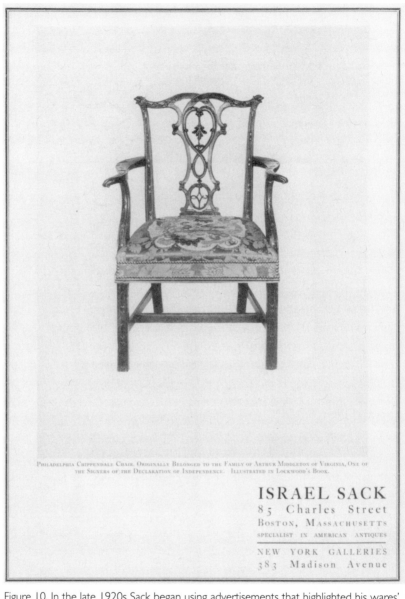

PHILADELPHIA CHIPPENDALE CHAIR. ORIGINALLY BELONGED TO THE FAMILY OF ARTHUR MIDDLETON OF VIRGINIA, ONE OF THE SIGNERS OF THE DECLARATION OF INDEPENDENCE. ILLUSTRATED IN LOCKWOOD'S BOOK.

ISRAEL SACK
85 Charles Street
BOSTON, MASSACHUSETTS
SPECIALIST IN AMERICAN ANTIQUES

NEW YORK GALLERIES
383 Madison Avenue

Figure 10. In the late 1920s Sack began using advertisements that highlighted his wares' aesthetic qualities. *The Magazine Antiques*, January 1928, inside front cover.

Flayderman. The move could not have come at a worse time. Economic recovery remained elusive, and both dealers and collectors began selling off their prize possessions in an effort to raise cash. In 1932 Sack was forced to liquidate. The auction, held at New York's American Art Association and Andersen Galleries, was a huge disappointment. As Harold recalled in 1986, "Choice pieces brought low prices, so low as to be unbelievable today."[54]

By the time of the stock-market crash, however, Sack had successfully used his business to gain an important measure of status. No longer just a Jewish immigrant, he was now a respected expert in American antiques, associating with the "best furniture" and the "best people."[55] Through the medium of antiques, he became a regular associate of some of America's top businessmen, including C. K. Davis, president of Remington Arms, and DuPont's Henry Francis du Pont, both avid collectors. When Henry Ford was asked whether he was anti-Semitic, he denied the charge, citing Sack as a friend.[56] Sack's philanthropic activities also challenged the boundaries that separated him from his wealthy clientele. When New York City was planning the Washingtonia Educational Exhibit, held in 1932 to mark the two hundredth anniversary of the birth of George Washington, Sack became a member of the advisory board and served alongside the wives of such wealthy New Yorkers as newspaper publisher William Randolph Hearst and railroad magnate Cornelius Vanderbilt. The fact that Sack's fellow board members were largely women and not their powerful husbands illustrates the limits of his ability to access the uppermost echelons of American society. Nevertheless, associating with Mrs. Vanderbilt was a big step for the immigrant from Lithuania.

Antiques also provided Sack with a real level of economic success. After the stock-market crash, he never regained the wealth he had in the 1920s, but he had used money from the good years to send his sons to college. Harold earned a degree from Dartmouth College (the alma mater of one of his father's antiquing friends), and Albert completed a year at the University of Pennsylvania. This investment proved to be Sack's most important. Armed with his knowledge of business strategies and a loan from a former college classmate, Harold bailed the family out of debt and established a new company, Israel Sack Incorporated, which maintained the family's position at the top of the antique business throughout the entire twentieth century.[57] Incorporation might have been beyond the means of an immigrant from Lithuania, but Israel Sack had used antiques to transform his family into successful Americans.

Supplying the Trade

In building their businesses and advertising their wares, Jewish dealers such as Israel Sack made many contributions to the culture of antiques, but one of the most fundamental was supplying collectors with new goods. Unlike other kinds of industries that flourished with the development of America's twentieth-century consumer culture, antiques could not be manufactured on the factory floor (at least not honestly). In this case, "production" was a laborious process that included locating the goods, separating them from their local context, and packaging and preparing the individual objects for market. While collectors acting as independent scouts did produce new finds, their contributions could not compare to those of dealers who dedicated themselves to the pursuit full-time. Henry Wood Erving, the pioneering Hartford collector, liked to recount the story of rescuing a Connecticut chest from a farmhouse cellar where it was being used as a potato bin. But Erving, a banker by trade, also admitted that it was more economical and efficient to let dealers do his searching for him.[58] Simply put, dealers' discoveries made antiquing possible.

Many collectors recognized the key role played by Jewish dealers. An article in the *Antiquarian* concluded that much of the work of locating and identifying New England's material heritage had been left to "the chosen race."[59] Famed collector Wallace Nutting agreed. In an unpublished manuscript written in the 1930s, Nutting vehemently denied the charge that Jews were "responsible for the evils and uncertainties connected with antiques" and concluded that antiquers needed to "thank the Jewish dealer" for his work. "The Jews have largely found the material, and very many of them have first discerned the merits of early periods," he wrote. "Were it not for them, perhaps even now we should find only here and there a pioneer calling in the wilderness of the depraved and the mediocre."[60]

The work of discovery could take many forms. In the early years of the antique market, driving through the countryside, identifying old homes, and knocking on doors was routine for dealers. Israel Sack pursued stock from old Boston families, but also made frequent trips outside the city, occasionally in the company of Eugene Bolles, a regular customer and friend. Thus an automobile was an early necessity for many dealers.[61] The activities of Jewish antique dealers were rarely covered in newspapers, but the *Boston Daily Globe* reported two separate automobile accidents, one in 1919 that took the life of Eli Jacobs and one in 1923 that resulted in the death of Louis Rosenthal and William Alpert, all area dealers conducting routine scouting trips.[62] Antiquing was obviously not without its dangers, but for dealers, heading out on the road was essential to the process of discovery. In order to plan more focused searches, savvy dealers read obituaries and established friendships with doctors, mail carriers, and others whose work brought them into people's homes. As antique dealer Zeke Liverant put it in the 1950s, "A medical man with an eye for a cabriole leg is handy to know."[63]

Dealers also cultivated relationships with old New England families. Often reluctant to sell a cherished heirloom, families might be courted for years by dealers patiently waiting for an acquisition. Soon after coming into his father's business, Zeke Liverant started developing contacts with his region's old families. These relationships could take years to develop, and they might pay off very slowly. One elderly woman, a Miss Haley of Bozrah, Connecticut, would summon Liverant to her house whenever she found herself in need of funds. On most occasions, the old woman sold him a few specific items or asked for an advance on his next purchase. One day, however, she left him alone in her living room and he used the occasion to examine an old journal sitting nearby. The journal turned out to be an account book of the early eighteenth-century Ipswich chair makers John Gaines II and Thomas Gaines. Not only was the woman a Gaines descendent, related through the Appleton family, but she also owned an original Gaines chair. Today the journal is in the collection of the Winterthur Museum; it is the earliest known account book of an American chair maker.[64] Rare though they were, such important discoveries were only possible through a dealer's careful and patient practice. No chance knock at the door would have brought the journal to light. Old families routinely guarded their treasures, selling only to a dealer who had proven himself through years of communication.

Jewish dealers also had the advantage of being close to a network of "pickers," small-time dealers who canvassed the countryside searching for stock. Known occasionally as "knockers" or "rappers" for their door-to-door techniques, pickers operated on the lowest rung of the antique hierarchy. Bad roads, mean dogs, and unreliable cars were a regular part of their lives, as were more serious problems such as cash shortages and lack of credit. Because of their marginal status, little is known about the lives of pickers. In Harold Sack's reminiscences of the Boston antique market, he cites a picker named Joseph Epstein, a Russian Jew whom he credits with almost magical powers when it came to making a buy. According to Sack, other pickers were so fascinated with Epstein's success that they would occasionally bet him a hundred dollars that he could not convince an owner to sell. As Sack tells it, Epstein always won.[65] Epstein clearly was skilled in acquiring new goods, but to what degree he should be considered a picker rather than a dealer is difficult to say. The 1924 *Boston Business Directory* credits Epstein with his own business address and lists him as a purveyor of antique goods.[66] While he was adept at locating new goods and bringing them to market, he most likely would not have appreciated the label of "picker," which many saw as an affront, an insult implying low status. When *Life* ran an article on Zeke Liverant's Colchester antique business, reporter Robert Wallace proposed calling the piece "Zeke the Picker," but found the title quickly rejected by his subject. The article ran with the title "Zeke the Seeker."[67]

Certainly there were many reasons why an individual would not want to be classified as a picker. Collectors frequently blamed the problems of the antique market on pickers. They were also closest to the nasty transaction in which a cherished family object became an ordinary commodity. They were portrayed as the embodiment of all market evils, people of unbelievable cunning who could trick almost anyone out of his or her possessions. One scheme reported in both American and English collecting journals described a picker who would offer the lady of the house huge sums for her old furniture. When he had her confidence, he would turn his attention to his mark, some pieces of glass or china. For these, he would offer only paltry sums, but the woman, pleased with her other profits, would quickly acquiesce. The picker would then announce that he would send his truck the next day and pay for the furniture at that time, but would take the fragile pieces right away. The woman would never see him or his truck again.[68]

While we will never know to what degree such stories were true, dealers and pickers did have to convince owners to sell, a process that broke the ties of local and family associations. If an owner believed that his or her antiques were junk, this could be easy. But if sentiment was involved, closing the deal would be much harder. Liverant told *Life* that he was often "obliged to buy a good deal of family history and sentiment along with the furniture." Sentiment cost him money but had no value what-soever once the goods reached his shop.[69] When owners resisted selling, dealers and pickers tried to help them see their possessions as a form of ready cash. In the *Romance of New England Antiques*, Edwin Valentine Mitchell told the story of a picker who responded to a man's unwilling-ness to sell his antique clock by placing a five-dollar bill in the hand of each of the man's five small children.[70]

The conflict between sentiment and money was often central to the process of separating an antique from its owner. A late nineteenth-century poem by Mary Brine told of a woman who sells her old furniture to some city dealers who come looking for what she calls "antiks." The woman is tempted by her desire for a new bonnet and shawl and unthinkingly agrees to part with what she believes is just old junk. But as the objects leave they become a representation of her family life: the spinning wheel she used as a young bride, the bed in which her children (who later died) slept, and the gateleg table that expanded as her family grew.[71] On this level the story provided a cautionary tale to those who were thinking of getting rid of their old things: old furniture matters; do not sell your memories. When the woman learned about the popularity of antiques from her wealthy granddaughter, who had bought the very same table that the old woman sold (at a greatly inflated price), the poem presented an alternative moral: know what your things are worth. Indeed, as time went on, pickers and dealers, like door-to-door collectors, found that their problem was not making people see their antiques as commodi-ties, but dealing with those who had already made the switch. As early as 1910, Walter Dyer wrote in *The Lure of the Antique* that "the old vil-lages have been scoured by collectors and dealers, and people who have antiques to sell nowadays have a pretty clear idea of their value."[72] By the 1950s, Zeke Liverant found this a constant problem. The old ladies who sold him their furniture played dealers against one another, researched prices in the local antique shops, and watched the dealer closely for any signs of deceit. According to Liverant, they often tested him by selling him a small object and then visiting his shop to make sure that his markup was not excessive.[73] These women had completely internalized the commodity system. If they saw their antiques as representations of family history or sentiment, they were also able to see them as market goods with a cash value.

By the mid-1930s the number of unidentified antiques hidden away in barns and attics was dwindling. With the publicity generated by the Flayderman and Reifsnyder sales, many antique owners, searching for ways to generate extra cash during the depression, scoured their attics and sold off their inheritance. With fewer finds available, Jewish dealers were among those who went to heroic efforts to locate new stock. Benjamin Flayderman, Sack's Boston competitor, turned to international markets in a quest of repatriation. In 1938 Flayderman took several trips to the West Indies with the intention of "locating examples of New England furniture, shipped there many years ago."[74] Reuben Margolis was another dealer who pursued antiques abroad. Like Sack, the Margolis family emigrated from what is now Lithuania, first moving to London before arriving in the United States. With the rest of his family, Reuben worked as a cabinetmaker in Hartford, Connecticut, but as an adult he bought and sold antiques along the eastern seaboard. In the 1920s he took his search further and began what became sixteen trips to London in search of antiques for the American market. Margolis, who also settled in England for extended periods of time, appears to have found a ready market for his discoveries, many of which were sold through the New York business of his brother Jacob. Jacob dealt in both American and English antiques, but Reuben also made trips at the behest of Sack, who usually limited his wares to American-made goods. It is hard to say whether dealers who purchased items from abroad passed off English-made goods as American, either knowingly or in error. Still, the fact that dealers turned to foreign countries in an effort to locate American antiques demonstrates the central importance of producing antiques for the trade. Just as New England dealers turned to the south for new stock in the first years of the twentieth century, augmenting the region's historic resources in the process, dealers in the 1930s would not be limited by geographical borders in their effort to find antiques. In the same way that many of the dealers who supplied collectors themselves originated abroad, Americana too could be imported.

Foreign travel did occasionally produce spectacular finds, but more often dealers turned to their old customers for new stock. Information Sack supplied to the Winterthur Museum on the history of its collections is instructive in just how many of Henry Francis du Pont's pieces were originally owned by early collectors. On a tour of the museum's collection, Sack repeatedly named the individuals who had owned these items: Arthur F. Kelly, George Palmer, Helen Temple Cooke, Samuel King, Arthur W. Wellington, all pioneering collectors and early Sack customers, as well as the Boston dealer Philip Flayderman. The paths du Pont's antiques took to reach him could be quite convoluted. Take Sack's description of a chest located in a room du Pont named the Flock Room for its dramatic canvas wall coverings flocked to emulate costly velvet: "This chest was in the Wallace Nutting collection which I bought and I sold the chest to Dwight Prouty. . . . Prouty sold his collection to Wanamaker's [department store] in New York. I bought the chest from them and sold it to Behrend. I bought the Behrend collection and sold the chest to Mr. du Pont."[75] In its life as an antique, the chest could claim at least five individual owners as well as three separate periods in Sack's possession.

By moving antiques from collector to collector, Jewish dealers not only supplied their customers with goods, they also established a history of ownership that worked to dilute local ties and construct a new kind of provenance based on the object's history as a collectible. An eyewitness to many early antique transactions, Sack often identified objects as having once belonged to a specific collector. For example, one Christmas Sack, who never balked at participating in his clients' religious traditions if it was good business practice, presented Henry Francis du Pont with a small pitcher. The pitcher was not especially valuable in and of itself, but it had been owned at one point by Charles Pendleton, the pioneering Rhode Island antique enthusiast who donated his collection of American decorative arts to the Rhode Island School of Design in 1904 to form one of the first art museum displays of American antiques. For Sack, the value of the gift was clearly its association with another collector. It was important not simply as a document of life in early America, but as a piece of the history of collecting itself.[76] In this sense, Jewish dealers did more than simply supply collectors—they helped shape the meaning of antiques and their value to the public.

Repairs and Reproductions

By locating and disseminating objects, Jewish entrepreneurs were instrumental to the rise of antique collecting in America. Simply put, their work ensured that there would be antiques for collectors to buy. But this was not the only contribution of these recent immigrants to the preservation and appreciation of American antiques. Indeed, the collecting community relied heavily on the work of immigrant craftsmen to repair, and sometimes even reproduce, early American furnishings. With today's reverence for the untouched object, early antique repairers and refinishers have received an undeserved reputation as bunglers who ruined ancient objects with overly invasive techniques. But, as I noted in chapter 1, early collectors expected, and even encouraged, restoration. This restoration required the work of skilled cabinetmakers, individuals familiar with traditional construction techniques. As furniture production in the United States became more mechanized, the industry began to rely heavily on semiskilled or unskilled labor, and by the beginning of the twentieth century experienced cabinetmakers were in short supply.[77] Against this backdrop, Jewish cabinetmakers, many trained abroad, provided the antique trade with a specialty workforce.[78]

Often the line between repairing and selling antiques was a thin one. Many antique dealers started as repairers, some moving back and forth between the two trades as circumstances dictated. As we have seen, Israel Sack himself, trained as a cabinetmaker in both Lithuania and England, started out by repairing antiques in William Stephenson's shop. Sack recalled that clients would gather to watch him work, constantly imploring him to be careful with their precious finds.[79] When Sack started his own business, he first concentrated on repair work, taking on odd jobs for his former boss, local dealers, and area collectors. As Jeanne Schinto has discovered, he was listed as a cabinetmaker, not an antique dealer, in the Boston city directories as late as 1917, at least eleven years after he had gone into business for himself. The listing should not be seen as evidence that Sack was slow to start dealing (something his family disputes).[80] Rather, it is further confirmation of the connectedness of the two trades.

The practice of combining repair work with buying and selling antiques was common in the early years of the trade. In fact, the biographies of several early dealers echo Sack's story, joining a European education in cabinetry with business ventures in antique repair and sales. Samuel Wineck was one. Born as Sack was in Kovno, Russia, an area known for its walnut forests and fine furniture production, Wineck immigrated first to Liverpool, England, and then, in 1888, to Hartford, Connecticut, where he established a furniture repair shop. As it did for Sack, repair work eventually led to buying and selling antiques, and Wineck expanded his business and moved into larger quarters in Hartford's former Armory building.[81] Never a big player in the national antique market, Wineck was nevertheless an example of a skilled immigrant craftsman who found a niche serving antique collectors.

The careers of Jacob and Nathan Margolis, two brothers who were relatives of Samuel Wineck, also illustrate the close connection between the skills of the cabinetmaker and the antique dealer. Nathan and Jacob immigrated to Hartford in the early twentieth century. They were brothers of Reuben Margolis, the dealer who traveled back and forth to England in an effort to locate American antiques. Like Sack and Wineck, the pair received their early training as woodworkers in Russian Lithuania and London. As young men they apprenticed in their uncle's cabinet shop in Yanova (also spelled Janova), a town adjacent to Kovno, where Wineck and Sack were born. While much of Yanova's furniture production was simple fare, intended for local sale, the region had also produced fine furniture for the Russian nobility who favored French designs. Nathan was the first to leave. In 1888 he immigrated to London where he began working for the cabinetmaking firm known today as Waring & Gillows, a company with roots in the eighteenth century. Soon after, he was joined by Jacob and their father, Charles, as well as several other family members. Here the Margolises learned about eighteenth-century English design, an excellent primer for the American antique trade.[82]

Arriving in Hartford in 1893, Nathan Margolis set up shop with his father (figure 11). Like Sack and Wineck, the Margolises started by repairing furniture, gradually moving into the business of buying and selling antiques as the market grew. From there, Jacob's and Nathan's careers diverged. Jacob became a dealer, first in Hartford, then in Albany, New York, and finally on Madison Avenue in New York City. Advertisements for Jacob's New York City business regularly appeared in the *New York Times* and *Antiques*; they show that he was specializing in high-end wares. A two-day auction staged by Jacob in 1926 at New York's Anderson Galleries netted an impressive $40,182 and included a carved mahogany Rhode Island block-front desk.[83] But even though Jacob successfully sold at the top of the market, he never abandoned the repair side of the business. In a 1923 *New York Times* advertisement, Jacob announced that he would give up his retail shop and sell only through auction specifically so he could attend to his repair work. Being a cabinetmaker served Jacob well. Not only did he offer his repair services as a complementary benefit for those who purchased his antiques at auction, but it also helped him win the confidence of collectors.[84] One of Jacob's most important clients was Francis P. Garvan, the Yale alumnus who donated his large collection to the university in 1930.[85] Garvan began by acquiring English antiques, but sold them promptly after learning that he had purchased some fakes. Unsurprisingly, he became particularly concerned about authenticity,[86] and as a cabinetmaker Jacob Margolis could help him guard against fakes. With their knowledge of woods, cabinetmakers often uncovered forgeries, embellishments, and other forms of deception. In this sense, they were essential to the antique trade, not only for their ability to make repairs but also for their skill in detecting deception.

The career of Jacob's brother Nathan illustrates another service immigrant craftsmen supplied to the antique trade, the work of reproduction. While antique collectors abhorred forgeries, reproductions were another matter. *Antiques*, whose advertisers included reproduction furniture companies, published an editorial in 1926 encouraging reproductions. While acknowledging that many manufacturers claimed a much higher level of authenticity than they actually attained, the magazine's editor praised reproductions because they helped cultivate an appreciation of early American design among the buying public.[87] In truth, the reproduction business ran the entire gamut from mongrel designs that only faintly suggested early American forms to faithful, and often costly, replicas. By the 1920s, furniture inspired by early American designs was a major component of the furniture industry. Fueled by the national craze for Colonial Revival design, which invaded all aspects of house construction and home decor, retailers as wide-reaching as the Sears catalog and regional department stores all featured furnishings loosely

Figure 11. Reproduction furniture craftsman Nathan Margolis. Photograph courtesy of the Winterthur Library: Joseph Downs Collection of Manuscripts and Printed Ephemera.

dubbed "colonial."[88] But high-end reproductions were much more limited in their availability. Beginning in 1917, Wallace Nutting used the
national sales network that he had constructed to market his hand-tinted
photographs of early American scenes to market a furniture line, largely
based on early American examples. Most reproductions, however, were
constructed by smaller-scale enterprises that combined modern machine
tools with hand craftsmanship.[89] For buyers, the high-end reproduction
industry performed several functions. First, reproductions made it possible for those of moderate means to participate in the fashion for antiques,
demonstrate their knowledge of period styles, and display their taste. In
this sense, reproductions democratized antiquing, allowing those who
could not afford the expense of authenticity to join the fold. But reproductions also served the needs of dedicated collectors. By its very nature,
antiquing was a limited pursuit, and few antiquers had the resources
to reach their collecting goals. This situation was exacerbated by the
fact that most collectors in the 1920s did not want simply to acquire
antiques. They wanted to use them, to set them out in their homes and
create a vision of early American elegance, an approach evident in a regular feature in *Antiques* titled "Living with Antiques," which examined
how people used antiques in their houses.[90] Decorating with antiques
reinforced their importance as aesthetic objects by emphasizing artistic
arrangements, but the demands of decorating created new pressures on
the antique market as collectors searched for pieces that would meet both
aesthetic and functional needs. For these collectors, reproductions were
essential. They allowed collectors to display full suites of furniture in
period style, even when authentic antiques remained unavailable.

Moving from a mixed business that combined repair work and
antique sales, Nathan Margolis built a reputation as a fine cabinetmaker
specializing in antique reproductions. His customers included members
of Hartford's old families, such as Morgan Brainard, chairman of Aetna
Life, and the architect Theodate Pope Riddle. In one of his most high-
profile jobs, Nathan reproduced and repaired furniture for the restoration of the former Connecticut State House building in Hartford. But as
Eileen Pollack has pointed out, Margolis's customer base also included
many local Jewish families who used his furnishings as a way to negotiate their dual identities as both Jews and Americans. Owning a piece of
Margolis furniture allowed them to support a local Jewish businessman

and at the same time display their appreciation of American heritage. Indeed, Pollack has shown that Margolis's Jewish customers continued to purchase the family's reproductions long after the fashion for Colonial Revival furniture had passed in Hartford's gentile community.[91]

Nathan headed the reproduction business until his death in 1925; he was succeeded by his son Harold. Nathan and Harold proclaimed their close attention to detail and careful measuring techniques, practices that ostensibly produced faithful copies. In reality, both Nathan and Harold often rescaled original designs to make them fit more easily into the smaller rooms and lower ceilings of many modern homes. The firm also constructed similar objects at different levels of embellishment, providing customers with a variety of price points. Chippendale mirrors, for example, could be purchased with simple scrolling or elaborate carving and gilding.[92] At times, building furniture for contemporary homes could take the Margolises down a decidedly modern road. In his obituary, Nathan was credited with producing the first cabinet for a radio, adapting the new creation from a refashioned dressing table.[93] Whether the story is true or not, the construction of radio cabinets remained a recognized part of the firm's production during Harold's tenure.

In order to produce for even a regional market, the Margolises relied on immigrant woodworkers (figure 12). Many employees were relatives, trained as Nathan himself was in his uncle's shop in Lithuania, and others were former residents of Yanova. From newspaper reports of an incident in which Nathan was fined for breaking Hartford's Sunday statute, it is clear that his employees included several Orthodox Jews who worked on Sundays and observed Saturday Sabbath.[94] As Harold recalled for an oral history conducted by the Jewish Historical Society of Greater Hartford, the city developed a sizable community of Jewish cabinetmakers, some who worked for Margolis, others who built businesses of their own. These men included Barney Rappaport, a cabinetmaker from Yanova, Abraham Aronovsky, a Margolis employee who eventually started his own business in East Hartford, and Joseph Rosen, a craftsman who worked in both the cabinetry and carpentry trades. By the mid-twentieth century, Harold Margolis began hiring outside the Hartford Jewish community, but he continued to rely on European immigrants. Referring to his employees as a "League of Nations," Harold remembered a shop populated by Danish, English, French, German, Italian, and Spanish cabinetmakers.[95]

Figure 12. During the 1920s, workers in Nathan Margolis's cabinet shop carefully reproduced period pieces. Photograph courtesy of the Jewish Historical Society of Greater Hartford.

Despite the increasing diversity of the woodworking trade, Harold Margolis's biggest competitor was another Jewish immigrant from eastern Europe, Abraham Fineberg. Like the Margolises, Fineberg first spent time in England before arriving in the United States. From there he traveled to Portland, Maine, where he set up his first shop. In 1929, he moved to Hartford and established a business there.[96] Less is known about Fineberg's output, in part because he did not consistently label pieces produced in his shop.[97] But while the details of these immigrant cabinetmakers' careers might be lost, their existence is important for what it says about the relationship between the development of antiquing and the need for a skilled workforce. As an early center of antique collecting, Hartford attracted cabinetmakers who quickly transformed their skills into new jobs and burgeoning businesses. The fact that these immigrant craftsmen recognized that they were working in the specialized world of the antique trade, rather than the general furniture business, is illustrated by an 1898 advertisement in which Nathan Margolis

Chapter 2

announced antiques for sale and reproduction services available.[98] This was an early date to use the word *antiques* in a business advertisement, but even though Margolis had arrived in Hartford only five years earlier, it was clear that he had defined his market. The existence of antiquers, as well as established businesses like Margolis's, worked to draw additional craftsmen and fuel a pattern of chain migration from areas such as the Yanova region of Lithuania.

Foot Soldiers of the Trade

Jewish dealers supported many aspects of the antique trade. Working the front lines, they identified antiques and brought them to market, used their skills as cabinetmakers to make repairs and detect forgeries, and constructed reproductions that popularized the antique aesthetic and provided aficionados with practical furnishings for daily use. Each service was essential to the growth of antiquing, both as a hobby and as a trade. For new immigrants who became dealers, associating with antiques provided an intimate knowledge of their adopted nation's artistic heritage and a claim on American citizenship. But while antiques provided Jewish dealers with a kind of cultural cachet, it was the fact that antiquing was a business that made the study of early American furniture a practical pursuit for recent immigrants. For Jewish dealers, antiques represented a means to financial security, the opportunity to be self-employed, and a chance to achieve the American dream. If antiquing had been merely a hobby, a matter of passion and not financial gain, early American furnishings might still have come to function as evidence of the nation's artistic spirit. But they would not have expanded their influence beyond the largely white, middle- and upper-class audience that formed the collecting public and would not have attracted recent immigrants into the antiquing community. For as much as many antique dealers loved the objects that filled their shops, they needed to make a living. They needed to see antiques as both aesthetic objects and commodities.

3
Jessie Barker Gardner and George Gardner
Making a Collection Permanent

George Gardner and his wife, Jessie Barker Gardner, were early twentieth-century antique collectors in Providence, Rhode Island. George was a surgeon, Jessie the descendent of an old New England family. The pair spent their adult lives in a middle-class neighborhood of Providence. They knew the famous Pendleton collection of American decorative arts at the nearby Rhode Island School of Design, and they traveled to New York to see the American Wing and the Brooklyn Museum's collection of nineteen period rooms opened to the public in 1929. They read *Antiques* and the *Antiquarian*. They consulted collecting manuals and decorative arts literature. But at a time when the antique market was burgeoning, George and Jessie were decidedly small-time. They did not lend items to the famous exhibition of American decorative arts organized by the National Council of Girl Scouts in 1929. George was not invited to join the Walpole Society, and the couple certainly never bid on blockbuster items at major auctions such as the Flayderman sale.

Still, George and Jessie's story is an important one, because they represent a class of antique collectors rarely discussed: dedicated amateurs who lacked the resources to collect at the highest levels, but nevertheless valued antiques passionately. History most often records the stories of wealthy, powerful collectors, individuals such as Henry Francis du Pont or Francis P. Garvan, who built extensive museums or attached their names to prestigious institutions with generous gifts. George and Jessie strove to imitate their more famous counterparts, but theirs is the story of what it was like to negotiate the twentieth-century antique market and create a legacy without the benefits of a bottomless pocketbook or professional advisers. They might not have always followed the recommendations of experts or achieved the most aesthetically pleasing results, but what they did do was to integrate collecting into their lives and find meaning, both personal and political, in antique objects.

Middle-class though they were, George and Jessie saw themselves as part of a philanthropic tradition. Jessie, born in Providence in 1873, was the daughter of one of the city's prominent families (figure 13). Her mother, Annie Cushman Tripp Barker, hailed from New Bedford, Massachusetts. Her father, Henry Rodman Barker, was a Providence native who served as the city's mayor from 1889 to 1890. Jessie attended Miss Abbott's School for Young Ladies, where she most likely knew Abby Greene Aldrich, the future wife of philanthropist John D. Rockefeller Jr. and benefactor of many art museums. After graduation, Jessie attended Brown University as a special student from 1892 to 1894, where she met fellow student George Warren Gardner, a native of Maine. The couple traveled frequently but made their home in Providence, where George worked for a short period as Brown University's physician and later as a surgeon at Rhode Island Hospital.

It is difficult to say when exactly George and Jessie began collecting. Some of their treasured artifacts were inherited; others were purchased at auctions, from antique dealers, and on travel vacations throughout the East Coast and abroad. But in the 1920s they came to an ambitious idea. They would make their collection permanent; they would make it into a museum.

Figure 13. Painted by artist Sydney Richmond Burleigh, this portrait of Jessie Barker Gardner hangs in Gardner House. Photograph courtesy of Gardner House, Brown University.

For most collectors, the hunt is the most dramatic phase of collecting, culminating in the moment when the object is located and secured. Collectors often tell detailed stories about their discoveries, of identifying an unrecognized treasure and rescuing it by adding it to their collection. George and Jessie's acquisition stories are important for what they tell us about how they negotiated aesthetic standards, functioned as consumers, and understood their relationship with the market. But as Leah Dilworth has argued, acquiring individual objects is only a small part of the process of collecting; the objects are also "amassed, selected, grouped, and displayed."[1] These "acts of possession" are important to the collector because they represent an opportunity to attach his or her own interpretation to the artifacts through ordered arrangements and display. But while objects themselves may possess solidity and relative permanence, a collection's integrity and arrangement can be quite fragile. Objects can easily be sold, resituated, or divorced from the context of other collected objects or period-room settings. Only the owner's continued custody or control assures the collection's permanence. In this sense, deposition represents the final act of possession. It is the only way collectors can continue to influence, albeit in a much weaker form, the use and interpretation of their collections after their own custody ends. George and Jessie understood that to maintain control over their collection and ensure its survival, they would have to move beyond collecting and become donors.

For George and Jessie, the fragility of their collection was brought home to them when a couple they knew died. They watched as their friends' antiques were "pawed over and auctioned off," and they found this process appalling.[2] How could a lifetime of work locating, selecting, and acquiring historic objects be undone so quickly and so crassly? Seized with idea that the collection they worked so hard to create would be ripped apart, they began to think about how to prevent their antiques from being "scattered," cast "to the four winds."[3] The couple had no children and George's health would soon begin to fail.

Building a museum was one of the few ways George and Jessie could secure the continuity of their collection. In the context of collecting practices, building a museum is an extreme act. It is one thing to donate objects to the care of an organization with the expectation of their preservation; it is quite another to establish one's own institution. Both actions are built on the owner's assumption, accurate or not, that their possessions are not just of personal but also public value. But a donation requires the donor to give up authority over the collection and place it in another's hands. By choosing to build their own museum, the Gardners were hoping to exert continued control.

According to Jessie, she and George considered establishing a museum at several universities and colleges. They liked Middlebury College, and they had long considered moving to a rural area such as Vermont. But only one place seems to have been seriously considered: Brown University in Providence. With Jessie's Providence ancestry and George's close relationship with the school, Brown seemed like a natural choice.[4] In addition, many of their antiques had Rhode Island roots, and it seemed only fitting that they should stay in the state.[5] By donating their antiques to Brown, George and Jessie would protect them from the auction block while aligning the collection with a prominent institution and establishing its value.

I do not claim that George and Jessie's story is a universal one. The couple was part of a category of middle-class collectors, but even though their experiences and frustrations were shared by many of those trying to assemble a first-rate collection in the age of rising prices and increasingly stringent standards of aesthetics and authenticity, their story is individual. My research on George and Jessie's collecting career is based on several detailed journals that Jessie titled "The Story of Gardner House." Written primarily by Jessie, with occasional contributions from George, the journals included favorite antiquing stories, correspondence, object lists, personal recollections, and summaries of their experiences establishing a historic house museum.[6] The material is related strictly from George and Jessie's point of view and contains notes inserted by Jessie years later in an attempt to amend her earlier opinions in light of subsequent events. The journals were a way for Jessie, who was clearly thinking about her legacy, to record her version of the museum's story and define its history. They also provide a window into the rarely documented world of middle-class, nonprofessional collecting.

On the Hunt

As we have seen, in the 1920s, when George and Jessie were actively collecting, the antique market had already taken its modern form, with specialized publications, networks of dealers, canons of taste, and concerns about fakes and forgeries. Even though they were small-time collectors, the couple experienced this new world fully and did their best to meet the new aesthetic standards. Jessie, the descendant of an old Rhode Island family, had plenty of reasons to favor antiques with historic associations. Building her collection locally, she had acquired many pieces of Rhode Island origin, some bought from the families that originally owned them, others inherited. But Jessie had absorbed the new collecting advice against "misplaced sentiment."[7] She cultivated her aesthetic skill and rarely celebrated her antiques as expressions of family or local history. Typical was her interpretation of a set of Lowestoft china that had belonged to her grandmother and several fine lacquered boxes brought from China by her grandfather.[8] She considered the Lowestoft one of her most prized possessions and referred to it repeatedly. But what made the china so valuable in her eyes was not the fact that her grandmother had owned it; she valued it because a dealer working for the Metropolitan Museum of Art once offered her $1,500 for the set.[9] Similarly, she did not acknowledge the value of her grandfather's boxes until an antique dealer labeled one "Maidou Longwood with burl amboyna panels," and declared it an artifact of the China trade.[10] In this case, Gardner allowed the market to create significance. An antique dealer's ability to identify and describe, a solid offer of cash, a connection to the established Metropolitan Museum of Art—these are the mechanisms she used to understand value.

Gardner put her faith in the importance of aesthetic classifications. She took great pride in being able to recognize period styles and showed contempt for those who could not. In her journals, she told the story of a woman who came to visit her collection. According to Jessie, she had a "slightly proprietary manner, evidently wishing to give the impression that while she did not possess such objects herself, she had what is better,—a knowledge and appreciation of them."[11] The woman gushed when she saw Gardner's English chairs, but her enthusiasm waned when she learned that the tall secretary was a Rhode Island piece. Since American collectors valued American-made pieces over their European cousins, to Gardner the woman's reaction was a significant faux pas. "Should I enlighten and perhaps embarrass her?" Gardner remembered thinking. "I really just couldn't resist." The appreciation of antiques, Gardner decided, did not necessarily follow the expected class lines. She thrilled when a grocery deliveryman correctly identified her Sheraton dining room and when an electrician was able to distinguish English from early American design. The fact that Gardner recorded such small incidents in her journal shows the extent to which she had internalized the new aesthetic standards. She believed the ability to identify period classifications was an important category of knowledge, one that corresponded with education and status, but also one that could be learned as a form of self-improvement.

While Gardner practiced her skills as a connoisseur, she also relied heavily on dealers for both goods and information. In Rhode Island, she used the services of an antique dealer, D. R. Sexton. Like Israel Sack and the Margolis brothers, Sexton had a background in cabinetry. Occasionally she bought specific antiques from him; he also repaired and refinished her finds.[12] More often, however, Sexton examined her purchases to make sure they were genuine. Like most serious collectors, Gardner saw fakes and forgeries. In the late 1930s, for example, she uncovered a modern nail hidden in the joint of a William and Mary dressing table, a sure sign that something was amiss.[13] In another instance, she paid over $1,000 for a pair of Chippendale chairs, one of which turned out to be a refashioned bedside commode. She had purchased the chairs from the reputable Parke-Bernet Galleries in New York, but after only owning them for only a day she learned of the falsification. "Before this unpleasant affair was settled," she reported, "I had hired three expert antique-detectives, an Englishman, a German (not Jew) and a Swede, and had threatened to sue the Parke-Bernet Galleries."[14] Jessie's anti-Semitism, apparent in her parenthetical comment, helped her blame fakes on Jewish dealers and made her wary of the Boston market. The fake William and Mary dressing table she pinned on a Jewish dealer in Boston.[15] Gardner appears to have tolerated the existence of fakes as one of the risks of doing business. But the market was a corrupt place for her, one that only a trusted dealer with the proper pedigree could help her navigate.

Gardner's preferred dealer was a woman named Katrina Kipper, who owned a shop in Accord, Massachusetts, and who counted Henry Ford and Henry Francis du Pont among her clients. Kipper's father came from an elite German family, and Gardner had high opinion of him. She described him as "an old school gentleman . . . possessing a mind and heart of rarest culture and beauty."[16] While his daughter's business was evidence of the fact that the family had long since lost its fortune, the antique business provided them with a way to attach themselves to a genteel past.[17]

Kipper was successful in her trade. In a single day, she sold $30,000 worth of antiques to the Rockefeller Foundation for the period displays being built at Colonial Williamsburg.[18] It was an impressive feat. Kipper's high-profile sales reassured Gardner of the value of her own possessions and allowed her to connect her small museum project with some of the nation's most prominent. "Katrina is an intimate friend of the American Wing people," she wrote, "and fortunately for us, a friend of ours." Later, when Gardner was constructing her university museum, she repeatedly reminded officials at Brown that "if anything should happen" to her before Gardner House was complete, she wanted Kipper to "superintend the interior finishing and furnishing." Indeed, Gardner relied on Kipper as a source of connoisseurship. Kipper helped her select individual artifacts, choose wallpapers and colors, and cultivate her knowledge of period styles. Kipper was Jessie's most trusted adviser.

Kipper was not the Gardners' only source for antiques, however; they corresponded with dealers in Maine, Boston, New York, and South Carolina, answered advertisements in *Antiques*, and even sent cables to dealers abroad. With prices high and specific styles rare, such networks were essential in locating specific pieces. George's search for a complete set of Chippendale dining room chairs took over a year and spanned two continents. Even a small-time collector had to be committed to his search.[19]

Like many collectors, the Gardners derived particular pleasure from "buying at the source," canvassing the countryside for old families willing to sell their possessions.[20] These seemingly innocuous country rides placed the Gardners squarely in the role of antique consumers, masterminding deals, exploiting unequal power relationships, and separating artifacts from their family context. The couple's collecting escapades took them into the homes of many old New England families who had fallen on hard times. If the two feared the same for themselves, they never mentioned it. Gardner portrayed her rural purchases as a kind of rescue mission, saving remnants of their past from families who could no longer appreciate them. In her journal, she wrote about Marguerite Gooding, a Bristol, Rhode Island, woman who epitomized the old New England family's decaying condition. Jessie and George met Gooding when they answered a newspaper advertisement announcing the sale of many fine antiques. When they arrived at the seller's home, they found it in disarray: the porch post gave way when George took hold of it, the roof was patched with pieces of tin, and the front porch was ready to fall off the building. "How could there be valuable antiques . . . in such a hovel?" Jessie recalled wondering.[21] Her first assessment of the house's resident was not much more favorable. She described Miss Gooding as an "unkempt" woman, wearing a man's shoes and of such "girth that she would scrape the jambs in passing through any ordinary doorway." "Repellent," was her verdict. But over time Gardner came to pity this young woman who was herself ill and caring for her infirm mother. Gooding, she learned, was from an old New England family that had arrived from England during the seventeenth century aboard a private ship. She possessed good breeding and a certain graciousness, offering Jessie presents of flowers, fresh eggs, and craftwork. She also showed respect for her antiques, polishing their hinges and carefully wrapping them for travel. What had caused the family's troubles? Gardner did not speculate, concluding that only Edgar Allan Poe could "unravel the mystery of the fall of the House of Gooding." Her focus was on the antiques—a Sheffield mug, a cabriole-leg dressing table, and the family's seventeenth-century bible box among them. They were the only residents she would try to rescue.

Collecting at the source was also a way for the Gardners to demonstrate their knowledge of antiques, self-reliance, and consumer skills. Armed with knowledge gleaned from collecting manuals, antique magazines, and regular columns in newspapers such as the *New York Sun*, door-to-door collectors made a careful study of antique forms and styles in an attempt to match the skill of pickers. Their goal was simple: subvert the market and capture antiques at bargain prices. Like many collectors on the hunt, Jessie and George were careful to distinguish themselves from what they perceived as corrupt dealers. "After I have knocked at a door I shall wait in fear and trepidation for someone to come, but I shall represent myself at once as a collector rather than a dealer," George recounted in one of several stories he and Jessie wrote to commemorate their rural finds.[22] This desire to distance himself demonstrates the uneasy relationship collectors had with the market. While owners might be pure in their love for objects, market transactions debased both the aesthetic and the associative value of artifacts, exposing the crude economic nature of the transaction. When money was changing hands, the antique was neither an aesthetic object nor a family heirloom; it was simply a commodity.

The predatory nature of antique buying was hard to deny. In the same story, George described the liberating rush he felt when approaching a potential seller's home. "No longer am I a doctor hampered by ancient and modern codes of professional ethics," he recalled; "I am a rapper, I go to the door and rap. I know what I want. I want to get in and have a look for antiques."[23] In their stories, the Gardners often denied any adversarial relationship between themselves and the sellers. In a typical anecdote, George emphasized his own generosity (and revealed his anti-Semitism) by noting that he doubled the offer of a Jewish dealer.[24] But even if the Gardners believed that they did pay well, their stories showed that manipulating the market was part of the appeal of rural antiquing.

One of George's most prized possessions was a shelf clock made by the early nineteenth-century Boston clockmaker Aaron Willard (figure 14). George first spotted the clock in a New Hampshire home being run as a boarding house. Displayed on a corner shelf in front of the great dining room, the clock was obviously a family heirloom. George offered the owner $150 for it, the price derived from the fact that another gentleman had offered $135 before. But the man refused to sell, saying that the clock had belonged to his great-grandmother. Time passed and George visited the boarding house again. When he arrived, the family was in the midst of building a new house and had evidently decided that selling the old clock could provide needed funds. They made the sale on one condition: George would also have to take an old mirror that hung nearby. The family had always displayed the two together. They set the price for both at $250. In George's telling of the story, he emphasized the owner's limited knowledge, noting that he insisted that the gears were made of wood, while George knew that Aaron Willard only worked in brass. He also mentioned that he purchased the clock without knowing whether it was in running condition, as if to call attention to the risk he took as a buyer.

But just as George's story portrayed him as the clock's rightful owner by establishing his superior knowledge, it also celebrated his command of the market and his ability as a dealmaker. George knew the clock's value far exceeded the innkeeper's modest expectations. He had seen another Aaron Willard clock sell at auction for $2,006. Indeed, price was an important component of George's antiquing tale: he recorded that one dealer offered him $1,500 for the clock after another potential buyer promised $1,250.[25] As museum makers, Jessie and George would forgo profits from such savvy purchases, but stories like that of the Aaron Willard clock belie the Gardners' claims that their interest in antiques

Figure 14. George Gardner purchased this shelf clock, made by Aaron Willard of Boston, along with an antique mirror, from a New Hampshire family for the bargain price of $250. Photograph courtesy of Gardner House, Brown University.

derived only from the love of beauty. Antiquing provided collectors such as the Gardners with the thrill of being skilled consumers. There was the excitement of the hunt, the satisfaction of the find, and the pride of crafting a deal. For George and Jessie, these were experiences to celebrate and commemorate in their journals.

An Ideal House

George and Jessie displayed their antiques at their home on 44 Orchard Avenue, which Jessie dubbed the prettiest in the neighborhood. Exhibited in the context of the house, the antiques became functional objects that were a part of the Gardners' daily lives, as well as a reminder of their collecting adventures. Clarence Cook, a student of landscape architects A. J. Downing and Calvert Vaux, had popularized this idea of decorating with antiques as early as 1875, in his articles on interior decor for *Scribner's Monthly*. Later collected together as *The House Beautiful*, Cook's articles touted antiques as part of an Arts and Crafts aesthetic that advocated greater simplicity and lighter lines for the home.[26] But while the notion of decorating with antiques was well established by the time the Gardners set up housekeeping in the first years of the twentieth century, there were still plenty of detractors. In a 1921 article for *American Cookery* suggestively titled "Heirlooms and Degeneracy," a Mrs. Charles Norman told the story of her own encounter with antiques after having inherited a "few heirlooms" from an "aged relative."[27] At first the gift was met with joy, since Norman had just married and was in need of furnishings for her new apartment. But then the heirlooms arrived: "There were andirons, tongs, and candlesticks. There were several boxes of books and a chest of papers and another of clothing. There was parlor furniture, solid mahogany, very large and uncomfortable and in perfect condition." Norman's final comment reveals her true feelings about these objects. At best she found them impractical; at worse, a burden. Describing herself as possessing a "broad streak of sentiment," Norman recognized and valued the family history these objects represented. She also acknowledged their aesthetic merit, depicting the silver serving pieces as "extremely beautiful." But sentiment and beauty would not change one fundamental fact: the heirlooms were "mere things."

Opinions like Norman's represented a real challenge to the antique-loving public. If antiques were ordinary material goods, then the art of collecting was only another form of consumerism. Dependent on the ever-suspect antique dealer and a ready participant in market maneuvers, collectors like George and Jessie were already in danger of being labeled consumers. By displaying their antiques at home, where they would be used alongside mass-market goods, they subjected their prized possessions to the risk of being conflated with ordinary retail purchases. The prospect of placing their antiques in a museum promised to alleviate this problem. By removing the antiques from daily use and honoring them with the promise of perpetual care, the museum would secure their public value.

According to their journals, the Gardners first thought about making the museum in the late 1910s, but it was not until about 1929 that they took action. Between the time that Jessie and George first considered museum making and the time when they actually started the project, the couple was beset by financial woes. The upper-middle-class Gardners had a lot to lose. George's income as a doctor provided them with financial security and the comfort of an extensive investment portfolio—until the stock market crash of 1929.

In many ways, it is not surprising that the Gardners began to concentrate on their antiques just as their financial status began to erode. The couple had originally hoped to leave several public bequests, including funds to create a small urban park. But when their deteriorating financial situation made such generosity impossible, they turned exclusively to the preservation of their antiques. Throughout the Great Depression, antique dealers tried to drum up business by arguing that antiques would always maintain their value and could weather any economic storm. They knew from their own pocketbooks that such a promise was hardly true. But even if sales figures belied dealers' claims, antiques still suggested permanency and endurance by their very nature. These historic objects had survived, and their continued existence was a testament to continuity in the face of change. For collectors such as George and Jessie, this permanency was part of the appeal of antiques.

Jessie described the museum that she wanted to make as "an ideal home." It was a phrase that acknowledged the origins of the museum in the couple's home display and also evoked the historic house museums established throughout New England by groups such as the Society for the Preservation of New England Antiquities and the Daughters of the American Revolution. George and Jessie believed their new museum would transcend financial struggles, ties to consumerism, and mundane problems. It would be a home in which culture and refinement ruled. But creating an "ideal home" raised its own set of challenges, challenges that would bring George and Jessie back to the world of commerce, loss, and uncertainty.

First, however, the Gardners had to find a sponsor for their museum project. With their limited finances, they could not fully endow a museum and provide for its perpetual care, so the couple approached friends at Brown University with a plan to donate their antique collection if the university would provide a building to house it. In May 1932 Jessie and George presented their formal written offer. "Three years ago we began to plan for the ultimate disposal of our possessions. Our idea was then, as it is now, to give our collection of antiques, bric-a-brac, paintings, books, etc., as an entity, a collection to be kept together, to some institution, preferably a college, that will appreciate, care for, renew and use them," they wrote.[28] As part of their arrangement with the university, the Gardners specified that they would donate their antique collection, valued at between $65,000 and $75,000, and establish an endowment for its upkeep. They would also deed their home on Orchard Avenue to the university so that the income generated from its eventual sale or rental could be used to support the museum. In exchange, Brown would purchase an old house adjacent to campus in which to house the collection. The Gardners would restore the house to reflect the date of its original construction and be allowed life tenancy. After their deaths, the house would become the sole property of Brown University and be used as a "guest house–museum."[29]

Brown was slow to accept the Gardners' offer; it took a full three years for an agreement to be reached. University officials were apparently disinclined to acquire another campus building, and they first suggested that some of the couple's best pieces be displayed in the student center, Faunce Hall, originally constructed in 1904 and expanded with funds donated by Brown alumnus John D. Rockefeller Jr. in 1930. But Jessie was adamant that her collections be shielded from rough use. No records exist that fully explain why university officials ultimately agreed to purchase a building to house the Gardners' collections, but Jessie was not wrong in her assumption that American antiques had value in liberal arts curriculum of the 1930s. In the 1910s and 1920s scholars such as Van Wyck Brooks, Vernon Louis Parrington, and Lewis Mumford were beginning to publish studies exploring the "American mind," the intellectual and cultural qualities that set Americans apart from their Old World brethren. These pioneers in the emerging field of American Studies saw little university support for their endeavors, but by the mid-1920s Yale University had established an interdisciplinary department of History, the Arts, and Letters, which offered courses in "American Thought and Civilization." Harvard followed in 1936 with an interdisciplinary graduate program in the History of American Civilization Studies, and the same year George Washington University opened its program in American Studies.[30] Formal, university-based studies in American culture tended to focus on great American writers, as opposed to material culture collections, as a window into the nation's psyche. By the 1930s, however, early American antiques had become so widely accepted as legitimate national art that several universities had established teaching collections. Most notable was Yale's acquisition of over five thousand items—prints, furniture, china, glass, silver, pewter, iron, and other metal works—from collector and Yale alumnus Francis P. Garvan.[31] One of the premier collections of the 1920s, heralded for its aesthetically accomplished examples of seventeenth-, eighteenth-, and early nineteenth-century decorative arts, Garvan's acquisitions bore little resemblance to the Gardners' proposed gift. Nevertheless, in a letter to Brown officials, Jessie and George cited Garvan's university donation as a precedent for their own.[32]

Brown would not establish its own program in American Civilization until 1945, but in 1932 the university received a Carnegie Corporation grant to foster public art education. Although the Gardners' donation does not seem to have played any direct role in the grant program,[33] the grant suggests an interest on university officials' part in the artistic traditions of early New England, an interest that might have made them sympathetic to the acquisition of American antiques. But it was most likely the Gardners' personal contacts that sealed the deal. In 1932, the year Brown finally accepted the Gardners' offer, A. D. Mead was the university's acting president.[34] Mead, a biologist, was not known as an antique aficionado, but he and George Gardner had been friends since their college days. It was during Mead's short tenure as acting president that the university agreed to accept the Gardners' donation and procure a structure to house it.

The couple deeded their Orchard Avenue house to the university to support their donation, but they did not consider it a suitable location for the new museum. The house was in the colonial style, but it was not old, having been built as part of an early twentieth-century development, and it was a mile or two away from campus. It was constructed of wood and thus a fire danger to the Gardners' precious collection. A new location was, therefore, in order. Jessie's first choice was that the university build a fireproof reproduction dwelling to house the museum. (She was most likely looking to the example of Pendleton House, just down the road at the Rhode Island School of Design. Charles L. Pendleton had given his antiques to the school on the condition that the it build a fireproof structure to house it. The resulting structure, like Pendleton's own Providence home, was of Georgian design.) But Brown instead purchased a dilapidated building at 106 George Street, near the campus center. Built by mason Joseph Haile in 1806, the three-story brick Federal-style house was elegantly designed, but it was in terrible shape. The roof leaked, the chimney was crumbling, and cracks marred the exterior brick walls. Inside, dirt, dust, and rubbish ruled. University officials cautioned the Gardners not to visit the house until they had hired contractors and had it cleaned out. But the couple could not wait and arrived to find a soot-covered kitchen, an upstairs bathtub filled with trash, and windows obscured by dirt and cobwebs.[35]

Jessie Gardner's approach to acquiring this old family house was very much like the one she used when acquiring antiques directly from owners. She erased its family history. What was locally known as the Peck House, for the family who had inhabited it for generations, quickly became Gardner House. By Gardner's account, the Pecks were an old New England family who had somehow become debased. The dirty house was all the evidence Gardner needed to justify her acquisition of the building and its history, but she saw Mrs. Peck as particularly contaminated. In a story she titled "When Ignorance is Bliss," Gardner painted an unflattering portrait of the old woman, describing her as the "lone remnant of a once fine family," who had "grown to enormous proportions and become infirm and bearded on upper lip and chin with long dark curls."[36] Denying Mrs. Peck femininity functioned as a way to erode her claim on the old house. Gender ideology dictated that, as a woman, Mrs. Peck should be able to make a house into a home. By portraying her with masculine characteristics, Gardner denied those abilities, ascribing the house's ramshackle condition not to poverty or the infirmities of age, but to Mrs. Peck's essential character.

Appropriating the house's history was the easy part; now the hard work of restoration began. Much of the work was structural. The roof had to be replaced, as did sections of the walls, the front porch, the plastering, two chimneys, the wiring, the heating system, and the plumbing. Over time the house had settled seven inches and required jacking, as well as new steel posts and girders to support it. "Almost nothing exists of the original house, not even the four exterior walls," Gardner wrote in 1933.[37] "It is only a shell of a house with a sieve of a roof and unstable foundation. Each day's destructive work, tearing out plaster and laths, shows the condition to be more and more serious, so that a large amount of money will have to be spent merely to keep the building from falling into its cellar," she told another correspondent.[38] Needless to say, the project was expensive. According to Jessie, Brown officials originally estimated $5,000 to $6,000 to "put the house in good condition." Gardner herself believed the project would be accomplished for $15,000.[39] But when all was said and done, the total was closer to $30,000.[40] "106 George Street has been a horror of anxiety to George and me," Jessie wrote, "like a beast with a great maw that devoured our fund."[41]

With their stock-market losses, $30,000 had become a lot of money for the Gardners. In order to secure it, Jessie turned first to the estate of her brother, Henry Ames Barker, who had died in 1929. An advocate of public parks and a theater enthusiast, Barker had set up a trust to encourage the promotion of drama, the presentation of plays, and the establishment of parks in Providence. At the time of his death the fund was worth over $100,000, but with the stock market collapse the value of the remaining securities had eroded to about $20,000. This money Gardner targeted for her museum. Convincing the trustees of Barker's estate that the limited funds could best support a more focused project, and that a public museum spoke to her brother's love of beauty and culture, she persuaded them to donate the stocks to Brown University as funds earmarked for the restoration of 106 George Street.[42] Her brother's money made her project possible, but Gardner knew from the beginning that her budget would be tight. Rather than hire an architect to supervise the project, she contracted with the Providence firm of Howe and Church to prepare plans at a fixed price. The arrangement meant that she had to pay for additional consultations and that she would do a considerable amount of design work on her own.[43] Even with such cost-saving measures, the Barker fund was insufficient, and by August of 1933 Gardner started to consider the possibility of renting out the building's top floor and also pleaded with the university to extend her a loan.[44]

The ideal home that Gardner wanted to construct, the house that would elevate her antiques from mere commodities to priceless cultural artifacts, a place that would be removed from the corrupt world of business, was pulling her and her husband back into market transactions and politics. A staunch Republican in the era of Franklin Delano Roosevelt, Gardner saw local government fall to a Democratic mayor, the advent of New Deal programs that threatened her Puritan self-help ideology, and the decline of Rhode Island's booming industrial economy. Such economic and political developments may seem far removed from the construction of a small guesthouse and museum, but Gardner saw them as a threat to her legacy. New Deal economic reforms were a case in point. Under the university's auspices, Gardner gladly employed city relief workers whose salaries were capped at $15 a week. She knew that these low wages meant major savings for the project, and she regularly used relief workers for routine tasks such as cleaning out rooms and taking down plaster. But at the same time, she constantly feared that government reforms would raise salaries and further erode her funds. Even her plan to build brownstone steps leading to her front door became a political drama in her eyes when the Republican city officials who had promised to ignore the fact that the design for the steps violated city ordinance were voted out of office.[45]

Then there was the business with her contractor, a local man named Preston Leeming. When Gardner hired Leeming in 1932, she described him as a "young man of taste and ability."[46] By August of 1933, she was accusing him of having "played horse" with her and inflating prices.[47] She began to watch Leeming's every move, and she demanded that he justify his prices. Typical was her complaint about his bill for rebuilding a section of wall in the cellar. According to Jessie, Leeming's charge of $37 was grossly inflated. Only two "boys," she claimed, had worked on the project and they were paid only 40¢ an hour.[48] Small incidents like this played out again and again. In August of 1933, her complaints about overcharging led Leeming to reduce his prices. Gardner saved $25 on brickwork around the front door, $21 on the copper roof, $50 on basement trim, and $28 on sidewalk repairs.[49] Such adjustments did not mollify Jessie but only convinced her that Leeming had been defrauding her all along. With encouragement from Dr. Hermon Carey Bumpus, secretary of the Brown University Corporation, she stopped all work on the house in September and opened the project to additional bidders.

Having rid herself of her exclusive contractor, Gardner declared she was "at last a free woman."[50] Certainly she used the new arrangement to her benefit. She hired a second contractor, a Mr. Barker, to provide competition, and she made it clear that Leeming had to toe the line if he wanted to stay. Gardner was thrilled with the results. She believed that Barker knew more about historic buildings, and he gave her advice on moldings. Faced with competition, Leeming seemed to lower his prices by up to half his regular fees. Gardner also felt Leeming to be more sympathetic to her needs, citing the fact that he fixed a set of previously installed garage doors and itemized his bills more clearly.[51] Still, financing problems always seemed to haunt the project, and Gardner constantly had to use her skills, not as an antique connoisseur, but as an accountant. In separate incidents she believed that she caught Leeming charging her for material she already owned, Brown University accountants failing to report dividends earned from stock in the Barker fund, and her architect billing her at a higher rate than they had agreed on.[52] Such incidents were, in Jessie's mind, acts of corruption, sullying her project. But managing stocks and juggling inflation rates was not any easier. At every turn, she seemed to lose to the fluctuations of a depressed economy. Lumber prices rose before she could purchase flooring.[53] Stocks were sold at their lowest value, and work lagged even as the salaries of her employees rose.[54] Eventually, Gardner had to place herself in debt in order to keep the project rolling. After Brown officials denied her request for a loan on the grounds they could not provide her with additional resources when they had just cut their own faculty's salaries, Gardner applied to the bank and subjected herself to unstable interest rates.[55] Everything had come down to cash.

Gardner's inventory is evidence of how much money matters concerned

Figure 15. George Gardner's portrait is displayed in Gardner House above the Dutch tiles he was admiring when he suffered his first stroke. Photograph courtesy of Gardner House, Brown University.

her during this period. Carefully preserved in the records of her house are pages and pages of itemized expenses, letters written to contractors, and detailed synopses of dealings with construction workers and university officials. It is clear that while she might have exasperatedly exclaimed, "Oh, I can't keep track of all of this," she did an admirable job.[56] It was hard work, certainly nothing like the connoisseurship she thought she would be doing. All was made harder when, in June of 1933, less than a year after the Gardners had started construction on the house, George suffered a stroke that left him weak, agitated, and upset. Objectively, George's illness had nothing to do with antiques, but for Jessie, her husband's decline was intimately attached to their shared struggle to create a legacy. In recounting the story of George's first "attack" in her journal, Jessie emphasized that it occurred while he was admiring a set of Dutch tiles they had acquired from a contractor who had removed them from a local house whose owners preferred modern brick (figure 15). The passage starts out as a classic antique rescue story, George "shrewdly" discovering the tiles "tucked face to the wall" and purchasing them for a mere $15 from the contractor, who did not appreciate their value. The Gardners had triumphed over the market, but their delight was short-lived. In the course of studying his new acquisitions, George suddenly fell from his chair. In the days that followed his right leg grew weak, and Jessie saw him walking in circles on the lawn, "an anguished look on his face."[57] Soon after, Jessie decided that the stress of their museum project was too much for George and placed him in a rural Maine camp where he could enjoy the beauty of nature. From that point, he had little contact with the Gardners' museum project, but Jessie continued to blame his ill health on their struggles with the university's bureaucracy.[58]

With the exception of occasional visits to Providence, George remained in Maine until his death in 1936.[59] It was a difficult time for Jessie be alone, especially since George had always taken such an active role in their collecting endeavors. But his absence only made her more determined. She was building not just a museum, but a memorial as well. Jessie was with George in Maine during his final days. They were far from their Providence museum, but Jessie reinforced his connection to the project by emphasizing in her journals that their last conversation was about the antiques.[60] According to Jessie, George took her on an imaginary tour of every room, making suggestions for furniture arrangements and new purchases. There was the Queen Anne desk he wanted moved, the maple or cherry chest he wanted purchased, and the sitting room that he wanted completely redecorated. "I wish I knew those rooms were going to be furnished as we planned," George told Jessie a few hours before he died.[61] It was clear that he was thinking of the house on George Street as a legacy. Jessie saw it that way, too. She treated George's final instructions as a source of divine insight. "His suggestions are remarkably fine," she wrote a few hours before his death. "He comes to the subject as fresh and free (unhampered by association and misplaced sentiment) as though he dropped from the moon. His aim is perfection, his judgment unerring."[62] Jessie transcribed the conversation with her dying husband and placed it prominently in her journal. Two years later, when she compiled a report evaluating her progress, George's dicta were still much in evidence. Typical was her description of a small room over their kitchen: "George wished to improve the appearance of this room by furnishing it with nice old pieces. I have brought in the maple flat-top highboy as he wished, but have not got rid of the brass beds and other modern pieces. I hope to do so."[63] Nothing seemed to anger Jessie more than the suggestion that George might not have been of clear mind when he dictated his final wishes. She was "boiling mad" at a local doctor's wife who told her George's advice couldn't be trusted since he had a "sick mind."[64] Antiques had literally become an issue of life and death.

All through George's illness Jessie pushed the museum project forward. Living alone in Providence, with the couple's household assistant, Marian, stationed in Maine to look after George, Jessie oversaw the restoration, made crucial building decisions, managed the accounts, steered her way through the university's bureaucracy, hired and fired workers, and negotiated with assertive contractors. It was not, by her own admission, a good period for Jessie. "Take a stimulant," she advised friends in a letter after subjecting them to a detailed list of her troubles.[65]

Gardner used her journals to record the difficulties she faced, as if she wanted future readers to recognize the obstacles that limited her ability to create the beauty she desired. But from the pages of her journals emerges the story of another struggle, her struggle to maintain standards of architectural authenticity. Authenticity was a relatively new concept in historic preservation. Through the beginning of the twentieth century, women controlled the field of historic preservation as an extension of their role as "moral and aesthetic guardians of the domestic environment."[66] These women emphasized the domestic nature of the buildings they restored, often cultivating "period" gardens or serving tea against the backdrop of the colonial fireplace, the symbol of early American home life. They came to the work of preservation from a sense of decor and love for the past, but not from a trained understanding of period styles. They were concerned with presenting an alternative to the present, and picturesque structures could fulfill that function just as well as historically correct ones. But the nature of preservation was beginning to change, and while Jessie lacked the formal training to understand building construction or identify historically correct features, she could not ignore the fact that such skills were now becoming essential. Not far from the Gardner's new museum lived the preservationist Norman Isham. Born in 1864, he was a pioneer in both the professionalization of preservation—he was one of the first licensed architects to join the movement—and the promotion of historic buildings as aesthetic objects. Isham helped move preservation from a female-dominated model, centered on buildings with patriotic associations, to one concerned with architectural design and structural analysis.[67] Working frequently with William Sumner Appleton, whose Society for the Preservation of New England Antiquities was dedicated to saving historic buildings, Isham became a preservation architect, restoring such buildings as Rhode Island's Eleazer Arnold House and the Clemence-Irons House, and also contributing to the period-room displays at the Metropolitan Museum's American Wing. As Gardner acknowledged, Isham was a recognized authority with the skills and knowledge to pursue historical accuracy.[68]

In October 1932 Gardner wrote Isham one of several letters soliciting his advice. "I wish George or I could speak with you for about five minutes to get the answers to certain questions." Not one to hold back, Gardner continued with her inquiries: "What kind of floors would you have in the front hall, dining room and bedrooms? . . . Are wall lighting fixtures correct?"[69] No reply exists in Jessie's records, and Isham appears to have provided little assistance. Two years later, Gardner described him as "a crab." "Great pity," she wrote, "if he doesn't give out more generously, much of his profound knowledge of early architecture and furniture will be lost at his death."[70] Despite Isham's brush-off, Gardner continued her search for professional advice that would help her meet the demand for accuracy. She wrote to George Francis Dow, then curator of the Society for the Preservation of New England Antiquities, and to R. T. H. Halsey, at the time a professor in the Department of American Culture at St. John's College in Annapolis but most well known for his work on the American Wing. Halsey wrote her an encouraging letter (which she quoted frequently), but both men ultimately referred her back to Isham as the recognized authority on Rhode Island architecture.[71] At times Gardner even tried to press the head of Brown's Art Department, Will Samuel Taylor, into service, apparently believing that his artistic sensibilities would translate into an innate understanding of early American design. Jessie was annoyed when he declined to offer free assistance, but it is hard to imagine what she expected a painter best known for his murals of the evolution of man in the American Museum of Natural History to contribute.[72]

For the most part, Gardner was left to her own devices. Describing her work in a letter to a friend, Gardner wrote, "Someone had to dig and delve for information as quickly as possible, and the only person to do it seemed to be myself."[73] Dig and delve she did. She consulted books on architecture (most importantly J. Frederick Kelly's *Early Domestic Architecture of Connecticut*, and Norman M. Isham and Albert F. Brown's *Early Rhode Island Houses*), clipped pictures of appropriate models (Yale University's Elihu Club being one of her favorites, but old copies of the magazine *House Beautiful* offered other possibilities), and studied the period rooms in museum displays (the Boston Museum of Fine Arts provided her with examples of "early curtain rods," at least until a "certain disagreeable guard" interrupted her inspection—which was perhaps just as well, since curtains would not have been found in a New England home of that period).[74] When these sources did not provide enough information, Gardner consulted extant buildings. In order to ascertain correct proportions for her front steps, she and George set out on an expedition through the streets of Providence, measuring the width, depth, and height of various steps, as well as the overhang of the stair platform, all to make sure that it would produce the correct "sun shadow."[75] The Federal-period houses of Salem, Massachusetts, proved particularly helpful. By the 1930s, Salem's Chestnut Street was widely celebrated as one of the most beautiful streets in America. Home to early nineteenth-century mansions attributed to the architect and carver Samuel McIntire, it was widely featured in architectural books and picture postcards. Gardner studied Chestnut Street's architecture in Frank Cousins and Phil M. Riley's 1919 book, *Colonial Architecture of Salem*, a work she dubbed "a staff to lean upon when wearied by doubts," and was excited by what she termed the "striking resemblance" between 106 George Street and McIntire's famous creations.[76] Before George's first stroke, the pair traveled to Salem to make a study of the houses. Armed with a yardstick and permission from the Essex Institute, owner of several historic house museums, they measured doorways and took notes. Salem houses soon became models for the restoration of 106 George Street. Replicas of the famous fanlight at the Peabody-Sillsby House, the sidelights of 10 Chestnut Street (figure 16), and a mantel from the West Parlor of the Peirce Nichols House were all added to Gardner House.[77]

As an amateur architect and interior designer, Gardner used historic designs to her advantage. Adopting a famous doorway or fanlight treatment in her own house helped buttress Jessie's confidence in the choices she made. Even though she lacked expert advisers, she could rest assured that she had the weight of history behind her. At the same time, choosing from the catalog of history provided her with a way to escape the mass-market sameness of contemporary design. When Gardner replicated the sidelights of 10 Chestnut Street, with their circles and diamonds, she did so precisely because they would be "fresh in Providence."[78] Similarly, nothing bothered her more than when her architect's proposed design resembled what could be found in a "popular magazine."[79] But while Gardner used history to escape contemporary consumer markets, her architectural research came to resemble an extended shopping trip. She treated historical models as a design catalog, an architectural sourcebook from which she could choose individual features, independent of their relationship to the integrity of a given building, and apply them to her own domestic setting. Indeed, Gardner assessed the diverse offerings of architectural design just as one would traditional consumer goods. She rejected her architect's design for the basement door as "absurd" and "pretentious."[80] His plan for the front entrance received similarly poor reviews. "The architect had gone ahead and made a full scale working drawing of an entrance too elaborate for our house according to my taste, and in a design that I detested," Gardner reported in her journal.[81] She never seemed to doubt her discrimination or question her methods of

Figure 16. The front door of Gardner House shows the fanlight and sidelights Jessie Gardner adapted from historic houses in Salem, Massachusetts. Photograph courtesy of Gardner House, Brown University.

selection. In her mind, being the custodian of a historic house was based on taste. Aesthetics were central to her understanding of history.

Still, Gardner understood that the kind of piecemeal design and slavish imitation that she employed could not hold up under rigorous standards of accuracy. She knew that some of her choices for the house were simply wrong. Such was the case when she decided to install paneling in the dining room. She had planned on paneling that room from the beginning and had commissioned her architect to draw up the plans. But she abandoned the idea when Isham, evidently providing the much-sought-after advice, informed her that the paneling was not in keeping with the period, since Providence houses built around 1800 would have most likely had plastered walls. Confronted with the voice of expertise, she desisted, but still longed for what she considered a "pleasing contrast" in her decor. Then a young architect working as a site supervisor found the plan and praised it. That was enough. Gardner ordered the chimneybreast paneled, even though construction was by then too far along to install the entire plan. "It is due to my own indecision and weakness of character that in the dining room we have an arrangement that is neither fish, flesh, fowl, nor good salt herring,"[82] she acknowledged.

Nothing embodied Gardner's desire to create authenticity gone awry than the seventeenth-century room that she installed in the basement. As she readily acknowledged, Gardner House was built about 1806 in the neoclassically influenced Federal style. These were the characteristics that made the house similar to those on Salem's Chestnut Street. Yet Gardner decided to convert her unused basement into a seventeenth-century tavern room, to be named in honor of her brother, Henry Barker, reasoning that he always preferred gateleg tables to Chippendale and Hepplewhite.[83] But building a seventeenth-century room in the basement of a nineteenth-century house was no simple task. Gardner made cardboard models of fireplaces in an attempt to adapt the "yawning" fireplace of seventeenth-century construction to the nineteenth century's "cramped flues";[84] she had the room's exterior door constructed in two separate styles (battened on the inside, paneled on the outside), so that each side would blend with its respective context; and, most dramatically, she lowered the floor to create a higher ceiling. When the contractor resisted this last plan on the grounds that it would undermine the building's foundation, George himself ordered holes dug along the walls to demonstrate its feasibility.[85]

Even as Jessie and George were compromising the house's physical integrity, Jessie was criticizing her architect's accuracy of design. Her list of criticisms included "walls of paneled plaster board and picture moldings like a remodeled attic," and a "dinky little fireplace" made to look antique by the presence of an iron oven door and crane. "Nonsensical," Jessie pronounced.[86] Clearly, adding a seventeenth-century room to an 1800s house was out of context, compromising the building's stylistic and structural integrity. But Gardner did not see it that way. For her, "authenticity" was a matter of consistency of design, not structure or originality.

How do we reconcile Gardner's professed concern for accuracy with her readiness to improve and remove? As an antique connoisseur, she had learned to accept the importance of authenticity, particularly when it came to furniture. Like most antique collectors, she prided herself on the genuineness of her pieces. "No fakes for us," she resolved.[87] But even though Gardner and her fellow collectors rejected modified or embellished antiques as inauthentic, the rules were not as rigorous when applied to buildings. Frequently modified to suit the changing requirements of their tenants, buildings simply could not claim the kind of organic purity that many household antiques could. When applied to a building, "in the rough" could only mean in disrepair. An important influence on George and Jessie's plan for Gardner House were the new exhibits of American decorative arts housed in existing art museums. In comparison to the traditional historic house museums dotting the New England landscape, these period-room installations were cutting-edge in terms of accuracy (even if the Boston Museum of Fine Arts example included apocryphal colonial curtain rods). Isham himself had designed the seventeenth-century rooms for the American Wing and had encouraged a rigorous attention to maintaining consistency in period style.[88] But even if these rooms authentically replicated early American design, they lacked one crucial feature: they were not buildings, merely rooms housed within a modern structure. For this simple reason, art museums tended to treat buildings as piecemeal collections of decorative features. They mocked up Federal-style fireplaces, installed seventeenth-century casement windows that looked out to the museum's interior walls, and removed interior paneling from existing houses for reinstallation in the museum's galleries. This final action angered many preservationists, such as William Sumner Appleton, who saw art museum installations as a threat to New England's architectural heritage.[89]

For amateur museum makers like George and Jessie, art museum period rooms had limited value as a preservation model. They encouraged consistency of period style, but for homeowners faced with the reality of an organic structure that had been modified over time, meeting such strict standards would require removing later modifications and building anew, even in the absence of archeological evidence revealing the structure's original appearance. At the same time, art museums were constructed around chronological and geographic surveys of early American design. They collected period rooms in much the same manner as one would collect furniture—a seventeenth-century room from Massachusetts might be followed by an early eighteenth-century one representing Philadelphia design. In this light, Jessie and George's plan to install a seventeenth-century room in their basement appears less outrageous. They were merely trying to imitate the chronologically comprehensive displays found at the nation's leading museums. That by doing so they compromised the integrity of the building they claimed to be restoring shows the compelling nature of art museum displays and the way in which they encouraged antique aficionados to place aesthetics over the history of an individual building.

The issue of George and Jessie's restoration tactics came to a head when Jessie set out to create a commemorative plaque for the building (figure 17). Unsure of how to communicate what she had done, she wrote Lawrence Vail Coleman, director of the American Association of Museums, for advice: "The great question is: just what did we do to this house which we call Gardner House? Did we reconstruct, reproduce, remodel, rebuild? Not exactly."[90] Eventually she proposed "transfiguration," a term she intended to mean "not so much a change in form, but as an exaltation and glorification of the outward appearance." Coleman countered with "reconstructed in period style," but Jessie's comments show that she understood both the value attributed to historically correct treatments and the invasive nature of her decision to improve on the past.

With the shell secured, Jessie turned her attention to the interior and its furnishing, the heart of her ideal home. From the beginning, Jessie and George had applied the idea of antiques as aesthetic objects to their emerging museum. Their furnishing plan took the form of strict period-

Figure 17. Jessie Gardner created this plaque to commemorate her and George's work restoring and furnishing Gardner House. Photograph courtesy of Gardner House, Brown University.

room displays, modeled on the art museum's examples of chronological and stylistic arrangement. As small as their museum house was, they pursued the comprehensiveness of a large survey museum with rooms designated "Pilgrim," "Queen Anne," "William and Mary," "Sheraton and Hepplewhite," and finally "Hitchcock Group." "Any gaps in the succes-

sion we will enthusiastically fill in," Gardner promised university administrators.[91] Ordering furniture into period arrangements in this fashion
provided Jessie and George with the opportunity to demonstrate their
knowledge of antiques and their ability to live up to established canons
of taste.[92] It required them to identify stylistic schools, assemble harmo-
nious arrangements, and maintain established standards of quality—in
short, to prove that they had the knowledge and taste to be considered
true connoisseurs. But living up to the demands of the antique-collecting
community was not easy for a pair of amateurs. The Gardners knew that
their antiques did not meet the aesthetic standards of elite collectors and
museum curators. "We have very few pieces of Class A-1," Jessie admitted in a letter to university officials at the time of her museum proposal.[93]
Even so, the couple did not give up, convinced that they could improve
the collection as their own level of taste increased. "The interesting thing
about this game is that the further you progress, the more discriminating
you become," Jessie explained.[94]

Committed to the idea of aesthetic standards, Jessie and George
embarked on a continued course of acquisition and elimination, a process
Jessie continued after George's death. There was always room for improvement. To upgrade the collection, George conducted a room-by-room critique, editing out inferior articles, encouraging new arrangements, and
identifying potential purchases. Jessie transcribed his suggestions and
used them as a blueprint for the developing museum, returning to them
in later years to record her accomplishments in the margins.[95] George's
instructions forced Jessie to do away with many possessions. It was not
easy for her; even though she did not value her antiques as family heirlooms, they still had associations tied to the life that she and George
had made for themselves and to their collecting adventures. But if the
couple were to live up to the dictates of connoisseurship, they knew that
they would have to practice selection. Jessie explained the situation to
university officials using clothing as a metaphor. "George says the contents of our house reminds him of a man whose suit is perfect, of the
finest material, and made by the finest tailor in the country, but whose
socks are from [the five-and-dime store chain] Newberry, and his tie
from Kresge."[96] Quality was clearly at issue.

In 1937, Gardner was finally able to report success in editing the collection: "Many hundreds of articles of long and tender association have

been discarded under the wise initiative and gentle guidance of George Gardner. Looked at in the new light of suitability to Gardner House, these objects, often beautiful in themselves and costly, were admittedly meaningless and commonplace; they represented 'stock,' the trite, the easy thing to acquire."[97] Gardner's comments reveal the degree to which aesthetic standards influenced her idea of the museum and forced her to forgo artifacts with personal meaning. They also establish her belief in the importance of taste over money. Costly objects, she maintained, were not necessarily good objects, especially if associated with easily available, mass-market goods. Gardner's belief in discrimination as a trait independent from wealth must have given her confidence in her ability to build a noteworthy museum collection. In truth, as we have seen, money was always a factor. In the years after George's death, Jessie tried to carry out her husband's final wishes by acquiring additional artifacts to replace those he found inadequate. But even though the market was still depressed, she could not afford the pieces she knew were necessary to achieve the kind of aesthetic display acceptable to antique connoisseurs, or to her own husband. "The library, supposedly Chippendale, is most in need of attention," she wrote a friend in 1938, "but Chippendale is costly and very hard to find."[98] Without the means to purchase high-quality antiques directly from dealers, Gardner relied on compromises and luck. Such was the case when she secured a Chinese Chippendale tea table at a bargain price from a house sale in Providence.[99] As we have seen, antique experts always cautioned collectors about bargains, claiming that inexpensive antiques usually merited their low prices. But for a collector like Gardner, such cautions were not practicable. Building a collection required her to be a bargain hunter.

The idea of connoisseurship greatly affected Jessie and George's approach to interior decor. But there was another influence on the way they furnished their house as well: the idea of "home." Since the mid-nineteenth century, the canon of domesticity had portrayed the home as a bastion of moral values, physically and spiritually removed from the corrupt worlds of business and politics, yet powerful in its own right. A proper home could promote piety, engender morality, and maintain traditional cultural values, and its influence extended far beyond its own walls. Early preservationists and historic house museum founders drew on this idea of the home as a site of cultural reproduction and connected the saving of individual buildings with the preservation and maintenance of traditional cultural values. For some, the connection was explicit. In Salem, Massachusetts, philanthropist Caroline Emmerton purchased the Turner-Ingersoll House, known as the House of the Seven Gables for its connection to Hawthorne's popular novel, and used proceeds from visiting tourists to finance a settlement house to serve the city's immigrant community.[100] Across the state, in Deerfield, local women used the historic Frary House as a setting for a "common parlor," a place to discuss community concerns and promote cultural growth.[101] For the Gardners, Jessie especially, the idea that their museum was to be housed in a home was an important element, not to be ignored.

As part of their arrangement with the university, the Gardners planned to occupy 106 George Street during their lifetimes. Inhabiting the new museum was, in one sense, another economic strategy for the couple. Selling their house would produce additional funds for the museum's restoration, and because the new building was owned by the university they wouldn't have to pay taxes on it. But living in the museum was about more than money. It was a chance to make the place a bona fide home.

Jessie's desire to build her own life into the very structure of the museum speaks clearly to her need to commemorate her contributions and build a monument to herself and George, but the idea of home was about more than Jessie and George as individuals; it was wrapped up in the project of museum making itself. By the early 1930s, over four hundred historic house museums had already been established in this country. Rhode Island could claim only fourteen, but nearby Massachusetts boasted well over a hundred.[102] Most of these buildings were owned by private associations, each operated according to the individual desires of the community volunteers who maintained them. In 1933, Lawrence Vail Coleman published his *Historic House Museums*. Recognizing the prevalence and importance of this new museum genre, Coleman set out practical advice about ownership and administration, financing, furnishing, and building restoration. For Jessie, Coleman's book was a rare source of professional advice. She read her own copy thoroughly, transcribed selected passages into her journals, quoted them in her correspondence, even incorporated them in her will. Of all Coleman's advice, Jessie cleaved to one dictum: "Historic houses must be made to LIVE again." "Houses," Coleman wrote, "appeal partly to the emotions, and this deserves to be strengthened by developing atmosphere. One of the commonest remarks of visitors in any well appointed house is that they enjoyed being there because the place is like a home and not like an institution."[103] After stripping 106 George Street of any remnant of the Peck family's ownership, Jessie could not claim that the museum had a homelike atmosphere. She would have to manufacture it, using her own life as its foundation.

From the beginning, Gardner had planned to donate, alongside her valuable antiques, mementos and keepsakes from her own life. These included not only antique furniture and art, but also silver, china, jewelry, and many decorative pieces that Gardner summed up as "bric-a-brac,"[104] all of which would help cultivate the homelike atmosphere she sought. The arrangement was a bit unusual. Gardner's friend and financial adviser, James Collins, assumed that Brown would not want the couple's jewelry and silver, but Gardner reprimanded him. "Perhaps they don't know enough to want the jewelry," she wrote, "but after all, Gardner House is to be a Historic House Museum and that means it is supposed to be personal and to have atmosphere with the beautiful things of the past that have belonged to the people who lived in it."[105] She remained committed to including decorative objects with her gift, but doing so created certain contradictions. On one hand, small artifacts and personal mementos provided homelike touches, but on the other hand, they could also resemble the "trite" objects George had encouraged her to avoid. Clutter was the issue. Victorian decorating practices tended to emphasize ornate interiors, heavy drapes, and a profusion of mass-produced ornament. It was a style clearly out of fashion, but one still found in many working-class homes.[106] If Gardner was not careful, her personal displays could easily be read as outdated, or even worse, lower-class. Gardner thought often about this problem, quoting Coleman in her journal as saying, "It is much better to have incomplete furnishings than to show an abundance of poor material. THE FEAR OF EMPTY SPACE HAS CAUSED MANY AN ERROR."[107] In an attempt to maintain aesthetic standards, Gardner instructed her contractors to build display cases into the fabric of the house. She saw their presence as central to her project, and worried that the money would run out before they were built. The display cases, as ordinary as they might seem to a visitor touring the house, were Jessie's attempt to reconcile the aesthetics of the art museum with the homelike atmosphere cultivated by historic house museums. In many ways, the two represented competing interpretations of the past, one defined by artistic display, the other invested in sentimentality and historic associations. But Gardner saw both as valid.

The fact that Gardner saw both "home" and "beauty" as powerful cultural forces helped her see antiques as a force for civic reform. Her interest in civic reform was a bit unusual for an antique collector. Many collectors in the 1920s and 1930s saw antiques as an inspirational testament to the American spirit, but Gardner envisioned a more direct, if still undefined, connection between public museums like her own and social progress. This focus on civic improvement was most likely inspired by her brother, Henry Barker. A businessman by trade, Barker was best known as chairman of Providence's City Plan Commission and executive officer, from 1905 to 1920, of the Metropolitan Park Commission. In his civic work, Barker collaborated on city traffic plans, worked to introduce zoning, and most significantly, helped establish a system of public parks for the city of Providence and its environs.[108] Speaking to the Rhode Island chapter of the American Institute of Architects, Barker made the connection between urban beautification and social progress by comparing what he saw as Europe's beautiful and artistically built cities with their less refined American counterparts. "There is little of the vulgarity, the rowdy obscenity of the gang on the corner, the hoodlum toughness that in some parts of all our cities is an unconscious protest against the life repressed and the soul imprisoned."[109] Barker's comments were typical of those associated with the City Beautiful movement. An architectural and urban planning style defined by Beaux-Arts planning principles, monumental structures, and classical design, the City Beautiful movement was founded on a belief in the power of beauty to inspire civic responsibility and social betterment. Often promoted by middle-class women who sought to apply their skills as domestic housekeepers to the city at large, City Beautiful proposals could be as simple as placing trash cans on street corners or as monumental as Daniel Burnham's 1901 plan for Washington, D.C., which was designed to place America's capital on par with the great centers of Europe. No matter how large or how small, at the root of such initiatives was a shared belief in the power of beauty to inspire moral rectitude, eliminate social problems, and reverse the ill effects of suburbanization on the urban core.[110]

By the time Gardner began her museum endeavors, the movement had already lost its luster after failing to make good on its lofty promises. But she nevertheless believed her antiques could have an elevating influence on the community as a whole. To that end, she planned to offer her house museum as a meeting space. It would not be one of those "do not touch museums," she pointed out proudly. Those encouraged to use it included groups interested in "Parks; Civic Improvement; Preservation of Natural Resources; Roadside Beautification; Preservation of Antiquities."[111] As in all things relating to the museum, Gardner would not leave anything to chance. She specifically omitted those "individuals who seek social prestige" from using the house, noting in the margins a "Mrs. Lustig" who evidently fell into this category.

When it came to Gardner House, Jessie rarely trusted anyone but herself to make decisions. Over the course of the years that she restored 106 George Street and installed her collections, her relationship with Brown University disintegrated. She was angry that university officials had stuck her with a decrepit house, that they had refused to give her a loan during her time of need, and that they had (in her opinion) mismanaged the stocks in her brother's fund. To make matters worse, university faculty did not seem particularly interested in Gardner House as a teaching tool or research facility. Since the project's conception, Gardner had assumed that the faculty of the Art Department would have a special interest in the building, but no record exists to show that it was ever used for classes or special projects. She did note in her collecting journal the rare visit of a Brown faculty member. Pleased with his apparent interest in the collection, she asked him if he would like to glance through the rooms, but he replied that he had come in search of a solution to his drafty office and only wanted to view the weather stripping on her windows.[112] If Gardner's journal is an adequate record of Gardner House's use by university faculty, then the university's acceptance of the donation had less to do with curriculum development and more to do with A. D. Mead's friendship with the Gardners and his position as acting president at the time of their proposal. In any case, by the mid-1930s Mead was about to retire as the university's vice president and Gardner no longer trusted the university to manage the museum when she was gone. "Can you believe," she wrote in connection to her will, "that after the years of complete absorption in this project, . . . I will sign away control and turn our precious Gardner House contents over to the indifferent, uninformed crew that is Brown

University to do with it as they see fit?"[113] As much as Gardner swore she would never give up control, there was little she could do. She was coming to the end of her life. Like George before her, Jessie had suffered a stroke, and the time when she could exert control over material goods would soon be over. What pained her now is that when she and George signed their initial agreement, they had given the university control over the collection, including the ability to add to it after their deaths.[114] In a note written in 1934 and inserted next to the original agreement reproduced in the journal, she claimed she and George had been pressured into signing the paperwork. They had been "rushed," she maintained.[115]

Antiques were everything to Jessie Gardner. They were sources of beauty, culture, and even civic improvement. But they were also fragile. To maintain their power, they must be treated correctly, arranged to show off their aesthetic qualities, and freed from the corruption of the mass-produced and the trite. Building a high-quality collection and exhibiting it according to the standards of aesthetic display had been a challenge for the couple. As amateurs, they lacked the knowledge, professional contacts, and monetary resources to fully succeed as collectors. But that did not mean Jessie trusted the university to carry on in her stead. Still, all she could do was voice her desires in her journal and hope that the university would respect them. "It is my earnest request that no changes be made in GARDNER HOUSE or its contents, that no furnishings be disposed of and none added except under the expert advice of persons of recognized conservative taste. No nouveau or modernistic notions should enter here. Nothing foreign to New England. Furthermore I direct that the house shall be a historic museum but never take on the appearance of collections, but shall be kept simple, spacious, personal, a historic house museum. I hope that it may be so."[116] This was her final wish.

Seeking

On April 14, 1935, Jessie Gardner staged a ceremony to dedicate the Henry Ames Barker Memorial Room, the seventeenth-century-style room created in honor of her brother. A. D. Mead, still Brown's vice president, spoke at the ceremony. Gardner immediately reported the event as an enormous success: "While Dr. Mead was speaking, the friends who had gathered in the memorial room for a cup of tea and the simple exercises to follow, sat with bowed heads and tears in their eyes; and when he had ceased speaking, there was a silence till he asked them to step forward to witness the ceremony of the hanging of the crane and lighting the fire. Everyone was deeply touched."[117] But when Gardner wrote to Mead several days later, her tone was more ominous. "All through that lovely ceremony, Sunday which your little talk made impressive and just perfect, I was depressed by what I knew was going on behind the scenes: the propagation of countless termites, traveling and chewing the side walls and over our heads."[118] A few months later she called the arrival of termites "the most tragic blow" next to "George's break in health."[119] Indeed, the insects proved a most persistent foe. They spread all through the Barker room in the basement, which was built on wooden sills placed directly on the ground, and from there throughout the house. Gardner swept up hundreds of wings. Termites were relatively new to the Northeast; possibly they had come from some of the old boards used to give a venerable patina to the Gardners' new construction. It was a disaster. Gardner had university entomologists consulted and hired a termite control company, but the problem continued, and she eventually wrote a detailed report commenting on all the infestations over a period of nearly ten years.[120]

As was the case with everything associated with her museum project, Gardner did not see the termites as simply a stroke of bad luck. She saw them as another sign of corruption, and she blamed the contractors, this time because they built the floor in the Barker room out of wood rather than stone and laid the sills directly on soil.[121] It is hard not to feel bad for Gardner: everything she had been working for was being literally eaten out from underneath her. It is also tempting to see the termites as a symbol of the tragedy Gardner perceived in making the museum. Indeed, the idea of struggle colored her interpretation of the experience for all time. Pasted at the beginning of her journal is a seemingly cryptic newspaper clipping: "Most of us go through life seeking something. We do not always find it, so we can end the tale with the happy cry: 'It is not too late.' Mr. Hilton seems very familiar with the baffling situation that faces most people either because of some lack in themselves or surrounding circumstances which make the accomplishment of their desires unattainable."[122]

Gardner saved this clipping as an obvious reference to the frustration she felt building her museum. In the simplest sense, she did succeed. She restored the building, installed her antiques, and turned the house over to the university, which has used it as a guesthouse for visiting dignitaries, a function outlined in her original donation. But the clipped quotation suggests that Gardner was not completely fulfilled by what she had obtained. Certainly she would have pointed quickly to the "surrounding circumstances" that compromised her project: the architect's lack of expertise with historic design, the contractor's constant price-gouging, and what she saw as the university's failure to appreciate her project and support it with expert advice and additional funds.

Throughout her journals, Gardner was quick to point the finger and lay blame, to take to task those who were not helping as she believed they should. But the quotation raises another question: Did she also perceive "some lack" in herself? I believe she did. The aesthetic standards of the collecting world, with their new emphasis on accuracy and authenticity, were difficult for an amateur to meet. Without the funds to buy at the highest levels, without the advice of experts or the services of dealers, Gardner would always be trying to live up to the ideals of decorative art museums. Indeed, it was an anxiety that ate at her. Many times she wrote in her journal that Gardner House would be a place that must withstand scrutiny, a place that would be judged by everyone in the antique field. The idea that the nation's most recognized connoisseurs would visit Gardner House was probably a bit of wishful thinking. Nevertheless, her comments speak to the ways in which new forms of antique collecting created canons of taste and forced individual collectors to relinquish authority and command over their own possessions. Gardner found the project of making a museum a huge disappointment. Repair bills, contractors, and termites consumed her project, taking her away from the practice of connoisseurship and filling her days with the most mundane of concerns. Only one thing was worse: the fear of failure.

Highboys and High Culture [4]

Adopting an American Aesthetic in Deerfield, Massachusetts

*I*n 1959 Henry Flynt, a New York lawyer and antique collector, wrote the editor of the *Saturday Evening Post* about an antique collecting and historic preservation project he was conducting in the small town of Deerfield, Massachusetts. "As a reader of your valued publication I deeply appreciate your stalwart efforts to stem the tide of softness in our national character and to bolster our citizen's morale and your thinking along the lines of our American heritage. I therefore have the temerity to send you a few pages I have written about Deerfield, Massachusetts for I feel the story that this stark village carries forward the ideals you urge in your editorials."[1] The editor's reply is not recorded, but Flynt's letter points to the connection collectors forged between historic objects and American patriotism at mid-century, as the nation sought to define itself against a communist Other. The end of World War II and the coming of the cold war signaled a period of renewed popularity in American antique collecting; antique prices rebounded from their depression-era lows and attendance at history museums soared. Just like the generation of collectors that preceded them, mid-century collectors used American antiques as evidence of the existence of a distinctly American artistic and cultural tradition. But for cold war collectors, antiques proved especially valuable in combating the communist critique of American capitalism.

Few mid-century collectors were as articulate in their ability to join history, antiques, and cold war ideology as Henry N. Flynt. Henry and his wife, Helen, first became involved with Deerfield in 1936, when they enrolled their son in Deerfield Academy, a private school for boys. They began to buy property in the town in 1942. In 1945 they purchased and restored the Deerfield Inn, and two years later they tackled their first museum property, the Ashley House. Thus began a relationship with Deerfield's history that lasted until Henry's death in 1970. While the couple worked on a scale that George and Jessie Gardner would have found unimaginable—in addition to establishing a library and twelve museum properties, which they filled with antique furniture and decorative objects, the couple razed existing structures, moved additional historic buildings into town, and erected new buildings in period style—their work was similar to the Gardners'. The Flynts too would make their own restoration decisions, purchase antiques, and ponder issues of interior decor. And, like the Gardners, the Flynts would pay careful attention to the aesthetic standards of contemporary antique collecting. Neither Henry nor Helen knew much about aesthetic collecting practices when they began their work in Deerfield. Both Henry's father and his uncle had been antique collectors, but Henry had deliberately distanced himself from the antique world as a young man, fearing that what he termed "Collectivitis," an uncontrollable state of hyperacquisition, was a family disease. When Flynt finally gave in to his passion and began purchasing antiques for his Deerfield museums, he soon adopted the aesthetic standards promulgated by established American art museums and national publications such as *Antiques*. Buying antiques of aesthetic quality proved useful for Flynt. Not only did they buttress his anticommunist message with evidence of a free market society's cultural and artistic worth, but they also helped him obtain national recognition—something to which Jessie Gardner could only aspire— for his project in Deerfield.

Flynt did not begin with a blank slate. Deerfield's residents, unlike those of many other small New England towns, had a long history of cultivating their past. The town first earned fame for its role in Queen Anne's War (1702–1713). On the night of February 29, 1704, a band of French soldiers and their Kanienkehaka Mohawk and Abenaki allies attacked and nearly destroyed the village. As Marla R. Miller and Anne Digan Lanning have noted, the so-called Deerfield massacre "provided New England colonists with a rallying image not unlike the Alamo, the Maine, or Pearl Harbor: the story of the surprise attack, the burning of the village, the murders of women and children, the forced march to Canada of 109 captives, and the failure and/or refusal of several captives to return was the stuff of which legends are made."[2]

The attack placed Deerfield squarely in the national consciousness. Sites associated with the 1704 raid became early tourist destinations, connecting Deerfield to a network of American landmarks. But while the attack provided Americans with a dramatic origin myth, Deerfield residents shaped the past to their communal needs. Inspired by the attention generated by their history, they restored family homesteads, constructed memorials to their ancestors, built a museum out of household keepsakes, and developed a thriving trade in traditional crafts. Deerfield's history provided a way to understand their community, face adversity, honor family ties, and even augment their income. Flynt's arrival, therefore, marked a decided shift in the community's relationship to its past. By focusing his collecting efforts on aesthetically accomplished antiques and by reaching out to a nationally based community of collectors and antique curators, Flynt undermined traditional patterns of valuing family stories and local heirlooms with a new emphasis on using Deerfield to define national values. Because Flynt not only collected antiques but also worked toward a larger restoration of the town, his work in Deerfield did more than simply create an alternative to earlier forms of history commemoration. It transformed the entire town and inscribed his vision of an aesthetically accomplished past on the landscape itself.[3]

The Past's Past

In 1955 Cornelius Vanderbilt Jr. described Deerfield as an "Extraordinary Village" and a "Natural Preservation." "When you walk down old Deerfield

Street you do actually feel you are in the eighteenth century. . . . I did not feel that I was in an exhibit, that I was seeing a site. For old Deerfield is not [an exhibit] in the sense that Williamsburg or Dearborn or other restored or preserved 'villages' are. . . . Old Deerfield is a 'natural' preservation." Vanderbilt went on to claim that "no historical society, no wealthy individual or organization assembled, restored, or preserved" the town.[4] He could not have been further from the truth. Deerfield owed the retention of its stately colonial homes and elm-lined streets not to coincidence, but to the hard work and deliberate acts of many individuals who made conscious decisions about which monuments to erect, which artifacts to collect, and which buildings to restore. When Henry Flynt came to town in the 1930s, what he found was not a natural preservation, but the result of many years' work preserving the past.

If in fact Deerfield was exceptional, it was for the extent and early development of its citizens' preservation efforts. In 1847, the Ensign John Sheldon House, commonly known as the Old Indian House because its front door retained hatchet marks made by Deerfield's eighteenth-century attackers, became the site of one of the first preservation attempts in America. According to the preservation historian Charles Hosmer, the Old Indian House had become a popular destination for tourists seeking evidence of the 1704 raid.[5] An article in the *Gazette and Courier* of nearby Greenfield reported that "the house has long attracted the attention of the antiquary, and at this time has become a relic of public interest, which few travellers omit to visit, on their passage through the village."[6] But despite the building's landmark status, its owner, Henry Hoyt, put the building up for sale in 1847. Deerfield residents passed a resolution calling for the building's preservation and appointed a five-member commission to publicize the cause. Although enthusiasm was high, money was scarce. Residents failed to collect $2,000 to buy the house on its lot, or even $150 to move the building. In 1848 the Old Indian House was demolished and Hoyt erected a new house on the property.[7]

Even though the preservation initiative failed, the Old Indian House remained an important community symbol. In the months before it was torn down, residents rushed to record its image. Paintings, such as the one made by George Washington Mark in 1848, provided a lasting link to the old house.[8] Pieces of the building, the most famous of which was its hatchet-scarred door, also became celebrated relics. According to Hosmer, members of the Hoyt family sold the door to D. D. Slade, a doctor and antique collector in Boston. In 1868, after years of trying, Deerfield residents bought back the door and returned it to the village (figure 18).[9] The loss of the Old Indian House also sparked the construction of new links to the past. In 1869 a group of Deerfield residents erected a monument on the site where Eunice Williams, wife of the Reverend John Williams and a prisoner in the 1704 raid, was killed by her captors for failing to keep up on the forced march to Canada. More monuments followed, including one recognizing Deerfield residents who lost their lives in the 1704 raid, another dedicated to Samuel Allen, who "held his ground" during an Indian attack in 1746, and still another commemorating the longest single-family holding of any estate in Franklin County.[10] Visitors who came to Deerfield saw a landscape marked to solidify its ties to the past (figure 19). Deeply grounded in a sense of memory and commemoration, these places drew their meaning from their connection to specific individuals and from the nearby presence of descendents. Taken out of context, the stone markers would be nearly meaningless. It was their location in Deerfield that made them important.

At the center of these commemorative endeavors was George Sheldon, a descendant of the original owner of the Old Indian House (figure 20). By the time of his death in 1916, at the age of ninety-eight, Sheldon had built many monuments, written a two-volume history of Deerfield, and established the Pocumtuck Valley Memorial Association (PVMA), a museum of which Sheldon became both president and curator.[11] In 1880 the PVMA acquired Memorial Hall, built in 1799 by Asher Benjamin and first occupied by Deerfield Academy. Sheldon soon filled the large three-story brick building with his collection, and he placed at its center the Old Indian House door. To enhance the museum, he created what is now commonly believed to be the first period-room installation in America, predating those constructed by antiquarian George Francis Dow at Salem's Essex Institute. The rooms included a colonial kitchen, bedroom, and parlor.[12]

As an antique collector, Sheldon had little interest in the aesthetically based collecting that emerged at the turn of the century, and rarely participated in the developing market. Indeed, Sheldon's period rooms had few aesthetic pretenses and bore very little resemblance to the ones that would be established years later in the Metropolitan Museum of Art.

Figure 18. The Old Indian House door, named for the hatchet scars left by French and Native American attackers during their 1704 raid on Deerfield, was displayed as a sacred relic in the town's Memorial Hall Museum. Photograph courtesy of the Pocumtuck Valley Memorial Association, Memorial Hall Museum.

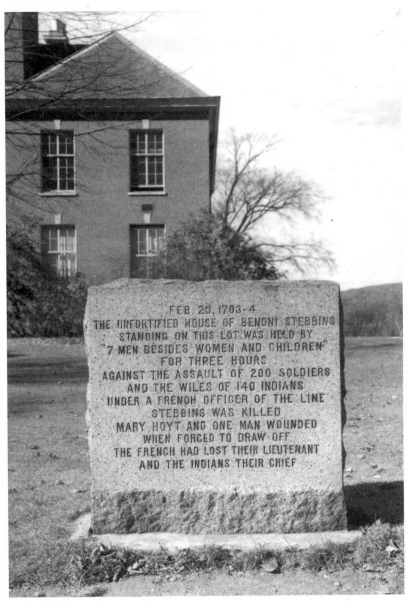

FEB. 29, 1703-4
THE UNFORTIFIED HOUSE OF BENONI STEBBINS
STANDING ON THIS LOT WAS HELD BY
"7 MEN BESIDES WOMEN AND CHILDREN"
FOR THREE HOURS
AGAINST THE ASSAULT OF 200 SOLDIERS
AND THE WILES OF 140 INDIANS
UNDER A FRENCH OFFICER OF THE LINE
STEBBINS WAS KILLED
MARY HOYT AND ONE MAN WOUNDED
WHEN FORCED TO DRAW OFF
THE FRENCH HAD LOST THEIR LIEUTENANT
AND THE INDIANS THEIR CHIEF

Figure 19. Deerfield residents used stone markers to inscribe their history on the landscape. This marker commemorates the resistance mounted by Benoni Stebbins and his household against French and Native American attackers during the 1704 raid. Photograph by Samuel Chamberlain, courtesy of Historic Deerfield.

Figure 20. Deerfield photographers Frances and Mary Allen took this picture of antiquarian George Sheldon in 1895 at Deerfield's Memorial Hall Museum. Just visible at right is a Hadley chest. Photograph courtesy of Pocumtuck Valley Memorial Association, Memorial Hall Museum.

"Not a single article is here preserved on account of its artistic qualities," Sheldon explained of his displays. "The collection is founded on purely historical lines and is the direct memorial of the inhabitants of this valley, old Indian and Puritan."[13] Rather than expensive furniture crafted for early American elites, everyday artifacts dominated Sheldon's collection. His prized possessions included ceramics, paintings, local furniture, tools, textiles, and Indian arrows, usually obtained directly from local families without the aid of antique dealers. In keeping with the Victorian approach to museum building, he acquired large quantities of items. Of Sheldon's collecting habits Timothy C. Newman, former executive director of the PVMA, has written, "If one pot was good, ten were better."[14] The colonial bedroom housed a jumble of furniture styles, and the kitchen was littered with more than eight hundred ceramic jugs, pewter plates, iron pots, and other utensils.[15] The result was an image of colonial domesticity and abundance, but not one of artistic design.

Sheldon's understanding of antiques was deeply tied to his reverence for place and for the local associations it engendered. As Michael C. Batinski has argued, Sheldon rejected broad historical narratives in favor of small details and individual facts specific to local life. For this reason, Sheldon rarely referred to himself as a historian, preferring to call himself a "local historian" or "antiquarian." In keeping with this local approach to the past, he embraced the study of genealogy, examining not only the history of his own family, but others in the area as well. The idea of family history thus became a natural tool for Sheldon to use in interpreting historic objects. In his accession records, he often included a detailed family history of the donor, as well as his or her story. "Bring in then those old mementoes before they are scattered and lost, and if you won't write the old stories, come in and tell them to me," he urged.[16]

Catalogs and guidebooks Sheldon compiled for the Pocumtuck Valley Memorial Association show clearly the kinds of artifacts he valued. Of the hundreds of items in Sheldon's 1886 catalog, few would be attractive to decorative arts collectors, especially on the merit of Sheldon's descriptions alone. Indeed, he defined most of the objects in terms of their associations. There was the "leather chair from the house at the Bars occupied by Samuel Allen who was killed by the Indians," the "door posts" from the Old Indian House, and a wooden pail "in constant use for more than 70 years." Even if the object was not tied to an incident or event, every item in the collection was associated with its donor, faithfully listed in the catalog entry. Deerfield donors are listed by name alone; those from neighboring communities are distinguished by their town of residence. Town identity was very important to Sheldon's collecting program. While almost all the artifacts in his collection were clearly connected to Deerfield or its local environs, Sheldon did accept objects from other states if they were donated by a local. Such was the case for Sheldon's "corn crusher," which W. O. Taylor of nearby Shelburne had brought from Fort Lincoln, Dakota.[17] In this way, an association with a local resident could transform a random artifact into a valued treasure.

Thanks in part to Sheldon, Deerfield ended the nineteenth century with a strong sense of its history and a material record of its past. But the town's retention of its historic buildings was also a symptom of its declining economy. By the late nineteenth century, Deerfield had no industry and no connection to the railroad, and it was quickly losing its male population to more prosperous towns. As Miller and Lanning have written, Deerfield's women recognized that continued development of the town's historic assets could solve their economic problems.[18] Between 1880 and 1920, these women embraced the craft revival that John Ruskin and William Morris began in Great Britain. Eileen Boris has argued that the handcraft movement in America represented the desire of white, Protestant elites for a preindustrial, preimmigration social order. Deerfield's craft movement exhibited many of the same class distinctions found in more urban handcraft schools. Employing the language of uplift, elite women, often summer residents from places such as Boston and New York, formed the movement's leadership. Joined by the matriarchs of old Deerfield families, these women found in craftwork a way to promote economic stability while reasserting their cultural authority. For the working classes, which included hard-up farming families from both old Anglo and new immigrant stock, crafting contributed important money to household income.[19]

Even though craftwork did not trade in historic objects themselves, the practice prefigured the antique market in the way it used history as a commodity. Using a guild system, craftworkers produced and sold artifacts that drew on both documented and fanciful images of old-time handiwork. Founded in 1896 by Ellen Miller and Margaret Whiting, the Society of Blue and White Needlework based its designs on embroidery in the PVMA collection. The society dyed its own materials and marked each piece with its symbol—a flax wheel superimposed with the letter D.[20] Raffia baskets had no precedent in Deerfield history, but members of the Pocumtuck Basket Makers made up for this lapse by invoking historic icons, such as the Old Indian House, in their designs.[21] Local men also contributed, replicating small pieces of Connecticut Valley furniture, such as Hadley chests. Other craft societies produced historically inspired textiles using handlooms, natural dyes, and old-time knotting techniques.[22]

While Deerfield's craftworkers did not commemorate local history with the concrete associations of Sheldon's museum guidebook, a sense of place was integral to their trade. To this end, they cultivated the historic resources of old Deerfield. Restoring historic houses was especially popular. Since many of the movement's leadership were women with attenuated ancestral connections to Deerfield, restoring historic houses not only provided them with fashionable summer residences, but also reaffirmed their family status and New England roots. At the same time, restored buildings supplied appropriate spaces for crafters to work and display their wares. Like most Colonial Revival restorations, these transformations were not intended to be historically accurate. Rather, they were romantic interpretations of the past. In 1890, C. Alice Baker, an educator, academy founder, and published antiquarian, restored the Frary House and opened it to the public as a type of common parlor for the promotion of an idealized Yankee past.[23] The house included an assembly hall where Miss Baker held dances in eighteenth-century dress. Around the same time, Annie Putnam of Boston restored the Barnard-Willard House and transformed "the little brown house on the Albany Road" into an art studio, complete with exposed beams and a large round-headed window.[24] Coupled with Sheldon's museum and monuments, the result of such an extensive program of restoration was a community tied to its past.

Leaving the Local

By preserving buildings, artifacts, and handicraft traditions, Sheldon and the Arts and Crafts community established a collection of historic resources grounded in local history and family stories. But it was a vision of the past that would not survive long into the twentieth century, as it would soon be supplanted by a new concern for forging an aesthetically driven history based on the standards of a nationally based antique community. After Sheldon's death in 1916 and the decline of the Arts and Crafts revival in the 1920s, Deerfield was without a historic leader. But that situation began to change in the 1940s, as Henry Flynt began to take an active interest in the town. Flynt fell in love with Deerfield's past. "Charm, architecture, history, courage—these are what make Deerfield different," he wrote in a statement prepared for visitors.[25] Like Sheldon before him, Flynt cultivated Deerfield's historic resources. Between the purchase of his first Deerfield property in 1942 and his death in 1970, Flynt restored or repaired dozens of the town's homes. He established a series of historic house museums, took over the presidency of Sheldon's Pocumtuck Valley Memorial Association, and built a library to service both organizations. But while Flynt saw his work as an effort to maintain rather than change Deerfield, his arrival was also part of a chain of events that transformed the village from an insular town that valued its old families and local traditions to a much more cosmopolitan community.

Well before Flynt arrived on the local scene, Deerfield Academy had begun to become increasingly attached to a national network of elite private schools and their supporters. Founded in the 1790s, the school had long catered to the needs of local students, but under headmaster Frank Boyden it was transformed into a premier preparatory school that drew its students from across the nation. Boyden had come to Deerfield in 1902. A recent graduate of Amherst College, he assumed the position of headmaster with only fourteen boys and girls enrolled. Officially, the school included the public Dickinson High School and received substantial financial support from the town. The students came from nearby farms and often received time off during the harvest season.[26]

In the 1920s Boyden began to distance the academy from its local community, in part because of an anti-immigrant and ethnocentric impulse to maintain the school as a Yankee institution. As Brian Cooke has noted, Boyden feared Deerfield's rising population of immigrant Polish farmers. Early in his career he decided that he "could not afford to become Principal of a school which would virtually be a Polish high school."[27] Determined to "maintain the school as an American institution," Boyden turned to boarding students.[28] As early as 1923, 80 out of 140 academy students were boarders. Their numbers included the sons of deans and professors from top universities, including the University of California, Harvard, the College of the City of New York, and George Washington University. Boyden also separated Deerfield Academy from the public high school in 1923. To maintain financial solvency, he appealed to the headmasters of Exeter, Taft, and Andover, who raised money among their own alumni. Other contributors included the presidents of Cornell and Amherst, and Dean Henry Pennypacker, chairman of the Committee on Admissions at Harvard.[29]

Historic preservation offered another way to cement Deerfield's Yankee appearance and advance the school's expansion. In 1924 Boyden contacted William Sumner Appleton at the Society for the Preservation of New England Antiquities about financing preservation in the town. "Somehow there should be found some way of securing money to buy these old houses as they are thrown upon the market," Boyden wrote, "as otherwise Deerfield will go, as Hadley and Hatfield have, into the hands of the Polish and other foreigners."[30] Purchasing buildings for academy use not only minimized demographic changes by taking individual buildings out of private hands, but also provided much-needed housing for students and faculty. In this way, promoting local history earned Boyden national prominence.

Boyden found a sponsor for his preservation initiative in Henry Flynt (figure 21). Having grown up in Monson, Massachusetts, a small town on the Connecticut border, Flynt knew Deerfield. During the Arts and Crafts revival, he and his family were among the many tourists who rode the trolley into town to view the old houses and purchase handmade goods.[31] But Flynt's connection to Deerfield was not cemented until his ties with Monson were broken. As owners of the local granite-mining company and general store, Flynt's parents donated their large Greek Revival house and nearby fields to Monson Academy. A few years later the Flynts returned to find the house replaced by new baseball fields, which, to make matters worse, were named after other donors.[32] In Flynt, Boyden recognized both a "real New Englander" and someone with the financial means to back the academy's expansion.[33] Already a trustee of his alma mater, Williams College, Flynt became a Deerfield Academy trustee in 1940 and chairman of the board in 1943. He and his wife soon donated money for tennis and squash courts, assisted with building a new dining hall, and funded faculty vacations.

Figure 21. Frank Boyden and Henry Flynt posed in the doorway of Deerfield's Sheldon-Hawks House for this 1962 photograph. Photograph courtesy of Historic Deerfield.

Flynt's wife, Helen, was a Cincinnati native with no personal connection to Deerfield or old New England, but her interest in the school soon made up for that. Indeed, it was Helen, a lover of sports, who donated the funds for the school's tennis and squash courts as well as faculty vacations. Helen's money also supported the couple's restoration work. The daughter of Fred A. Geier, founder of the Cincinnati Milling Machine Company, Helen had the benefit of a family fortune, a Vassar education, and a cultured upbringing. Her parents owned two splendid Victorian homes, one of which was furnished with English antiques bought from the New York firm of Ginsburg & Levy. With style and money, Helen was the perfect partner for Henry and his preservation interests.[34]

Reluctant to become a collector, Flynt undertook his first restoration projects solely in the name of the academy. After refurbishing the eighteenth-century Manse as the headmaster's house, the Flynts purchased the Manning House in 1942 and donated it to the academy as a dormitory. This was followed in 1944 by the purchase of the Rossiter House, and in 1945 the Deerfield Inn, Ashley property, and Allen House. In each case the academy profited. The Flynts rented the restored Rossiter House to the school, refurbished the inn to attract a more affluent class of students, prevented a liquor store owner from occupying the Allen House, moved one of the Ashley houses to the academy's grounds, and installed a faculty apartment in the other. These purchases insured that the academy would have ample space to grow, freedom from intrusive neighbors, and a beautiful streetscape to welcome prospective students and their families.

As the Flynts bought more properties, they became increasingly interested in antiques, historic architecture, and professional preservation methods. They hired local talent to research their properties, but unlike the Gardners, the Flynts had the money and connections to acquire furnishing and restoration advice from nationally known experts such as Joseph Downs, a former American Wing curator who in 1949 became curator of the Henry Francis du Pont Winterthur Museum, and his Winterthur colleague Charles Montgomery.[35] The Rossiter House provided one of the Flynts' first opportunities to practice restoration. In the 1930s the house's previous owners, Wynn and Sarah Rossiter, had restored the building to their own version of colonial by covering it in wooden shingles and paneling the dining room with knotty pine. Basing their restoration on a 1907 description of Deerfield's home lots, the Flynts removed the shingles, clapboarded the house, and painted it pink.[36] Thus, what the academy received was not simply a dormitory, but a revised colonial aesthetic.

The Ashley purchase was the Flynts' first museum property. In 1869 the Ashley family moved the eighteenth-century home of their ancestor, the Reverend Jonathan Ashley, to the back lot and constructed a new house on the old foundation. The Flynts reversed this process. They moved the 1869 house to the academy where it became a dormitory. Then, after razing a nearby twentieth-century bungalow, they returned the Reverend Ashley's house to the front lot and began the demanding job of reconstruction. After years of use as a barn, the house had lost clapboards, windows, doorways, interior molding, paneling, and partitions. Flynt approached the problem with the intention of creating an authentic restoration. He hired local women as researchers, interviewed Ashley family members, and even asked one of the academy teachers to excavate the original cellar hole. In addition, Flynt's contractor, William Gass, searched within the house for evidence of its former appearance.[37] In the end, Flynt lacked enough evidence to create an exact reproduction of the house as originally built, but his dedication demonstrated a deep interest in Deerfield history and its architectural heritage (figure 22).

Flynt's money and social standing connected him to a national network of authorities in collecting and preservation. In an oral interview conducted by Charles Hosmer, Flynt told the story of his reconstruction of the fireplaces in the Sheldon-Hawks house. The old fireplaces were important to Flynt's vision for the house, but they and the central chimneystack had long since been removed. He set out to reconstruct the chimney, but without the benefit of extant examples he had a hard time deciding what the fireplace lintels should look like. "There was a great discussion whether the lintel should be a wooden lintel, sandstone lintel or a steel or iron one," Flynt later recalled. "We couldn't decide." For guidance, Flynt turned first to his network of national antique experts and enlisted the advice of Vincent D. Andrus, curator of the American Wing. Andrus voted for sandstone, but before Flynt committed, he consulted with Helen. According to Flynt's account of the story, Helen quickly put things in perspective. "Why don't you fellows go over in Memorial Hall and look at the fireplace that Mr. Sheldon restored to exhibit kitchen utensils and you'll find a wood lintel there with a great big sign on it in big

Figure 22. The Ashley House provided a gracious setting for this 1948 photograph of Henry and Helen Flynt. Photograph courtesy of Historic Deerfield.

bold letters, 'This was taken out of the Sheldon Hawks House after it had been there 125 years.'"[38] Flynt's telling of the story emphasizes his respect for Deerfield's traditions and his appreciation of Sheldon's preservation work. But the story also points to another fact in the Flynts' preservation work: their readiness to consult with experts on the national scale.

The Flynts saw their work as an act of preservation, but in truth their efforts brought great changes to town. Not only did they employ museum professionals to do the kind of restoration work once reserved for residents, but their purchases took many houses out of local control. A 1945 document shows that Flynt and Boyden together considered altering over sixty buildings on the town's mile-long main thoroughfare, which was always known as "The Street." Their plan included tearing down thirty houses and moving or remodeling many of the others. To accomplish these goals, the pair estimated that they would have to buy thirty-eight houses for an estimated $533,000.[39] Flynt and Boyden never

Highboys and High Culture

completed this grand plan, but by 1969 Deerfield had changed from a village of local homeowners to a town dominated by museum and school interests. In 1969, the Academy, the Bement School, the Flynts, and the Heritage Foundation (an organization Flynt established for his museum properties) combined owned thirty-seven of the fifty-six houses along Deerfield's main street.[40] Flynt himself had some interest in twenty-six of these properties.[41] As a result, Deerfield became more closely identified with its nationally based student body and its restored houses than its local families.

Reinventing the Nation

One of the most dramatic ways the Flynts changed Deerfield was through their reconfiguration of its symbolic value. While men like Sheldon had found meaning in honoring ancestors and preserving local stories, Henry Flynt discovered a political message in Deerfield's restoration. Flynt understood Deerfield as not just a physical construct, but as an ideological construct, defining America as a nation through a representation of its past. In his essay "From Tomahawks and Arrows to Atomic Bombs," written in 1969 for the *Delaware Antiques Show Catalog*, Flynt explained his motivations for investing in Deerfield in terms of its ideological impact: "It is with a firm belief that the future of America can be favorably influenced by a delineation of the daily lives of the people who made this Village that a resolute attempt has been made to preserve and restore their homes."[42] In another essay, titled "Deerfield, Massachusetts: Its Meaning," he was more specific, urging readers to "reaffirm our sense of perspective" by emulating the rigorous lives, joyful worship, and dedication to education displayed by New England's first European settlers.[43] By reconstructing the culture and traditions of early America, Flynt's Deerfield offered a model for contemporary American society.

The cold war made Deerfield's message all the more urgent. In 1967 Flynt told *Yankee Magazine* that "the more people in America who know the background of the country, the better off the country is. You won't get a lot of isms and all kinds of fake notions going on if the American public knows its own history."[44] Flynt also believed that history would teach Americans how to face down Soviet aggression. In "From Tomahawks and Arrows to Atomic Bombs," he urged his readers to learn from the colonial past: "During these days of fears of atomic bombs it may be good to think of the American Indian Wars and the settlement of the New England village. Let us strengthen our determination, courage and spirits by recalling that our forebears did not give in because of swiftly soaring arrows and cruel tomahawks."[45] For Flynt, the cold war and the Indian Wars represented a pair of "red attacks." By learning about one, Flynt believed, Americans could prevent the other.

Flynt most strongly stated his anticommunist philosophy in the book he co-wrote with photographer Samuel Chamberlain, *Frontier of Freedom: The Soul and Substance of an American Village*, published in 1952. In truth, Chamberlain did most of the work—taking photographs, writing articles and captions, designing the layout, and adding pen-and-ink drawings. But Flynt reviewed every detail with such exacting standards that Chamberlain threatened to withdraw from the project.[46] As a result, the finished work closely mirrored Flynt's own ideas and values. Congratulating Chamberlain on the book's introduction, Flynt wrote: "It is splendid and I wouldn't even dot an 'i' or cross a 't'. Boy, if I can be associated with a book that has that as a Foreword I am ready to work for the U.S.A. and I think anybody that reads it should feel the same way."[47]

In *Frontier of Freedom*, Flynt and Chamberlain reinterpreted the story of Deerfield's massacre to send a message to contemporary Americans. Deerfield held strong in the face of Indian attack; contemporary Americans must hold strong against the new red threat. Chamberlain's introduction makes the comparison between past and present explicit: "This village heard the beat of the tom-tom two-and-a-half centuries ago, and met the challenge as we are meeting it in Korea today, with the lives of brave young men and women."[48]

Flynt was not alone in using history to combat communism. In the late 1940s, the National Archives and the Justice Department organized a mobile exhibit of American documents called the Freedom Train. The train visited 322 cities, and the exhibit, which included the Bill of Rights, the Emancipation Proclamation, and Jefferson's draft of the Declaration of Independence, was seen by more than 3.5 million people. Under the leadership of John D. Rockefeller III, Colonial Williamsburg was also actively promoting nationalism. Beginning during World War II, Rockefeller sponsored a series of patriotic radio programs, held tours for

Figure 23. Samuel Chamberlain illustrated *Frontier of Freedom* with photographs of beautiful homes, like this image of the interior of the Allen House, the Flynts' Deerfield residence. Photograph by Samuel Chamberlain for *Frontier of Freedom*, courtesy of Historic Deerfield.

military trainees, hosted foreign dignitaries, and organized a conference series on international affairs.[49] Flynt appreciated narratives of American history that celebrated the nation's democratic traditions. Indeed, before becoming an antique collector, Flynt built a collection of American manuscripts and historic documents—letters from Supreme Court justices, presidential autographs, and documents related to political history. But what defined Flynt's work in Deerfield was his attention to issues of aesthetics. After a brief introduction offering historic Deerfield as a model for contemporary society, *Frontier of Freedom* was filled with images of stately houses, fine furniture, and beautiful tree-lined streets. In order to assure the inspirational value of these images, he fussed about photographic quality. In letters to Chamberlain and to the book's publisher, Flynt pushed for additional close-ups and color photographs, despite the increased cost.[50] He understood that Deerfield's power was in its visual representation. More than anything else, elegant houses spoke to America's cultural superiority and to the rewards of patriotism (figure 23).

Certainly the idea of using antiques as evidence of America's cultural value was not new. As we have seen, turn-of-the-century antique collectors also valued their finds as evidence of the nation's artistic accomplishment, but against the backdrop of communism's implicit critique of America's economic and social disparity, aesthetically accomplished antiques offered proof that wealth could produce a higher good. Elites had taste and the ability to create beauty. Interestingly, Flynt's narratives tended to downplay the existence of economic inequity in the past. In the narratives he constructed, Flynt gave the leading role in Deerfield's history to well-to-do professional men and ignored the existence of individuals of lesser means. Few laborers, women, or slaves appear in any of Flynt's written accounts of Deerfield's history. Indeed, even though the town's economy was predominantly agricultural in the seventeenth and eighteenth centuries, Flynt rarely mentioned farmers. Jonathan Ashley the minister, Asa Stebbins the businessman and gristmill owner, Joseph Barnard the doctor, and Samuel Pierce the pewterer represent the type of men Flynt celebrated through his restorations and historical writings. By grouping together artisans, intellectuals, and businessmen, Flynt constructed what he saw as the colonial precedent to his own professional class. In addition to representing the achievements of their age, these individuals were of the class that owned the kind of expensive objects Flynt would celebrate as evidence of American cultural superiority.

Purchasing a Past

Flynt's vision of Deerfield as an aesthetic antidote to communism influenced his approach to collecting. If elegant homes and fine antiques were the proof of America's cultural superiority, then antiques represented a kind of aesthetic resource, a resource to cultivate by buying them. On its own, the town of Deerfield could certainly claim the presence of many antiques. Some were preserved in Sheldon's museum; others remained in family hands. But as Flynt became more deeply involved with the world of antiques, his understanding of aesthetics changed. No longer would Deerfield's local collections be enough. Rather, he would be influenced by the now entrenched aesthetic standards promulgated by the elite collecting community. Like many collectors before him, George and Jessie Gardner included, Flynt would add to his existing collection, work to refine his aesthetic sensibilities, and purchase additional objects in an effort to produce a more aesthetically accomplished collection. Such actions might not have been necessary if Flynt had retained Deerfield's local focus. But Flynt's nationally based collecting community demanded it.

Deerfield's redevelopment meant that Flynt, after years of avoiding antique shops and auctions, would enter the market in full force. The market was not completely new to him; both his father and his uncle had been collectors. Both were particularly interested in antiques as expressions of Yankee ingenuity, and clocks were their specialty. Flynt's father, George, left the restoration work to his brother, an avid tinkerer, but he knew the local market. A 1922 advertisement in *Antiques* notified readers that George C. Flynt had sold over one thousand chairs in the past year.[51] His reputation was strong enough that when Henry Ford came to Monson in search of a stagecoach for Greenfield Village, Henry's father brokered the deal. According to the younger Flynt, Ford had authorized his father to offer as much as $600 for the stagecoach. But knowing that farmers did not value such pieces and that $200 would be adequate payment, the elder Flynt proved himself a savvy consumer.[52]

When George Flynt died in 1929, the family collection was sold at auction.[53] As he established his home with Helen, Henry turned first to European antiques. Like many of their class, the Flynts started to collect English antiques. Their interest in European decorative arts was serious enough that they built their new house in the English style as well. But English goods were of little use in their Deerfield projects. Their first opportunity came with the purchase of the Deerfield Inn during World War II. Unhappy with the inn's furnishings, the Flynts decided to redecorate in a style in keeping with the town's historic atmosphere. Helen was in charge of finding antiques, and she approached the task from the perspective not of quality, but quantity. "I went to Sloane's in New York," she remembered. "I wanted ten beds, ten dressers, etc." The firm could not fill her order, but they did provide her with pine boards from which they fashioned dressers. Next, Helen went to an antique dealer in Greenwich, Connecticut. There she found many double beds, which she proceeded to have cut down to twin. Helen's first attempts at antiquing demonstrated her ignorance of contemporary collecting practices. Even though her purchases were intended for practical furnishings rather than components of a formal collection, her sins—fashioning new antiques from old wood and radically altering genuine stock—would have been seen as egregious by any serious collector. Looking back on her first foray into American antiques, Helen herself would denounce her actions as "silly."

As the Flynts became more serious about American antiques, they began to purchase simple pieces with connections to Deerfield and the Connecticut River Valley in an effort to maintain a sense of place. They frequented antique shops in nearby Northampton and relied on longtime Deerfield residents, such as Margaret Whiting, Margaret Harris Allen, and Mary Fuller and her daughter Elizabeth, for advice. The 1946 estate auction of Mrs. Susan Hawks, granddaughter of the historian George Sheldon, was an important purchasing event for the Flynts. They also acquired pieces from Louisa Billings's estate, despite the fact that she saw the couple as outsiders and expressly forbade her heirs to sell to them. The Flynts were sometimes misled, however; for example, some of the pieces at the Hawks auction came from Mrs. Hawks's antiques business rather than her ancestors.[54]

The Flynts' early interest in buying locally showed a sensitivity to place and associations rarely celebrated in contemporary collecting circles, but local antique sources could only supply so many goods. To fill their newly acquired properties, they began to cultivate additional collecting sources and to buy from major dealers. But like many collectors, Flynt found it hard to stomach the cost of his purchases. Whether he worried that dealers were taking advantage of him or that his Deerfield projects would outpace his pocketbook, his anxieties manifested themselves in a propensity to haggle. Encouraged both by the one-on-one nature of the antique sale and the fluidity of prices, haggling has a long tradition in antiquing. Still, high-end dealers have often resisted the practice, which implicitly undermines their authority and the value of their wares. As Elizabeth Stillinger reports in her history of the Flynts' work in Deerfield, Henry's insistence on negotiating price could lead to conflict. After trying, and failing, to secure a discount from New York dealer Bernard Levy on several pieces of antique furniture, Flynt made one last attempt, subtracting fifty dollars from the combined purchase price on the grounds that it was easier to write the check if he simply rounded down. Fifty dollars was not a large amount, considering that Flynt was purchasing an expensive Connecticut high chest, a Chippendale desk, and matching bookcase, but the act was a symbolic form of resistance to the dealer's ability to set price. Levy refused to sell until Helen pressured Henry into paying the full amount. It was then that Levy made his own symbolic display. From the wall, he removed a mirror, valued at $850, and presented it as a gift to Helen. The message was clear: the dealer would control his own wares.[55]

Suspicious of dealers and always anxious to secure the best price, Flynt most often bought from John Kenneth Byard, who had been a fraternity brother during their years at Williams College.[56] Originally from upstate New York, Byard attended Columbia Law School. In the 1930s he retired from his legal practice and purchased an old house, a mill, and several other structures along the Silvermine River in Norwalk, Connecticut. The area was home to a burgeoning art colony, and Byard saw the opportunity to build a small business. Dubbing the complex the Silvermine Tavern, he established a restaurant, an inn, and an antique gallery. With antiques only part of his business, and a second career at that, Byard lacked the expertise of longtime dealers such as Israel Sack or Jacob Margolis. Indeed, Byard's records show that he rarely gave his customers a guarantee of authority based on his own word, preferring to rely on the knowledge of other dealers. Typical was a note added to a receipt for a pair of Sheraton mirrors sold to Helen Flynt in 1958, which offers as proof of their American origin the fact that the New York antique firm of Ginsburg & Levy had advertised them as such several years before.[57] In other instances Byard could be even less assuring. In a notation on the receipt for an "Oak Brewster chair," for which Henry Flynt paid $475 in 1958, Byard conceded that "some might consider the chair to be of foreign origin," but nevertheless counseled Flynt that the chair could "just as well be considered a New England Brewster chair."[58]

However dubious Flynt may have felt about his friend's statements of authenticity, he had no cause for complaint about Byard's pricing polices. Byard's records show that he sometimes disclosed his purchase price to Flynt or passed on pieces at a fixed percentage. If Byard felt that an item was particularly important to Flynt's collection, he might even sell it to him at cost.[59] During the late 1950s Flynt bought antiques from Byard in great quantity. Purchases ranged from inexpensive objects—an iron hook priced at $27.50 or a $15 pair of candlesticks—to much more serious acquisitions, such as a $6,000 pie-crust table or a seventeenth-century New England chest on which Flynt spent almost $4,000.[60] As a result of the pair's close relationship, Byard had a significant influence on the process of history making in Deerfield. In many ways, the dealer's stock became the foundation for Deerfield's historic furnishings.

Flynt did not limit himself to Byard's wares, however, nor did he limit his collecting adventures to American soil. Like the Gardners, Helen and Henry used their European vacations as an opportunity to increase their collection. Many of the antiques they acquired abroad were costumes, bought in Paris or London and earmarked for Helen's emerging textile museum.[61] Henry used travel to locate American silver. His search led to the purchase of a large collection that had originally belonged to Lionel Crichton of London and was owned by his son-in-law Victor Watson. Watson insisted on selling the collection as a whole, and Flynt agreed. The purchase, ninety-two pieces in all, greatly enlarged not only Flynt's personal collection but also the amount of silver in Deerfield. Indeed, with the Flynts as active collectors, Deerfield was becoming more than a quaint old town; it was becoming a major repository for high-end antiques. For the Flynts, collecting during a period that valued the most aesthetically accomplished artifacts, this kind of aggressive acquisition was natural. But as an approach to preserving the past, it deviated from the traditions of Deerfield. Sheldon had ransacked local attics; the Flynts ransacked the world.

An Education in Taste

Flynt's willingness to supplement Deerfield's historic resources with purchased antiques was also tied to his increasing concern for aesthetic quality. As the Flynts progressed in their Deerfield project, they became accepted members of an elite collecting community made up of nationally known curators, dealers, and collectors. Among their many friends were curators Charles Montgomery and Joseph Downs, Metropolitan Museum of Art director Francis Taylor, Yale University silver expert John Marshall Phillips, and the editor of *Antiques*, Alice Winchester.[62] The Flynts also began to socialize with other collectors. They attended parties at the home of the fashionable collector Katherine Prentice Murphy, who inscribed her vision of eighteenth-century high style in period rooms all over the East; rubbed shoulders with folk art collector and preservationist Nina Fletcher Little, whose home, Cogswell's Grant, is now a museum property owned by Historic New England; frequented the collections of Shelburne Museum founder Electra Havemeyer Webb; and attended antique forums with the Texas oil heiress and patron of the arts Ima Hogg. According to Winchester, many of these collectors held social gatherings where they entertained among their prized possessions.[63] Such experiences initiated the Flynts into the world of high-style, contemporary collecting.

One of the most important acquaintances the Flynts made was Henry Francis du Pont. As a collector, du Pont sought the most beautifully proportioned, elaborately decorated, and finely crafted items, but only to the extent that they would harmonize with his other possessions.[64] Du Pont regularly refused artifacts because they were the wrong color, the wrong size, or the wrong quality in comparison to other items in his period-room settings.[65] Typical was his reply to dealer Isabella Barclay's offer to sell him an antique stool: "I'm sorry to say that the stool entirely dwarfs my coiffeuse and therefore I am returning it to you very reluctantly. It is most trying, as it is a lovely piece."[66] The Flynts' 1946 visit to du Pont's house at Winterthur was a revelation in the refinement that could be achieved with American antiques. Thanking du Pont for his hospitality, Flynt wrote: "You personify in this home the art of gracious living and graceful thinking. What a tonic it is to see a place like yours! . . . Our humble little effort to preserve old Deerfield, Massachusetts has taken on renewed zeal because of our trip to Winterthur."[67] According to Deerfield curator Philip Zea, the Flynts apparently mimicked du Pont's designs by adapting his famous Port Royal parlor to their own Allen House. Both rooms employed twin settees flanking the fireplace, brilliant yellow silk upholstery, and paired tall chests.[68]

Antique dealers also proved to be an important source of aesthetic education. To Mrs. Frank Thomas, a dealer in Oriental rugs, Flynt wrote: "What an education you have provided for us along a line in which our knowledge is so meager. . . . Our taste has been educated by your taste, your splendid descriptions and gracious courtesy so now we want only the best."[69] While Henry claimed that he did not have the funds equal to his desire, the Flynts nevertheless began replacing their simple hooked rugs with much more refined and elegant Orientals.

A comparison between the 1952 and 1970 editions of *Frontier of Freedom* reveals that the Flynts had refined their aesthetic sensibility. While the newer edition included the Flynts' most recent purchases, such as the opulent Dwight House, the most striking thing about the book is the number of photographs retaken to reflect slight changes in decor. For example, both editions include a picture of the front hall of the Ashley House. Both show the same scene: a staircase on the left, a tall clock, and a table against the wall flanked by two chairs. Closer inspection, however, reveals a small but significant change: The two vase-backed chairs with Spanish feet have been replaced with more elegant serpentine types. The text has also has been modified to reflect Flynt's increasing connoisseurship and his interest in a national audience. Rather than simply stating that the clock comes from Connecticut, the 1970 edition points out that it resembles the much-sought-after Newport type. Likewise, the new text fails to mention the print of Massachusetts governor Jonathan Belcher, who helped orchestrate the Native American peace conference held in Deerfield in 1735. A similar transformation can be observed in the Allen House, the Flynts' private residence in Deerfield. Photographs taken from almost identical angles reveal crewelwork curtains replaced by yellow damask, hooked rugs by Orientals, and simple vase-back chairs by ornate Chippendales. Many of the missing pieces can be found in photos of the second floor, which, according to the book, are deliberately furnished in a "less sophisticated style." Such changes demonstrate that Flynt was responding to aesthetic standards of the age.

As the museum's self-proclaimed curator, Flynt was careful to justify his elaborate furnishings with documentary and material evidence. In a 1952 letter to Deerfield resident Elizabeth Boyden, Flynt defended his decorative choices: "It is sometimes difficult for people to appreciate that the residents of this village in those far off days had the splendid examples of furniture, fabrics, china, glass, portraits, prints and other items, now on display there. . . . Inventories, accounts, and letters and other data of the Deerfield people of the eighteenth century and actual pieces of furniture, spreads, china, glass and fragments of material handed down from generation to generation of its loyal residents established the basis of the collection now available to the public and proved beyond the peradventure of the doubt, that the eighteenth century was one of culture, refinement, and taste."[70]

Since Flynt based his furnishings on documented examples, his errors were in the form of quantity more often than quality. To produce period rooms with an atmosphere of comfort and style, Flynt filled his houses to the point of excess. For example, the Reverend Jonathan Ashley likely owned a tall chest, but three was out of the question. Indeed, one of the main tasks of contemporary curators at Deerfield has been to scale back Flynt's elaborate rooms. Curators of the Wells-Thorn House now interpret a once opulently furnished room with only three pieces of furniture, no curtains, and no rug.[71] For Flynt, the excess had an important function. It allowed him to depict the past as a period that contemporary visitors would see as cultured and refined.

Like the Gardners, the Flynts had difficulty separating taste from authenticity. They believed that if a piece looked right in its surroundings, then in fact it must be accurate. Helen especially believed that she had an innate knowledge of colonial style: "I can see right away at the outset whether I like it or I don't like it, whether it's right or it's wrong, whether it's pleasing, whether it's accurate or whether it's not accurate. I have an eye."[72] The Flynts also believed that they knew what colonial residents would have wanted. In informal notes to his guide staff, Henry explained that he had decided to limit the use of eighteenth-century Italian raw silk in the Ashley House to the parlor because he believed that "no gay colors should unduly distract the parson from his conscientious duty in the preparation of his Sunday sermons."[73]

Taste was also something that Flynt sought in his contractor, William E. Gass. Although Gass lacked formal training in architectural history or design, he had grown up in the construction business, learning as he worked on surviving local examples of colonial architecture, studied preservation jobs, and assisted his father with a replica of the Old Indian House. But this kind of experience had limits, and Gass often built according to his own tastes and mistaken ideas about colonial buildings. For example, he favored unpainted wood paneling, large kitchen fireplaces, and slate roofs—all inappropriate for the period. Many of Deerfield's famous doors are Gass's loose interpretations of Connecticut Valley doorways; some residents called them "Bill Gass originals."[74]

Gass's sense of style made him a popular restoration carpenter. Commenting on his work at the Old Indian House, Jennie Maria Arms Sheldon, second wife of George Sheldon, wrote: "The replica . . . is a remarkably accurate reproduction. Mr. Gass, the father, has not the historic instinct but his son, William Gass, Jr., has it to an unusual degree."[75] Flynt agreed: "[Gass has] the sense of proportion, the feeling for the lines and things like that."[76] Flynt trusted Gass to such a degree that he used him on nearly every restoration project in Deerfield, despite frequent conflicts over money.[77] In fact, Flynt often encouraged Gass to exercise his sense of style. In a 1947 letter, Flynt suggested that Gass use Samuel Chamberlain's book *New England Doorways* as inspiration for his work on the Allen House.[78] Likewise, when Deerfield Academy hired the Platt architectural firm to build new dormitories for the school, Flynt paid Gass to go over the plans and make them fit in with the village architecture. The process elevated Gass's sense of colonial style over the Platt brothers' book knowledge of historic architecture.[79]

The Flynts did not completely abandon family histories or craft traditions in the move to emphasize Deerfield's aesthetic qualities. In a 1956 review of the museum's curatorial practices, J. T. Wiggin reported that the Heritage Foundation fell somewhere between art and history museums. "The historic houses maintained by the Heritage Foundation tend toward the latter [art museums] although they actually stand at the meeting point . . . where the tendency towards thorough-going connoisseurship is tempered by a historical perspective."[80] Indeed, Henry Flynt created a number of historical vignettes designed to illustrate work in early America. For example, the Sheldon-Hawks House included a sewing room in which a costumed mannequin sat surrounded by needleworking tools.[81] Likewise, the Wilson-Dickinson print shop included a working reproduction printing press, while the Parker and Russell silver shop juxtaposed a display area with a metalworking bench, forge, and bellows.[82] Such illustrations of craft processes provided a historical context for Flynt's aesthetic displays and allowed him to maintain the tradition of local stories.

Flynt also emulated Deerfield's tradition of celebrating family history, and even created a place for his own ancestral heritage, by moving the Dwight-Barnard House to Deerfield from nearby Springfield in 1950. While the house had no history within the village, its former occupants had genealogical ties not only to the Williamses of Deerfield, but to the Flynts as well. An undated history of the house attributed to Helen and Henry Flynt explains that "the present owner of the house, Henry Flynt, is distantly related by marriage to Josiah Dwight through Anna Flynt for he is descended from one John Flynt, a brother of Anna."[83] With his own family connection established, Flynt set out to give the house a Deerfield pedigree, enlisting the aid of Deerfield resident Elizabeth Fuller, whose mother descended from the Williamses, a family of Deerfield doctors. Fuller loaned medical equipment, family portraits, and furnishings for the house.[84] In return, Flynt dedicated one room as a memorial to Fuller's mother and published a genealogy of the Dwight family detailing their connections to the Williamses.[85]

Flynt also emphasized the aesthetic qualities of the Dwight-Barnard house. One of the final houses he restored, Dwight-Barnard was also one of the most elaborate.[86] The elegant south parlor included a bombe chest, Chippendale chairs, and a gold camelback sofa. Ernest LoNano, Henry Francis du Pont's favorite upholsterer, furnished the room's elaborately valenced silk curtains.[87] According to Peter Spang, the Flynts' first curator, even the decision to move the house was based on aesthetic considerations.[88] Indeed, Flynt considered salvaging only the building's elaborately paneled second floor and using it to construct period rooms. In this way, even Flynt's interest in local history and family connections was colored by his desire to create refined and elegant interiors.

The Flynts' ever-increasing appreciation of fine, high-style antiques provoked them to contest the standards and taste of Deerfield's earlier preservationists. Most notable was their reinterpretation of the Frary House, which was at the center of Deerfield's Arts and Crafts revival. C. Alice Baker had bequeathed the restored house and its contents to the Pocumtuck Valley Memorial Association with the stipulation that the building be kept "intact and unaltered with the furnishings as typical of the Colonial period."[89] By the late 1940s Henry Flynt was president of both the PVMA and his own Heritage Foundation, and he began to see the Frary House's furnishings as "creating a very bad impression." Flynt, a lawyer himself, had Baker's will reinterpreted using the argument that her furnishings were not authentic and thus violated the spirit of her wishes.[90]

In truth, Flynt's redecoration of the Frary House was simply the replacement of one age's aesthetic with that of another. For the refurbishing of the tavern room, Flynt accepted a sizable gift of almost seventy-five pieces from John Kenneth Byard, ranging from pottery mugs and wooden candle stands to eighteenth-century oil paintings and a New England corner cupboard.[91] Flynt noted that "Mr. and Mrs. Byard, realizing that some of the rooms in the Frary House have architectural charm but lack both the tasteful touch and the ring of the spirit of the Colonial Days which Miss Baker . . . spoke of in her will, decided to furnish the room on the south side between the old tap room and the dining room." While the Flynts considered these furnishings "tasteful," contemporary curators have discovered that many were fakes.[92] The Flynts took total control of Frary House in the late 1960s when the PVMA, desperate for funds to repair Memorial Hall, sold it to the Heritage Foundation.

Cultural Arbitrator

In many ways, Flynt's redecoration of the Frary House represented the pinnacle of his power as Deerfield's cultural steward. With the Frary House, he did not just add to the town's historic resources, but literally transformed them to conform to his aesthetically driven expectations. Flynt's aesthetic vision served him well in support of his cold war agenda, but the maintenance of that vision, and particularly its application to the village of Deerfield as a whole, proved problematic. For while Flynt ostensibly saw his work as important for a broad American public, allowing Deerfield to become a tourist destination threatened to undermine its quiet beauty.

From the beginning, Flynt thought of his work as educational, and the proximity of Deerfield Academy provided him with a ready audience for his ideologically charged history. As one of his prime reasons for restoring Deerfield, he often cited his desire to "impress the boys who go to school there with the heritage of America, the story of Deerfield and its massacre, the courage of our ancestors, [and] their appreciation of the finer things in life."[93] He was particularly fond of the academy's motto, "Be Worthy of Your Heritage." In keeping with this education mission, Flynt also opened his museum to college students. In 1953, he organized a conference of New England college art departments to encourage them to use Deerfield as a laboratory for their classes.[94] He instituted a summer fellowship, limited to men, to introduce undergraduates to work in the museum and decorative arts field. Under the sponsorship of a

Massachusetts woman, three spots were reserved for West Coast boys, on the provision that they see America on the way.[95]

Extending his educational mission to a wider public proved difficult, however. As part of his pursuit of a refined aesthetic environment, Flynt was determined that Deerfield would retain the appearance of a pastoral New England community. While he himself had done much to restore buildings, and even had the town's telephone lines buried underground, much of the town's charm lay in its quiet streets, unsullied by crowds or excessive traffic. The historic tourism boom of the 1950s threatened Flynt's ability to protect Deerfield from such ugliness. The outdoor museum visitation statistics for 1957 show that tourism to Old Sturbridge Village increased by 17.06 percent, to Mystic Seaport by 17 percent, and to the Farmer's Museum in Cooperstown, New York, by between 20 and 30 percent from the previous year's figures.[96] Flynt admired these places for their ability to introduce a large number of people to American history, but he did not want that many visitors in Deerfield.[97] Annoyed when his own attendance jumped 25 percent, he wrote, "This may sound snobbish but we are not equipped to run a 'Freedom Land' and don't care to."[98] In order to control the types of visitors who came to Deerfield, he closely regulated press coverage.[99] Before his restorations were complete, he denied reporters access on the grounds that the "wrong impression will be obtained" and that he did not "wish to have our efforts get off on the wrong foot as to authenticity."[100] In response to *Life*'s request to do an article on Deerfield, he cited the risk it posed to Deerfield's small-town character: "We are a humble community carrying on a way of life based on a history of which we are proud and are anxious to be worthy of our heritage, undisturbed by 'trippers,' curiosity seekers, or others who we fear your article will inevitably bring."[101] Similarly, Flynt refused the local tourism office's offer to include Deerfield in its press releases and films.[102] He summed up his attitude to the press in a letter to Samuel Chamberlain: "Magazines have endeavored to get in and take pictures and write articles but so far we have warded them off."[103] Flynt's success in discouraging daytrippers caused a writer for *Yankee Magazine* to remark that "old Deerfield is remarkably free from the grosser aspects of commercialism."[104] With hardly any press coverage and only a simple directional arrow indicating museum's location from the main highway, tourists had difficulty finding it.[105]

Having given up trying to educate a broader public, Flynt cultivated an audience that shared both his class position and his aesthetic appreciation of antiques. Beginning in the 1950s, he began a forum for "invited guests" each spring and fall. The guest list, limited to between thirty-five and forty, included prominent figures in the antiques field, such as Katherine Prentice Murphy and Rhode Island collector Ralph Carpenter. The events resembled a grand house party. The Flynts served cocktails in the silver vault, Hall Tavern, and their own Allen House. Special events included candlelight tours and street rides in carts pulled by oxen

When Flynt did write articles about his restored village, he courted publications with a more elite audience. The year 1950 was a turning point. Having assembled a significant portion of the collection, he began seeking appropriate venues to display his accomplishment. In addition to starting the book project with Samuel Chamberlain, Flynt develop a relationship with *Antiques* editor Alice Winchester, who featured his collection in many articles.[106] He also published in magazines that targeted elite collectors, such as the *Connecticut Antiquarian* and *Art in America*.[107]

On the rare occasions that publications with larger audiences did cover Deerfield, Flynt did everything he could to control its image. Authors and editors were routinely taken to task for what he considered slipshod coverage. The *Christian Science Monitor* received an eight-point letter listing inaccuracies ranging from incorrect impressions created by their descriptions to spelling and grammar mistakes.[108] Likewise, Flynt chastised the *New York Herald Tribune* for a lack of "accuracy and completeness" in its coverage of Deerfield in an article on preservation work in New England.[109]

Not surprisingly, Flynt was most concerned with Deerfield's visual image. He critiqued photographers at such reputable magazines as *Antiques* and *Life* over dull silver, late afternoon lighting, and smudged lampposts.[110] But even more, Flynt hated pictures that deviated from the refined and elegant image he favored. Flynt hotly contested photos taken for *American Heritage*: "Your photographer tried to impress me with his international reputation in the museum world. All that was beside the point. He apparently carries on his independent ways in other places where he has visited. . . . The pictures I saw are not representative of Deerfield; furthermore, they look as though a country auction was being held. You must appreciate that we are the ones responsible for what the present and future image of Deerfield should be, not Mr. Newman."[111] Having carefully constructed Deerfield's visual image through his restorations and refurnishings, Flynt was not about to let a photographer suggest a different interpretation.

Ugliness threatened in other areas as well. In the 1950s several companies began to market Deerfield-inspired home furnishings. Both B. Altman & Co. of New York and Sprague & Carleton of Keene, New Hampshire, offered furniture inspired by colonial Deerfield.[112] Sprague & Carleton's "Deerfield" furnishings were part of a larger campaign connecting their products to various New England towns famous for their colonial heritage. By appropriating the "ingenuity of our early craftsmen," Sprague & Carleton hoped to suggest quality, durability, and timeless style.[113] Likewise, Fieldcrest created a "Deerfield" bedspread advertised to capture the "spirit and charm of early America."[114] Even Ivory soap got into the act in 1961 with a proposal for a television commercial shot on location in Deerfield's Ashley House. With the tagline that Ivory "treats nice things as if they had to last forever," the commercial not only suggested that Deerfield's historic textiles could be safely washed in Ivory soap, but also that the soap itself would make heirlooms out of everyday sheets and curtains.[115]

In many ways, the use of Deerfield and Deerfield antiques to sell modern goods signaled an acceptance of the past as a model for both aesthetic quality and consumer culture. But while Flynt's cold-war patriotism implicitly celebrated the free market economy that produced mass-market goods, Deerfield's association with mainstream suppliers threatened its ability to symbolize the nation's artistic achievement by eroding its aesthetic quality. Not surprisingly, Flynt fought Deerfield's connection to such commercial goods. In a letter to Sprague & Carleton, he wrote, "I've looked these pictures over and can't seem to find where the inspiration for them can be said to have come from Deerfield."[116] He was correct that the furniture had little resemblance to examples at Deerfield. Rather than reproducing historic pieces, Sprague & Carleton used symbols of colonial style: splayed-leg tables, corner cupboards, turned legs, and scalloped boards. Retailers had many reasons to avoid reproductions; as we have seen, colonial production methods were unsuited for modern factories. Even Fieldcrest's Deerfield bedspread was not made on a jacquard loom, but screen-printed for mass production. But by basing the value of antiques on issues of originality, workmanship, and design, Flynt denied middle-class Americans the ability to embrace colonial styles. Most mass-marketed goods could not live up to the exacting standards he required. While their symbolic use of colonial design elements provided purchasers with a link to the past, it was not the aesthetically refined past he envisioned.

Yet Flynt himself promoted commercialized reproductions of Deerfield antiques, as long as they lived up to his aesthetic standards. In the late 1950s he formed a partnership with the interior-decorating firm Scalamandre to sell expensive replicas of eighteenth- and nineteenth-century wallpaper and fabrics adapted from patterns shown at Deerfield.[117] After Flynt's death, Heritage Foundation officials extended their commercial ventures, marketing reproductions of Deerfield furniture. The twenty-five-piece collection differed from earlier commercial offerings in both price and meticulous attention to detail. The Mary Hoyt Williams chest, for example, was copied from a museum chest right down to the solid brass pulls. According to a press release, "the wood was planed, the drawers joined, dovetails made, and the finish applied by hand, as in the original piece."[118] The fact that Flynt encouraged the construction of these commercial products shows that his concern was not commodification. What was at issue was Flynt's own interpretation of aesthetic quality.

A Town with a New Past

When it came time to name the foundation that Flynt established to maintain his museum, he did not select "Historic Deerfield," as it is called today, but rather chose the name "Heritage Foundation." Former Deerfield Academy teacher Richard Hatch, a friend of Flynt's, liked the name specifically for its patriotic implications. Hatch wrote: "My reaction so far to the name Heritage Foundation is that it is excellent. It strikes me that to call it either the Deerfield or New England Heritage Foundation would be wrong for, although it preserves a priceless heritage that is local in flavor, the great value of the enterprise, as I see it, is that . . . [it] symbolizes . . . a spirit and integrity that are the heritage of all Americans."[119] The name is indeed an apt sobriquet for the historic preservation and antique collecting project Henry and Helen Flynt brought to Deerfield, not only because it placed the town's history in the service of a national cause, but also because it symbolized the couple's deep involvement in shaping the representation of the little community's history. Indeed, the name Heritage Foundation was also intended as an allusion to Henry and Helen Flynt's initials—H. F.[120]

Through their museum village and support for the academy, Henry and Helen Flynt made great changes in Deerfield.[121] No longer dominated by privately owned homes and rural farms, Deerfield had become a museum and academy village catering to an elite, and nationally based, community. History had also changed. Inspired by wealthy American collectors such as Henry Francis du Pont, Flynt transformed Deerfield's historic houses into carefully crafted aesthetic environments. While nineteenth-century collectors such as George Sheldon had favored mementos of family and community life, Flynt prized ornate textiles and elegant furniture as symbols of American cultural superiority. The changes Flynt implemented represented not only a new chapter in Deerfield's historic commemoration, but also the influence of aesthetically driven standards of antique collecting on New England's history.

5
Exhibiting the Ordinary
History Making at the Smithsonian

*I*n a 1951 *New York Times* article, Israel Sack warned potential collectors against buying so-called country antiques, pieces made by early American craftsmen who, because of their rural origins, lacked the design sophistication of their more cosmopolitan urban counterparts. "You can't judge a country by its backwoods," he was quoted as saying.[1] Sack's advice was typical of the dominant mode of collecting that valued antiques as aesthetic expressions of seventeenth- and eighteenth-century period styles. But not everyone was listening. In the nation's capital, C. Malcolm Watkins (figure 24), a curator at the Smithsonian Institution's U.S. National Museum, was busily constructing a collection that included the very kind of rural pieces Sack decried. Watkins came to the Smithsonian in 1949 as an associate curator. He was thirty-eight years old at the time, and he had grown up in Massachusetts, where he

Figure 24. Taken in 1979, this publicity photograph shows Malcolm Watkins inside the Smithsonian exhibition "A Nation of Nations." Photograph courtesy of Smithsonian Institution Archives.

worked as a professional collector, curator, and antiques writer. While Sack encouraged museums to build their collections with furnishings from the homes of colonial America's wealthiest households, Watkins filled the Smithsonian with old tools, simple furniture, kitchen utensils, and lighting devices. These were decidedly humble objects, antiques that could be defined most often by their function and rarely by their aesthetics or inherent craftsmanship.

In choosing cracked fragments of redware pottery over fine Chippendale chairs, worn agriculture tools over stately block-front secretaries, and crude oil lamps over elaborately inlaid chests, Watkins presented a powerful ideological challenge to the dominant collecting model. While Sack's customers tended to focus on antiques' aesthetic qualities as opposed to their history of ownership, there was no getting around the fact that most of the objects praised for their artistic accomplishment had originally belonged to America's ruling class. In contrast, Watkins's collecting was a means of exploring the daily life of those he would classify as "ordinary"

Americans. Reflecting on the art exhibits that dominated national displays of colonial artifacts, Watkins wrote: "The up-until-then museum approach to American material culture was usually in terms of decorative arts and this turned me off. It seemed to me an elitist put down that limited the choice to how well an object ornamented its setting (or its owner's ego)."[2] As emphatically as Watkins rejected the aesthetic antique, he did not embrace earlier traditions of acquiring objects because of their associations. Just like his counterparts in the decorative arts movement, he decried family or local associations, seeing them as too provincial to have any value in the construction of a national culture, a goal just as important for Malcolm Watkins as it was for Henry Flynt, even if Watkins did not frame his agenda in such clear cold-war terms.

In his attempt to create a new kind of historical object, Watkins was responding to some of the same pressures that influenced the development of social history among university-trained historians, especially the desire to include ethnic and racial diversity as part of the American story. But Watkins's "everyday" or "ordinary" history did not emerge from the halls of academia; his collecting was inspired by middle-class New England collectors he knew from his youth. These locally based collectors did not have the resources to buy the Sack family's best finds, but that did not deny them the experience of becoming antique collectors or connecting with the past through historic objects. Some focused their efforts on relatively inexpensive ceramics, while others took up collecting more recently produced (or even mass-produced) collectibles, such as pressed glass manufactured by the Boston and Sandwich Glass company in the mid-nineteenth century or hand-colored lithography inexpensively made by the nineteenth-century firm of Currier and Ives in their assembly-line-style factory. Still others ignored the aesthetic market altogether and collected outdated kitchen utensils, old farm equipment, and obsolete craft tools, objects interesting for their functions but often without any artistic pretenses. By the 1940s several organizations had formed to support these collectors. They included groups such as the Rushlight Club, whose members dedicated themselves to the study of ancient lighting devices, as well as the Early American Industries Association, founded in 1933 around the collecting of obsolete tools. The presence of these collectors and their organizations demonstrates the prevalence of alternative forms of collecting that rejected the dominant aesthetic antique. While individuals such as Jessie Gardner slavishly worked to imitate high-end collecting, others invented their own antiques.

Smithsonian administrators supported the ideological and social messages embodied in Watkins's collecting program, but cultural politics was not the only impetus for the Smithsonian's backing. Just as market forces encouraged the transformation of antiques from associational into aesthetic objects, so too did financial pressures push the Smithsonian to acquire everyday objects as the basis of its early American collections. Indeed, both Watkins and his superiors recognized that collections of American decorative arts were popular with museumgoers and that they lent themselves to the construction of a kind of national culture based on aesthetic accomplishment, a particularly important attribute for a museum charged with representing the nation. But imitating the kind of high-style presentation found at such museums as Henry Flynt's Deerfield was impossible for them.[3] The Smithsonian simply did not have the kind of economic resources necessary to collect aesthetically accomplished antiques. In fact, Watkins's budget was so restricted that not only did he have to limit his purchases to inexpensive objects, but he also had to rely on donors to supply many of his acquisitions. Compared to museums such as Flynt's Deerfield, in which a single individual provided the institution's direction, Watkins's Smithsonian was much more dependent on the values and desires of donors.[4] For Watkins, the experience of collecting was less about negotiating the antiques market and more about identifying and cultivating donors sympathetic to his vision of the past and reinterpreting objects previously collected to fulfill his new agenda. Watkins's everyday antique was built around a different set of social values from its aesthetic predecessors, but it was also the product of a different kind of financial pressure.

A Curator from New England

Watkins came to his position steeped in the history and collecting traditions of New England. The only son of Charles Hadley Watkins and Lura Woodside Watkins, he belonged to an established, but not especially prominent, New England family that included a Methodist minister and at least one shipbuilder. Reflecting these modest origins, Watkins never pursued genealogy with the fervor displayed by many elites, nor did he use antiques as status symbols. He learned to appreciate New England's past by touring old cemeteries and historic houses in his home state of Massachusetts. So frequent were these trips that Watkins later speculated that he had "gone through every old house in Essex and Middlesex [counties]."[5] Watkins's maternal grandfather also helped engender his interest in history by bequeathing him a collection of historic lighting devices, a gift that prompted young Watkins to join the Rushlight Club.[6]

Watkins began his education in antiques literally at his mother's knee. Lura Woodside Watkins was an experienced collector, active in groups such as the Early American Industries Association, a frequent contributor to such magazines as *Antiques* and *American Collector*, the author of several books on pottery and glass, a founder of the historical society of Middletown, Massachusetts, and a consultant to both the Brooklyn Museum and the Toledo Museum of Art. Trained as a composer and pianist, Lura gave up her musical career after marriage, but needed a compelling hobby to engage her sharp mind.[7] Like many other antique lovers during the depression, Lura Watkins first turned to glass as an affordable collectible.[8] Her 1930 book, *Cambridge Glass: The Story of the New England Glass Company*, became an important reference text in the field.[9] But Lura Watkins's most important collection was her New England redware.

As a collectible, redware was most unusual. As early as the late nineteenth century, collectors pursued old ceramics such as Staffordshire china, ornamented with transfer illustrations of American views. Even though the pieces were manufactured in England, the images provided them with an association suggested by the locations depicted. As the antique market expanded, ceramics continued to be desirable. Henry Francis du Pont actively added ceramics to his collection in the late 1920s. He acquired common pieces, such as a blue-edged plate for $10, but prices could shoot up into the hundreds for a fine example of Chinese export porcelain. In 1928 du Pont purchased such a piece, a punch bowl decorated with scenes of the East India Company's Canton offices and the American consulate in China, for an amazing $1,000.[10] In the ceramic market, considerations of rarity, aesthetic quality, and patriotic associations fostered by the presence of American symbols and imagery were directly tied to price. But condition was also a particularly important source of value. The collector Dudley Brown was not unusual in insisting that everything he purchased be "proof." "Some of these so called would be collectors that occasionally visit our home, 'make a mountain out of a mole hill' when they notice a piece with a crack, discoloration, etc.," he explained to Pennsylvania ceramics dealer Samuel Laidacker. "I find it is possible to have 100% proof pieces, so in one way of looking at it, why should I buy pieces that are not proof."[11]

For redware, however, "proof" was a most elusive quality. During its active life, redware had provided colonists with an inexpensive pottery, but because of its low firing temperature it was quite brittle. Since whole pieces rarely survived, Lura Watkins's collection was based on shards, fragments she collected at former Massachusetts kiln sites. For her, collecting in no way resembled the negotiations between dealer and buyer associated with the antiques market. She began her collecting in the town hall and local library. Using ancient records, she identified individual potters and located their original kiln sites. Often accompanied by her husband, she then journeyed to these sites and conducted surface excavations. Her son would later boast that she was a practicing historical archaeologist before the field even existed.[12]

Unlike those who collected ceramics for their decorative and aesthetic qualities, Lura Watkins saw objects primarily as historical documents, valuable for their ability to unlock information about the past. Nevertheless, she was deeply influenced by the kind of scholarship attached to the high-end furniture market. Like decorative arts scholars, Lura focused her research around issues of production and craftsmanship, ignoring later histories associated with ownership to focus on the single moment of creation. By classifying each shard according to the location in which she found it and its distinguishing features, Lura identified the makers of many unmarked pots and uncovered regional variations in manufacture produced by European settlement patterns. The results became her most important book, *Early New England Potters and Their Wares*, published in 1950, just as her son was assuming his position at the Smithsonian.[13] Praised by such authorities as collector Nina Fletcher Little and *Antiques* editor Alice Winchester, the book downplayed issues of aesthetics, but also ignored associations in favor of craft processes and manufacture.[14]

By the time Malcolm Watkins graduated from Harvard he had become such an expert on antiques that he was able to convince A. B. Wells, the founder of Old Sturbridge Village, to hire him as a curator. Like the

Rushlighters, Wells focused on collecting objects as expressions of Yankee ingenuity, a trait prized by the Wells family. His father, George Wells, made the American Optical Company a financial success by inventing an automation system that produced six pairs of glasses at once. As a collector, A. B. Wells had the resources to buy expensive antiques and regularly purchased costly European collectibles, such as English-manufactured Rockingham ware, which he Americanized by referring to it as "his Bennington," for a Vermont town known for its nineteenth-century ceramics adorned with a similar brown glaze.[15] But Wells's favorite collectibles were preindustrial tools and farm equipment. According to Watkins, Wells delighted in "the simple, direct, or the ingenious."[16]

Wells's collection was most important for its size. Packed to the gills, the thirty-nine rooms of Wells's house contained carved knitting needle sheaths, sewing birds and spool boxes, shoemakers' tools, iron kitchen utensils, tobacco paraphernalia, and hundreds of lighting devices ranging from candlesticks to tin lanterns.[17] In his later years Watkins remembered the collection as helping him think "in terms of many kinds of objects; related to each other and to social patterns, customs, and skills within cultural boundaries."[18] Indeed, the comprehensiveness of Wells's collection was seductive. While large collections based on an individual object category, such as lighting devices, enabled Watkins to understand a specific technology and its relationship to a larger pattern within cultural and social history, Wells's collection suggested the ability to recreate the past itself.

Except for a four-year interruption during World War II, Watkins worked for the Wells family from 1936 to 1948. During that time, Watkins saw Wells's historical interests grow from a modest collection housed within his own mansion to an emerging museum village. Wells purchased the land that would become Old Sturbridge Village in 1936. Located on the Quinebaug River outside of Sturbridge, Massachusetts, the property contained the remains of an old mill complex, but no New England village. Wells used the mill's raceways to power a reproduction gristmill and sawmill, and he and his family also collected buildings to construct their interpretation of a New England community circa 1800. Soon after the village opened to the public in 1946, it included several houses arranged around a town common, a general store from Stafford, Connecticut, a church from Fiskdale, Massachusetts, and a number of new buildings reproduced from prototypes located within twenty miles of the museum. Wells employed George Watson, one of his draftsmen at American Optical Company, to move the buildings, but it was Watkins's job as curator to install the collections.[19] The experience helped Watkins develop an exhibition philosophy that used period rooms to contextualize artifacts and build recreations of everyday life. Looking back at his work at Sturbridge, Watkins told an interviewer that he became aware of the "marvelous story" that period rooms have to tell. As exhibits, he believed that "they make it possible for the visitor to walk into human spaces of other eras and sense a special time and way of living."[20]

Antiques in the Attic

When Watkins arrived at the Smithsonian in 1949, he did not find a blank slate. The new curator inherited a small collection that included textiles, ceramics, lighting devices, and musical instruments. While Henry Flynt had the funds to ignore, or at least minimize, the influence of his predecessor's collections, Watkins could not turn his back on past collecting practices. His limited resources meant that he would have to put those objects to good use. In many ways, Watkins liked what he found. Ceramics and lighting devices were his specialties, and had certainly been a reason for his getting the job. But along with the objects came the specific cultural meanings their donors attached to them, meanings bound up with ideas about family, nation, and progress.

One of the first of these collections had arrived in 1894, when John Brenton Copp, the last descendent of a middling family from Connecticut and Massachusetts, gave to the Smithsonian artifacts that had been handed down by his ancestors. Copp described them as "family articles and relics which had been used and also preserved by our family for upwards of two hundred years."[21] With merchants and shopkeepers among their numbers, the Copps had acquired some fancy textiles from Europe and imported china, but the majority of their collection was decidedly simple: eighteenth- and early nineteenth-century household utensils, tableware, books, quilts, woven coverlets, embroidery samplers, and other assorted textiles, both hand-worked and commercially produced.[22] For the family, these everyday objects represented a tangible expression of their ancestry. In 1893 John Copp loaned his family patrimony to the Connecticut Women's Auxiliary for display at the Chicago World's Fair. Most likely exhibited in the Connecticut State Pavilion, a fantastically oversized Georgian mansion, the Copp Collection joined over 250 artifacts loaned by the state's oldest and most prominent families.[23] Displayed with brief labels primarily identifying the lenders, these objects secured a place for their owners in one of the most important cultural events of the century.[24] John Copp believed the collection would serve a similar function at the Smithsonian. As a condition of his gift, he stipulated that the collection be exhibited in its entirety in no more than four cases labeled "The Copp Family Relics" (figure 25).[25] To comply with this demand, curators had to pack the cases. They folded the coverlets and stacked them one on top of another, arranged the lace and fringe work in decorative patterns, and hung numerous dresses from small pegs. While the layout prohibited visitors from appreciating the textiles' delicate handiwork, the close grouping reinforced the idea of a family memorial by emphasizing association over utilitarian value and solidified Copp's vision of a genealogically defined history.

As a national museum, however, the Smithsonian sought objects that would transcend local or family stories and appeal to a wider audience. A. Howard Clark, the U.S. National Museum's first historian, prized artifacts with patriotic associations. Among the many treasures Clark displayed were George Washington's tea set, Daniel Boone's pocketknife, and an array of Revolutionary War uniforms, flags, and weapons. Clark built his collection around relics, objects more important for their associations than for themselves. An ordinary tea set, because of its association with Washington, functioned as a symbol of the nation. Clark's relics took on an almost mystical significance. A display of locks of hair from fourteen presidents, "from Washington to Pierce, inclusive," bore a striking resemblance to the reliquaries of medieval saints.[26] Clark also displayed models. A nineteen-foot-tall plaster cast of the *Statue of Freedom* dominated the central rotunda, while ship models, including the Mayflower, told a story of European colonialism. Dedicated to collecting such symbols of state, Clark had no use for a little-known New England family's textiles and china.

The Copp Collection certainly did not possess the kind of national associations that Clark demanded, but the U.S. National Museum's director, George Brown Goode, had another plan for the Copps' simple objects.

Figure 25. In 1900 Smithsonian curators displayed the Copp Collection alongside George Catlin's portraits of Native Americans and a world map. Significantly, artifacts of both of Native Americans and white colonial settlers were assigned to the Department of Anthropology. Photograph courtesy of Smithsonian Institution Archives.

Trained as a natural scientist at Harvard under Louis Agassiz, Goode believed that history should record technological progress. As Gary Kulik has observed, Goode "had come to intellectual maturity in the great age of evolutionary positivism. Like others of his generation, he believed that science was the motor of history and scientific method the key to the truth." In practice, Goode created a patriotic history that testified to American achievement. He acquired such icons of industrial progress as Samuel Slater's spinning and carding machines, the John Bull locomotive, and Tiffany lamps.[27] For Goode, the Copp Collection played a key role in this historical narrative by providing a benchmark for technological progress, providing physical evidence of how people lived in the past. The handcrafted laces, simple textiles, and clumsy utensils all suggested a more primitive time, even if John Copp's prescribed arrangement made careful examination impossible. As Copp later wrote, Goode believed the artifacts were valuable "not alone for their attractiveness," but also as a source of "information relative to early Colonial Families' household utensils, attire, decorations, etc."[28] In this sense, Goode's histories were very different from the kind of family or associational histories that had inspired the Copps to save and protect the objects for generations. Even though the artifacts were displayed together and the case labels attributed them to the Copps, Goode severed these family associations by assigning the collection not to the U.S. National Museum's Department of History, but to the Division of Ethnology in the Department of Anthropology. There, curators displayed it alongside George Catlin's portraits of Native Americans and a world map.[29] Goode's decision to group colonial artifacts with those of racialized Native Americans attests to his readiness to denigrate the past as primitive. For him, the simple technologies were not so much to be understood as to be transcended.

The next set of objects Watkins would inherit came in 1924, when a Vermont collector and antique dealer, Gertrude Ritter (later Webster), presented the Smithsonian with interior paneling from an eighteenth-century house of Massachusetts origins.[30] According to Ritter's wishes, the paneling became the basis for a period room, the Smithsonian's first, furnished with artifacts from her own collection and installed in what is now the Natural History Building.[31] Ritter's donation was layered with meaning. Like the rooms in the Metropolitan Museum of Art's American Wing, which opened the same year Ritter made her donation, the paneling had both a pedigree and an aesthetic value. She purchased it for approximately twenty thousand dollars from the New York antique dealer Charles Woolsey Lyon, son of Irving Lyon, the Hartford doctor and pioneering antique collector.[32] Lyon had already sold another room from the same house to the Brooklyn Museum, and he told Ritter that the pine paneling came from the eighteenth-century house of cabinetmaker Reuben Bliss in Springfield, Massachusetts.[33] While Smithsonian curators have since discredited Lyon's information, the woodwork was highly decorative, with fluted columns, a generous crown molding, and multiple panels. Ritter was clearly looking to the aesthetically based past found in the American Wing, and she attributed this kind of artistic accomplishment to her native New England.

Ritter clearly understood the power and importance of aesthetic design, but her Smithsonian installation departed from the period rooms found in art museums in one important way. The room was cluttered. Displayed with the elegant woodwork were kitchenware, bedroom furnishings, and craft tools. The list included mortars and pestles, a candle mold, a spice grinder, a tin coffee pot, a simple iron lamp, a child's cradle, and a spinning wheel—hardly the furnishings of a stylish parlor designed for entertaining and formal display.[34] Ritter was particularly interested in the spinning wheel she placed next to the parlor's fireplace.[35] In order to highlight its function, she purchased flax and asked Smithsonian curators to display it on the wheel as if it were being spun.[36] If curators had carried out her plan, the room would have looked much different from the way it was originally intended. Fancy parlors with fully paneled walls were a rarity in the mid-eighteenth century, the time represented by Ritter's woodwork. Its owner would have used the room to impress visitors and establish his social standing, not to perform household chores. After inspecting the flax, Smithsonian curators informed her that it was "full of chaff which must be removed by the process of carding" and therefore "not in a proper stage of development to be placed on the wheel."[37] Ritter's spinning demonstration never materialized, but even without the flax, the room remained crowded with utilitarian wares.

What did this cluttered room mean? Did Ritter deliberately flout the conventions of aesthetic design or did she simply misjudge its requirements? She never made her intentions explicit, but there are clues. In her will, Ritter described the donation not as a "period room," implying a consistency in furnishings and design, a goal to which Providence's Jessie Gardner aspired, but rather as an "ancestral home," a looser term suggesting a multilayered and subjective interpretation of the past.[38] The distinction is a significant one. Instead of trying to capture or reproduce an individual moment in time, Ritter set out to forge ties between generations. Her room was a place for lost generations to dwell, and in that sense she used associations to infuse the room's furnishings with cultural value. Some of these were specific. Included among the furnishings was a mirror owned by the descendents of the eighteenth-century minister Jonathan Edwards, known for his fire-and-brimstone sermons. Others were more abstract, such as the bonds of sisterhood represented by the kitchen tools and spinning wheel awkwardly displayed in her fancy parlor.[39] But associations did not need to be explicit. Ritter intended her room to function as a national home, a role underscored by the fact that she established this room in the nation's capital at a time when similar rooms were being erected in New York City.

Ritter's paneling was only the first step in her plan to memorialize New England in Washington. In her will, she provided funds for a "complete Early American House" to be erected on the National Mall, west of the Natural History Building.[40] She hoped that the pine paneling she donated in 1924 could be incorporated in this new building. As part of the deal, she also promised to give her antiques, including a collection of American glass appraised at the time of her death at $70,000.[41] Smithsonian officials, however, never reconciled Ritter's "ancestral home" with the predominantly political and public histories that continued to dominate the institution's exhibits. Curators displayed the paneling with no window frames or panes and no integral ceiling. C. Malcolm Watkins later recalled that in the 1940s "it was set up . . . with some sort of chintz material as window curtains, and, of course, the wall, the height of the wall paneling was not the height of a museum structure's ceiling. Between the top of the paneling and the ceiling there were lugubrious black curtains hanging, and some two or three electric focused lamps illuminated what was there."[42] In 1930 Ritter was upset to find not only dirt and dust, but also excessive shrinkage of the paneling, and she began sending her chauffeur to inspect the room on a regular basis.[43] The final straw came when Smithsonian officials balked at erecting the colonial house on the Mall because of problems associated with high visitation. As a result, Ritter withdrew support from the institution and willed her collection, including the valuable glass, to her alma mater, the University of Michigan at Ann Arbor.[44]

Finding a Donor

Early acquisitions such as the Ritter Room and the Copp Collection provided more than the foundation for Watkins's future collection. They were directly responsible for the creation of his position at the Smithsonian. With so much mismanagement, the Ritter Room was removed from the History Department and reassigned to the Division of Ethnology where, with the Copp materials, it contributed to a small collection of historical artifacts that included ceramics, lighting devices, and musical instruments from Europe and North America.[45] Once directly under the care of the director of the Department of Anthropology, the collection grew large enough by the late 1940s to require its own curator. Thus Watkins was not hired by the History Department; he joined the staff of the Department of Anthropology's Division of Ethnology.

When Watkins arrived at the Smithsonian, he was dismayed. The Ritter Room was badly furnished, the ceramic collection had scarcely changed since the 1880s, and the Ethnology Division owned more European than American materials.[46] In comparison to Old Sturbridge Village, the Smithsonian looked like a poverty-stricken cousin. Private museum makers like Henry Flynt and Jessie Gardner built their collections through individual acquisitions. They sought out specific kinds of objects, evaluated the market, and made personal decisions. Watkins did not have that kind of freedom; as we have seen, the Smithsonian was forced to rely primarily on donors. This did not mean that Watkins lost control over his collection or the decision making process, for he always had the final say. He could cultivate specific donors, accept or decline objects, exhibit a gift prominently or condemn it to obscurity. But working with donors represented a much more complicated process than collecting as an individual. It was a process that required negotiation.

Watkins's first major donor was Edna Hilburn Greenwood (figure 26), who had had begun collecting as a student at Smith College in western Massachusetts and pursued the passion until her death in 1972.[47] She was not a wealthy woman, but she received support from her mother's relatives, the Filene family, founders of the Boston-based department store.[48] As a young mother and wife in the first decades of the twentieth century, Greenwood experienced firsthand the growth of the consumer market. Her diary records shopping trips to department stores, including her family's new Filene's outlet.[49] But she most often satisfied her desires with antiques. Reading widely, she cultivated a deep knowledge of the antique market, one that allowed her to estimate an object's fair market value or identify specific ceramic forms.[50] Still, she rarely bought expensive items. When a friend wanted to sell a chaise lounge at the height of the antique market in 1928, she longed to buy it, but she passed it by, acknowledging that the $1,500 asking price could buy a new car.[51] So she filled her house with less expensive goods: an old pine washtub ($12.00), a set of eighteenth-century carpenter tools ($6.00), a yarn winder (50¢), and a set of marked Hartley Greens & Co. Leeds ware ($100.00—a real splurge).[52] While collectors such as Jessie Gardner worked to emulate the high-style room arrangements in antique magazines and art museums, Greenwood

Figure 26. In 1956 Smithsonian Secretary Leonard Carmichael made Edna Greenwood an Honorary Fellow, allowing her to consult on the installation of her donation. Photograph courtesy of Smithsonian Institution Archives.

relished her independence. Although her diary records at least one visit to New York's Anderson Gallery, she seems to have avoided many of the most celebrated antique dealers.[53] On one of her rare visits to Boston's Charles Street shops, she complained that she had fallen into the "spider web," an obvious reference to what she perceived as market corruption.[54]

Turning instead to rural auctions, individual antique owners, and regional shops, Greenwood centered her collection on inexpensive and often underappreciated country artifacts, such as agricultural tools and rustic furniture. A family friend described her collection as eclectic and wide-ranging: "It is difficult to say what was not collected. The majority of furniture is late seventeenth- and early eighteenth-century with a smattering of Shaker and some early nineteenth-century pieces. Woodenware, pewter, silver, glass, English ceramics, pottery, iron, and drawers full of textiles are to be found at every turn."[55] In addition to these domestic artifacts, Greenwood owned a large collection of books, especially children's books, a barn full of farm tools, and a number of early vehicles, including a "nineteenth-century hulled-corn wagon, numerous farm wagons, sleighs, and even a fine early nineteenth-century hearse."[56]

Greenwood's interest in the past did not stop with the objects themselves. In 1925 Greenwood and her first husband, Amos Little, bought Time Stone Farm, located on the boundary between the Massachusetts towns of Hudson and Marlborough. The purchase was the result of an intensive search for a historic New England farm to provide a setting for Greenwood's burgeoning antique collection.[57] Built in 1702 and enlarged thereafter, the house had been occupied by the Goodale family since its construction, and boasted distinctive stenciling on the second floor.[58] Committed to creating a complete historic environment, Greenwood hired preservationist George Francis Dow to restore the house to its earliest appearance. Greenwood knew Dow from her volunteer work at the Society for the Preservation of New England Antiquities, where he was collections curator and publications editor.[59] Dow, who would soon begin building a replica of a 1630s village in Salem, Massachusetts, for the state's tercentenary, was already an authority on first-period architecture. His restorations included the Essex Institute's Ward House and the Topsfield Historical Society's Parson Capen House. Employing his brother Eugene to carry out the construction work at Time Stone Farm, Dow applied a first-period aesthetic to the main structure. He replaced sash windows with diamond-paned casement windows, decorated the central chimney with stone pilasters, and sheathed the house in short lengths of unpainted clapboards secured with imitation hand-wrought nails (figure 27). Inside, Dow installed unpainted vertical sheathing, removed later fireboxes, and tore out a plaster ceiling to expose the floor joists above.[60]

The restoration provided Greenwood with the place to enact country life. At the farm, she shunned modern conveniences such as electricity and central heating, preferring antique lighting devices and open fires (figure 28).[61] Antiques played an important role in her production. Celebrating the acquisition of two eighteenth-century looms, she wrote in her diary, "I'm going to set them out at the farm and use them!"[62] She took the same active approach to the farm itself, planting an "old-fash-

The Magazine ANTIQUES

PRICE 65 CENTS

June 1951

Figure 27. In 1951, *Antiques* pictured Edna Greenwood's house in Marlborough, Massachusetts, on its front cover. *Antiques*, June 1951.

Figure 28. At Timestone Farm, Edna Greenwood avoided modern conveniences to create a carefully constructed vision of old New England. *Antiques,* June 1951, 462.

ioned" garden and assembling a fully equipped cider mill and blacksmith shop.[63] As the architectural historian Alexander J. Wall recalled, guests were always treated to a historical pageant:

> Dining at the farm with a small group of historically minded fellow workers can truly be described as an adventure in hospitality and the ways of antiquity. Provided with early costumes and wigs, of which her collection has many, the group makes a jolly presentation at the long table-board where the meal is served, prepared entirely according to seventeenth and eighteenth-century recipes, and well-seasoned with herbs from the garden which is kept up, as in old times, for this purpose. The food has been cooked in a fireplace and brick-oven, . . . and is eaten from wooden trenchers and pewter plate. The table is a single pine board seven feet ten inches long, 2 1/2 inches thick and thirty-three inches wide. As you look about you from your vantage point while seated on a wooden form you can trace the progress of cooking, lighting, clothing, even of romance, in the things about you.[64]

While easy to dismiss as simple fantasy, elaborate productions like the one Wall described provided Greenwood with a way to promulgate her particular interpretation of the past.

The motivations behind Greenwood's intense dedication to the past are more difficult to pinpoint. She saw herself as someone who "tried to make life as big as possible."[65] Her son Edward remembered her as a "highly adventurous and imaginative" woman.[66] But why would she choose the past as her playground? While Henry Flynt's and Jessie Gardner's commitments to the past were bound up in traditional social values and conservative politics, Greenwood exhibited no such leanings. Indeed, her personal life was quite unconventional. As a young woman, she married Amos Little, an attorney from a traditional Boston family and a cousin of the notable collectors Bertrand and Nina Fletcher Little. In her memoir, *Little by Little*, Nina Little credits Greenwood with introducing her to antiques.[67] But Amos was not very passionate about either collecting or country living.[68] Although Amos Little's name appears on the deed to Time Stone Farm, Arthur Greenwood, a nearby doctor, began investing both money and time in the operation.[69] He helped with the chores, spent money on the house's restoration, and occasionally bought for Edna a piece of coveted furniture.[70] The situation must have been awkward. In a series of letters in which he threatened divorce, Amos complained about having to "share his woman" and being "looked upon . . . as a fool."[71] But the arrangement persisted for several more years, with Amos and Edna's four children accepting Arthur as a regular part of their lives. Edna saw her unconventional marriage as part of a New England tradition. "Amos," she wrote in a 1928 letter, "think back into the old pioneering days a little—when they first settled these old places like ours out here—there were women then who just made everyone they could part & parcel of their household."[72] Still, contemporary concerns eventually triumphed. In 1934 she divorced Amos Little to marry Arthur Greenwood.[73]

For a free spirit such as Edna Greenwood, the past provided an arena of individual expression outside of the mass-market consumer world that her relatives were building. She loved all aspects of antiquing—the research, the hunt, and the display. In many ways she was not unlike Lura Watkins, an educated and intelligent woman who turned history into a vocation. Like Lura Watkins's books, Greenwood's Smithsonian donation provided her with public affirmation of her accomplishments. According to Malcolm Watkins, it was Greenwood who initiated the gift. The two knew each other through their involvement in the Rushlight Club. After seeing the poorly furnished Ritter Room on a trip to Washington, Greenwood reportedly turned to Watkins and said, "Malc, we can do better."[74] In 1951 Greenwood donated over two thousand artifacts to the Smithsonian.[75] The gift gave Watkins, for the first time, an extensive collection. Most notable for its preindustrial tools and domestic utensils, Greenwood's gift emulated the Wells collection in its comprehensive recording of daily life. In the category of wooden kitchen equipment alone, Watkins listed "plates, burl bowls, ladles, mortars and pestles, bottles, spoons, stirring sticks, racks in the shape of sleds for use in brick ovens, an egg beater that works on the bow-drill principle, and numerous other classes of specimens."[76] In many cases, Greenwood's collection could illustrate an entire home industry. The textile collection, for example, contained not only spinning wheels, spool racks, and quilting blocks, but also dye recipes and packages of colorant.[77]

Greenwood relished the opportunity to make history in the nation's capital. In a letter to Smithsonian secretary Frank Taylor, she wrote, "I do so want you to have the best demonstration of what America was that makes it what it *is*."[78] The bequest came at significant personal expense. Forgoing income from the sale of her collection, estimated at over $500,000, she spent her final years trying to "sweet-talk her banker into larger loans."[79] But for her, the chance to make history was paramount.[80] In 1954 she offered the main house at Time Stone Farm to the Smithsonian with the suggestion that government officials erect it on the Mall, a proposal reminiscent of Gertrude Ritter's "Early American House" and one similarly rejected by Smithsonian officials."[81]

Making History Modern

Watkins accepted the Greenwood Gift, as it came to be called, with an eye to exhibition.[82] Still dominated by the old cabinet of curiosities model, which grouped objects according to strict classifications and ignored interpretive design, the Smithsonian was embarking on a program of exhibit modernization, an effort to increase museum visitation through interactive exhibits and professionally designed displays. For Watkins, the program represented an opportunity to make his mark and build his own exhibition. But what would make history modern? Watkins believed the answer could be found in the period room.

Of course, the period room itself was hardly new. Deerfield's George Sheldon had installed some of the nation's first museum-based period rooms in the 1880s, and earlier precedents could be found in the "Olde Tyme" kitchen displays at Civil War sanitary fairs.[83] But despite similarities in structure and design, all period rooms were not alike. Early examples often followed the principles of the Ritter Room. They were memory spaces, important not for their historical accuracy or intrinsic beauty, but for their ability to evoke contemplation and promote traditional values. Beginning in the 1920s, antique connoisseurs like Jessie Barker Gardner began imitating the new displays at the Metropolitan Museum's American Wing, which reinterpreted the period room to emphasize aesthetically pleasing environments and specific design forms. Both varieties had specific goals: one provided a mechanism to connect with the past; the other celebrated its aesthetic accomplishments.

On the surface, Watkins's period rooms looked much like those that had come before. Installed in the museum environment, they utilized antique furnishings, interior architectural features, and domestic settings. Indeed, the only distinctly modern elements were dimmer switches that enabled visitors to view rooms by "daylight" and "candlelight."[84] But Watkins did not set out to create an aesthetic statement or a memory room. Rather than simply remind visitors of what had come before, his goal was to transcend time itself, to recreate a piece of the past in the present. Drawing on the title of his group within the Division of Ethnology, Watkins called this approach to the past "cultural history," but by that he did not mean the kind of high culture constructed by elite institutions such as the American Wing and Deerfield's Heritage Foundation. Rather, Watkins employed the term "cultural history" to suggest that artifacts be used as evidence in uncovering social and cultural life—an idea today implied by the term "material culture."[85]

While the term "cultural history" never had a lasting impact outside the Smithsonian, where it continued as a division name within the National Museum of American History, the idea of recreating history represented an important shift in the way many collectors and curators had begun to think about historic objects. Inspired by the model of science, historians like Watkins came to see objects as primary source documents of history, vessels that contained a narrative of the past—if only one could interpret their inherent meaning. This approach was fundamentally different from that of collectors who valued antiques as aesthetic objects. For them, the object's meaning was wrapped up in its ability to express a kind of cultural achievement. Nevertheless, the two groups shared an important perspective on historic objects. Both rejected the idea of the antique as a family heirloom or storied object that derived value from its history of ownership, championing the intrinsic value of the object detached from sentimental tales or local associations.

The design features that differentiated Watkins's rooms from those that had come before were subtle, but significant. He deliberately mixed objects from different periods, as if a family had acquired them over time. The goal was both to distinguish his rooms from those celebrating specific aesthetic styles and to create a more realistic living environment. Yet he was careful to make sure that every object was appropriate for the region and room type being displayed, and that nothing anachronistic slipped through. Such precautions might sound too fundamental to be of any interpretive significance, but early period rooms were notorious for ignoring issues of accuracy. When Watkins first inspected the Ritter Room in the 1940s, he found at least twenty-seven artifacts that were inappropriate because of either age, use, or area of origin. Ritter's elegant colonial parlor had contained not only simple kitchenware and bedroom furnishings, but also nineteenth-century ceramics and a number of artifacts local to Pennsylvania.[86]

Contemporary museum theory tends see the respect Watkins and his generation had for accuracy as a fundamental contribution to the profession and the basis of its modern practice. Certainly their rigorous standards have pushed museum-based historians to see a complexity previously unacknowledged. But this drive for accuracy represented more than a new form of historical practice; it signaled a shift in Americans' relationship to the past. History has long drawn its power from encounters with "the real." Relics, such as the rocking chair Abraham Lincoln was sitting in when he was shot, were important because their authenticity (real or perceived) allowed viewers to transcend time and loss.[87] Nineteenth-century antiquarians embraced this connection with the past, but modern historians were not content with authenticity alone. They advocated a more rigorous adherence to the real, in which every aspect of the object and its display was tested for accuracy. It was not enough for an object to be old; it had to be precisely identified by its age, origins, and function, exhibited in a historically correct context, and conserved using techniques that would maintain its structural and physical integrity.

As Jessie Barker Gardner knew from her own experience renovating an old house, accuracy was becoming increasingly important to collectors involved in the preservation of historic structures. No longer was the appearance of age enough; "historically correct" was the new charge. This concern with accuracy took many forms across the history profession. In the late nineteenth century, academic historians, many of them trained at German universities, used the idea of objectivity and scientific method to distinguish themselves from amateur practitioners.[88] The idea of historical truth had come under attack among university scholars by the 1930s, but for those whose exploration of the past took place in the context of museums, historic preservation, and collecting, the idea of detached, scientific truth continued to be useful as a way to elevate their endeavors. The decorative arts market had also made accuracy a priority, rejecting reconstructed or altered antiques and using the requirement that objects be "in the rough" to guarantee authenticity.

The new standards of accuracy particularly affected women. As scholars such as Kevin Murphy and Gail Lee Dubrow have shown, the professionalization of public community history projects, and especially the historic house museum movement, forced many women from positions of power.[89] But even though women lacked the professional degrees and specialized education increasingly necessary to obtain leadership roles, they were hardly immune to the demand for accuracy or its impact on their relationship to the past. Edna Greenwood's story is a case in point. An avid reader, Greenwood saw it as her responsibility to research the objects she collected. She read popular antique manuals and she imported more specialized texts from England. Her library was so extensive that Watkins gladly accepted it as part of her Smithsonian gift.[90] In the late 1920s Greenwood began volunteering for William Sumner Appleton and George Francis Dow at the Society for the Preservation of New England Antiquities. Her duties were typical volunteer fare—cataloging accessions and driving Appleton, who did not own a car, to historic houses.[91] But Dow encouraged her to read widely, giving her copies of his own books, and he urged her to keep a journal of her collecting, a task Greenwood did only sporadically.[92] Dow became such an influence on Greenwood that she wrote in her diary "I told G.F.D. that since my advent at the S.P.N.E.A. 'B.C.' stood for Before Curating and 'A.D.' for After Dow."[93]

Greenwood's relationship with Dow was important, both for its impact on her personal approach to collecting and for what it said about the changing nature of historical understanding in New England. Dow was never trained as a historian. As a young man, he attended commercial schools in Boston and began his working life in the wholesale metal industry. But by the time he met Greenwood at SPNEA, he had already forged an impressive resume in historic preservation and museum management. As the Essex Institute's secretary from 1898 to 1918, he had installed some of the institution's first period rooms, a kitchen of 1750 and a bedroom and parlor of 1800. He also moved the 1685 Ward House to the grounds of the Essex Institute and restored the interior in seventeenth-century fashion, a project he followed with a similar restoration of the Parson Capen House in nearby Topsfield.[94] In each case, he cared deeply about primary source evidence. Describing Dow's restoration of Time Stone Farm, architect Frederick Kelly wrote that Dow worked by "minutely inspecting every nail-hole, every mortise or cut in the old frame-work, or prying beneath later applications of lathe and plaster in order to seek out patiently each shred of evidence."[95]

Research was a way of life for Dow. According to Charles Hosmer, Dow spent several hours a day "scanning ('gleaning' as he called it) eighteenth- and nineteenth-century newspapers for advertisements and news items that illustrated everyday life. He was particularly interested in descriptions of household furnishings, table settings, and comments on food."[96] Dow collected these observations in *Everyday Life in Massachusetts Bay Colony*, a book he published in 1935.[97] They also became the foundation for Pioneer Village, a full-scale reproduction of the settlement John Winthrop encountered when he arrived in Salem in 1630. Built to celebrate the Massachusetts Bay Tercentenary in 1930, the village included not only homes, agricultural fields, and animal sheds, but also tools and equipment for such early industries as salt-making, pit-sawing, fish-curing, iron-working, and woodworking.[98]

To be sure, Dow was not an objective historian by today's exacting standards. Like many of his generation, he believed in the influence of heredity on individual character and he saw family bloodlines as a way to access the past. For many years, he seems to have maintained a small genealogy research business, uncovering family histories for a fee. "I shall be deprived of my 'deaths,'" Ogden Codman wrote to Dow when he feared his newspaper obituaries would not arrive in time to take them to his summer home in Newport, Rhode Island.[99] When it came time to cast actors for a historical pageant designed to bring Pioneer Village to life, Dow turned to the descendents of Salem's original settlers, claiming that they added to the production's accuracy.[100]

As conflicted and complex as Dow's ideas about accuracy were, Greenwood took the new standards as her own. When a crew from *Antiques* that included Samuel Chamberlain, the photographer for Henry Flynt's book *Frontier of Freedom*, took pictures for a cover story, she bemoaned the fact that they showed the hooked rugs in her bedrooms. "I apologize for the hooked rugs upon the floors—they are our only anachronism! For warmth—," she wrote Smithsonian officials on a copy of the published piece.[101] For his part, Watkins recognized what he saw as Greenwood's sophisticated approach to the past. In order to take advantage of her expertise and allow her to retain some control over her collection, Watkins made Greenwood an adviser to the new exhibition, and she rented an apartment in Washington. She cataloged items, wrote exhibit labels, made decisions about what would be displayed, and loaned additional materials as it suited her purposes.

Watkins also recognized the limitations of Greenwood's knowledge and carefully controlled her participation. For example, when Greenwood insisted on carpeting the floors of the rooms with bearskin rugs, he removed them after the exhibition's opening (but not before the official photographs were taken). When she insisted that Watkins accept a late nineteenth-century tin peddler's cart, which she believed to be much older, Watkins dutifully took the cart to Washington but relegated it to a remote storage area.[102] Still, Greenwood exerted her influence over the final exhibition. Note cards in her coarse handwriting remain scattered throughout the Smithsonian's files, outlining exhibition suggestions and label text. Watkins acknowledged that he planned to stay true to Greenwood's vision in an article describing the exhibition for *Antiques*: "It is the intention of museum officials to exhibit [Greenwood's donation] ultimately in a manner that will create a vivid reconstruction of the past and so convey to the public as far as possible what it did initially did to Time Stone's guests."[103]

Figure 29. Malcolm Watkins moved this seventeenth-century house from Edna Greenwood's farm in Massachusetts and installed it in the U.S. National Museum. Photograph courtesy of Smithsonian Institution, Division of Home and Community Life.

The fact that Watkins modeled his exhibition after Time Stone Farm suggests the extent to which he valued not only Greenwood's knowledge and expertise, but also the idea of placing objects in a domestic environment. In essence, Watkins saw Time Stone as a model period room. From the moment Greenwood first suggested her donation, the two worked to define the rooms they would include. Early plans included a so-called English Wigwam, a kind of temporary shelter used by the first European colonists and, not incidentally, reproduced by George Francis Dow as part of his Pioneer Village in Salem. Watkins and Greenwood also set out to construct a 1630–1650 hall and 1650–1720 keeping room, both all-purpose rooms in which kitchen functions mixed with other family needs, as well as an eighteenth-century bedroom and an early nineteenth-century parlor.[104] The final exhibition bore little resemblance to these early plans, but still showed Greenwood's influence. Included were a refurbished Ritter Room, a nineteenth-century schoolroom to display Greenwood's early school materials, a circa-1720 New England interior, and a bedroom based on the 1820 Charles-Gilman house in East Brimfield, Massachusetts,

Figure 30. Malcolm Watkins used the seventeenth-century house shown in figure 29 to create a scene of early American life. Photograph courtesy of Smithsonian Institution, Division of Home and Community Life.

stenciled with patterns copied from those at Greenwood's farm. Most important, at least from the standpoint of size, was an entire seventeenth-century house originally built in Malden, Massachusetts, and restored by George Francis Dow's brother Eugene for use as a library at Time Stone Farm (figures 29 and 30). Installed at the U.S. National Museum, the structure was so ill fitted to its new home that museum technicians had to cut away a portion of its roof. The fact that Watkins was willing to compromise the building's physical integrity to allow for its display shows that he did not value the building in and of itself. Rather, he saw it as an interpretive tool, a context for the objects on display.

Locating a Nation, Defining a People

Nicknamed "Hall 26" for its location on the second floor of what is now the Smithsonian's Natural History Building, Watkins's new exhibit was officially titled "Everyday Life in Early America." But while it claimed to represent a nation, the exhibition's geographic scope was predominantly New England and entirely East Coast. Indeed, five of the exhibit's period rooms celebrated the history of New England, and only one, an eighteenth-century Virginia parlor donated by Miriam Hubbard Morris, represented the South.[105] If Watkins's superiors took issue with these limitations, there is no record of their opposition. Watkins was not, of course, the first New Englander to equate the region's history with that of the nation. Henry Flynt used the small town of Deerfield to embody the nation's cultural heritage. Gertrude Ritter assumed that a New England house should stand on the National Mall, and antique dealers, such as Israel Sack, regularly sold New England antiques to Western art museums that saw them as important national treasures. But Watkins struggled with equating New England and America. As a native of the region, he valued New England's past and upheld its importance to the nation, but as a curator working in the national museum, he also recognized that New England was a small piece of the whole.

Soon after Greenwood gave her gift, the Smithsonian began to expand. In 1958 Congress approved the construction of the National Museum of History and Technology (NMHT), the predecessor of today's National Museum of American History. The new museum resulted in the removal not only of all history exhibits located in the Natural History Building, but also of the history collections from the Anthropology Department's administration. As a result, Watkins transferred to the NMHT and became a curator of cultural history, a division title retained from his old administrative unit in the Division of Ethnology. The new museum also meant the closing of Hall 26 and the construction of a new exhibit, the Hall of Everyday Life in the American Past (HELAP).

HELAP provided Watkins with the opportunity to expand his vision of the past. Since his arrival at the Smithsonian, he had believed that it was the museum's responsibility to create an inclusive history. He regarded Greenwood's donation as the "beginning of an American cultural history group which could logically extend in similar fashion and according to the same standards to include rooms illustrating Pennsylvania Dutch life, the western frontiersman's, the southeastern estate owner's, the cotton planter's cottage of the Deep South, [and] the Spanish settler's hacienda."[106] After his marriage to Joan Pearson, a ceramic specialist from California, Watkins became especially interested in the history of the

American West. In the early 1960s the two traveled the California coast, where Watkins observed indigenous building practices and imported architectural styles. Summarizing his trip to Alice Winchester, Watkins wrote, "I can report that there is a great deal that is historically and antiquarian (if you allow of such a word!) fascinating in the West."[107]

In his search for a more geographically inclusive past, Watkins defined his area of interest as the "arts, crafts, folkways, living habits, and even spiritual and religious aspirations" of the American people.[108] In practice, he acquired domestic interiors that illustrated how people lived as opposed to the aesthetic qualities of their furnishings. Working with the Smithsonian's Anthropology Department, he obtained a Southwest adobe room and Hispanic-American crafts. In addition, Henry Francis du Pont's Winterthur Museum helped him locate an eighteenth-century log house from Delaware. Watkins pursued the study of traditional crafts by collecting the material possessions of ethnic immigrant groups such as the Spanish in the Southwest, the Germans in Pennsylvania, and the Dutch in New York. Like his mother had before him, Watkins also turned to pottery as a way to identify variations in regional cultures. In addition to pieces obtained through his own archeological excavations in the Middle Atlantic and South, Watkins displayed pots made by Hispanic Americans, Chinese Americans, and even a Western "frontier potter."

But moving from region to nation was not so simple. On the most fundamental level, Watkins's collections, scholarly interests, and professional contacts were grounded in New England. With bequests such as the Greenwood Gift, the Copp Collection, and a donation of pottery from his own mother, Watkins's second exhibit highlighted the New England past in much the same way as his first. Indeed, while Watkins used a single interior and accompanying case to represent the American Southwest, New England claimed at least seven period rooms, eight cases dedicated to the Copp Collection, and numerous others celebrating New England's craft traditions.[109] In part, Watkins's tendency to replicate the structure of his first exhibit was based on sheer practicality. Having just completed Hall 26, Watkins reused not only eighteen cases, but also the refurbished Ritter Room and Greenwood's New Hampshire schoolroom.[110] To these, Watkins added even more New England materials. Taking advantage of his New England acquaintances, he collected paneling and woodwork from the eighteenth-century Thomas Hancock House in Worcester,

Massachusetts, a building at one time owned by patriot John Hancock; another set of paneling dating to the 1740s from the Richard Dole House in Newbury, Massachusetts; a finial salvaged from the steeple of Boston's Old North Church; and architectural woodwork carved by architect Samuel Field McIntyre for the circa 1813 mansion Oak Hill in Peabody, Massachusetts.[111] Both the Hancock paneling and the Old North Church finial had special significance to New England preservationists, as the destruction of John Hancock's Boston residence and the restoration of the church both fueled the region's historic preservation movement.[112] For Watkins, such materials complemented and extended his existing collections by providing additional examples of New England's craft traditions.

Watkins also wanted a New England kitchen to display early furniture donated by Edna Greenwood.[113] In Hall 26, Watkins had used Greenwood's Massachusetts Bay House, but with the opening of the new museum, Anthony N. B. Garvan, a curator in the division of Civil History, appropriated the house for his exhibit "Growth of the U.S.," a textbook-style survey of American history from the period of discovery through the first half of the twentieth century.[114] Garvan's interpretation of history was somewhat different from Watkins's. While Watkins used the Greenwood Gift to illustrate how people lived, Garvan wanted the Massachusetts Bay House to demonstrate the transfer of building traditions from England to the United States. To serve his ends, Garvan planned to strip the house of its sheathing and expose its post-and-beam frame construction. As it turned out, however, the Massachusetts Bay House did not prove to be a very good example of seventeenth-century construction methods. When Smithsonian technicians began dismantling the house, they found that its seventeenth-century frame was incomplete, most likely modified by Eugene Dow, who had moved the house from its original location in Malden, Massachusetts, to Time Stone Farm. As curator Peter Welch explained, the house was an excellent vehicle to "convey seventeenth-century life," but not an authentic "document" of the period.[115] The house was returned to Watkins, but he had already been assigned an exhibit hall, and its ceilings were too low to accommodate the two-story building.

Despite the loss of the Massachusetts Bay House and the difficulty associated with locating a similar specimen, Watkins believed a seventeenth-century building was essential to his exhibit. In May 1954 Watkins's friend and former Old Sturbridge Village colleague, George Watson, alerted him to the existence of a 1675 tavern built in Boston's Roxbury district and recently dismantled to make way for a supermarket. Watson, who had seen the house before its destruction, described it as having chamfered beams, gunstock cornerposts, and feather-edged sheathing. In short, it boasted "the best features of a New England kitchen of the period."[116] Reduced to a pile of structural members, the house was in the possession of Jorge Epstein, a Boston jeweler with a side business in architectural salvage. Watkins arranged to buy enough pieces from Epstein to assemble a kitchen. But when the pieces arrived, Watkins found that they were neither sufficient to construct a room nor of the quality Watson had seen. The summer beam had been cut, the sheathing was rough, like floorboards, and there were no ceiling girts included at all.[117] After visiting Epstein's storage lot, Watkins concluded that he was a con artist who had probably sold the desired pieces to another customer. Describing his visit in a Smithsonian report, Watkins noted that Epstein pointed to a single timber in his front yard and commented, "If I put seven or eight of these out there at once, no one will look at them, but if I put out just one, I'll get a customer right away."[118] Disgusted, Watkins returned to the Smithsonian, canceled the contract, and ordered Epstein to remove his property immediately.[119] Even the everyday objects Watkins sought were clearly becoming part of the antiques market and thus subject to fraud.

Undaunted by Epstein's dishonesty, Watkins continued his search. In 1957 he learned that Henry Francis du Pont had purchased a first-period house built by the Story family in Essex, Massachusetts, to use in his museum at Winterthur. Watkins was very familiar with the property. In the 1940s his parents had considered purchasing the building to restore and use as their home.[120] Hearing of du Pont's purchase, Watkins contacted Winterthur's director, Charles Montgomery, about his plans for the kitchen. Montgomery replied that du Pont wanted to keep the kitchen for himself, but was willing to sell (at cost) a bedchamber that retained a large section of original wall-plaster.[121] While Watkins would have preferred a kitchen as a more suitable backdrop to many of the domestic activities of colonial life, he believed the rare wall-plaster an important find and decided to exhibit the simple bedchamber with pieces from the Greenwood Gift. In comparison to the Massachusetts Bay House, the small Story Room diminished New England's physical presence in the Smithsonian. But the change was not a philosophic one. Given the difficulty of obtaining seventeenth-century buildings, the Story Room represented Watkins's continued commitment to New England's past.

In contrast to the directed search Watkins conducted for the seventeenth-century room was the somewhat haphazard fashion in which he collected materials outside New England. Overwhelmed with the task of representing the entire nation, Watkins based his exhibit largely on the availability of regional period rooms. To represent the South, Watkins retained the Virginia Room donated by Miriam Hubbard Morris for Hall 26 and displayed artifacts from his own archeological excavations in Kecoughtan, Virginia.[122] Other period rooms came because of their imminent destruction. Watkins incorporated a confectionary shop from Washington's Georgetown neighborhood (later used as a backdrop for the museum's working coffee shop) after the business closed, and rescued the Victorian-era Comegys Library in Philadelphia from the wrecking ball.

Only Watkins's California kitchen came as the result of a specific search. In 1965 he added a post–gold rush kitchen of California origin to his new exhibition. Dismantled board by board and shipped three thousand miles from its original location at the base of Mt. Shasta, the kitchen was built by George Washington Arbaugh, a gold miner turned rancher who had immigrated from the South. As an exhibit, the kitchen was exceptional only in its ordinariness. Arbaugh was not a prominent man; after fighting in the Mexican War and marrying a woman from his native Alabama, he journeyed west to try his luck in the gold mines of northern California. His kitchen testified to a life of hard work and few comforts. Scars on the wall indicated where the family stacked wood and scoured the counter with strong soap. When Watkins found the kitchen, it was empty, but he furnished it to emphasize its simple origins. Installing a squat wood-burning stove, a gold miner's pan, and a pair of original Levis made by Levi Strauss of San Francisco, Watkins sought to portray the everyday life of an ordinary West Coast family in the third quarter of the nineteenth century.[123]

As one of Smithsonian's first western exhibits, the kitchen opened to much fanfare. One newspaper announced "Gold Rush Kitchen Is on Display in East."[124] Indeed, the exhibit was deemed so successful that the director of California's Oakland Museum asked Watkins to help him create a similar exhibit.[125] But while it represented the West, Watkins's California kitchen also bore a strong resemblance to many of the museum's eastern, especially New England, exhibits. The similarity was deliberate. In a press release announcing the opening of the California kitchen, Watkins wrote, "In many ways as primitive as eastern colonial kitchens of a century earlier, the simple but comfortable room symbolizes the survival of domestic life and civilized values on the Western frontier."[126] Watkins's decision to construct a kitchen exhibit was not surprising. A staple in New England history making, kitchen exhibits provided female preservationists with a way to establish the focus of history in the home.[127] By adapting this type of exhibit to a western context, Watkins expanded his geographic scope, but he did so in a way that replicated an understanding of the past cultivated by New England historians.

While Watkins achieved a modicum of geographic diversity, he did not produce a unified national story. Indeed, he used antique objects and period rooms to create regional patterns of representation. Central to Watkins's vision of America was the idea of an immigrant nation infused with traditions and technologies transferred from other parts of the globe and adapted to local surroundings. In both Hall 26 and HELAP, Watkins included a section titled "European Backgrounds," which cataloged the contributions of Spanish, French, British, Dutch and Flemish, Scandinavian, and German settlers by identifying their ethnic crafts.[128] As Watkins expanded his geographic scope, the idea of cultural transfer became even more useful. He interpreted the Delaware Log House as a Swedish architectural form and pointed to Spanish decorative motifs in HELAP's eighteenth-century adobe house.[129] By focusing on immigration, Watkins acknowledged groups that had traditionally been left out of national narratives. In 1965 he added a case to HELAP titled "Chinese in California." Revolutionary in its recognition of Asian Americans, the case illustrated Chinese craft traditions, especially pottery, a favorite of Watkins's wife as well as his mother.[130] Watkins also interpreted the California kitchen as a kind of eastern immigrant. Explaining his theory in a 1965 Curator's Report, Watkins wrote that the kitchen exemplified "both the transfer of traditional eastern folk concepts of farm-house architecture and the adaptation of design to new Western conditions."[131] But finding artifacts to illustrate the survival of ethnic or regional traditions could sometimes prove difficult. Responding to the social pressures of the Civil Rights movement, Watkins tried to incorporate African-American history in HELAP in 1968, but made little progress, lamenting that "African cultural expressions of Afro-Americans are rare" and that it was "quite difficult for us to find objects."[132]

By celebrating immigrant contributions, Watkins's exhibits exemplified a kind of nascent multiculturalism. When viewed through the lenses of race, region, and ethnicity, his was a diverse America, a patchwork quilt, rather than a solid nation. But it would be a mistake to assume that Watkins did not believe in a coherent national past. Like many other collectors and curators of his generation, he believed the objects he put on display represented the nation as a whole. As pieces from the country's past, they were evidence of its true character. For him, the issue was one of class, and class was implicit in his vision of history. Just as decorative arts collectors and dealers believed that elite culture could stand for the whole, Watkins placed his faith in his inexpensive ceramics and humble farm tools to exemplify the American spirit. Employing words like "ordinary" and "typical" to describe his intended subjects, Watkins celebrated the achievements of what he perceived as average Americans.[133] Describing HELAP, he wrote, "Although we propose to touch on poverty and slavery at one end of the scale and wealth and aristocracy at the other, the stress will be upon the material environment of those most responsible for the building of America—the anonymous farmers, artists, artisans, ministers, seafarers, shopkeepers, ranchers, and homesteaders, who comprised the dominant American middle-class."[134] To a large degree, Watkins's middle-class bias was an expression of the artifacts he employed. As the Copp Collection, the Ritter Room, and the Greenwood Gift reveal, Watkins obtained his collections from prosperous New Englanders whose donations reproduced their class status. But as Barbara Clark Smith has argued, Watkins's preference for the middle class also followed a pattern common to many histories written in the 1950s. Ignoring internal division and social conflict, these histories constructed the idea of an average, white, middle-class family that had existed since the Revolution and endured, unchanged, through the present day.[135] Visitors were also quick to recognize these class dynamics. Dubbing the brightly stenciled bedroom in Hall 26 a "middle-class room," a newspaper reporter made a judgment many were sure to follow.[136]

Watkins's belief in the average American affected the way he treated artifacts as well. When he found the Delaware Log House, its interior was badly damaged by fire. A neighboring house, however, almost identical in size and floor plan, contained hand-planed paneling. Watkins's decision to install the paneling in his exhibit meant that he did not have to risk creating an erroneous or inauthentic interior.[137] But it also destroyed the house's historic integrity. No longer was it an individual artifact, shaped by the experiences of the people who inhabited it, but an amalgamation of materials, joined in an effort to achieve typicality.

In order to emphasize the "ordinariness" of his antiques, Watkins always maintained their anonymity. He regularly identified rooms only by their region of origin, even though he often used ownership and probate records to research how they were furnished.[138] For example, Watkins referred to the room he believed to have been built by Reuben Bliss as the "Springfield Parlor," while the one constructed for Henry Saunders became the "Virginia Parlor."[139] Writing to a fellow curator in 1957, Watkins discouraged the practice of naming houses according to the families who lived in them: "Please, let us forget the *Shute* family, now somehow become *Schute*. Their association with the house is meaningless and late in its history. We call it the Massachusetts Bay Colony House, which defines pretty well its origin and its exhibit function."[140] Watkins's refusal to distinguish rooms with family names stands in sharp contrast to the practices of genealogically motivated collectors such as George Sheldon and John Brenton Copp, but ignoring histories of family ownership was also something he shared with decorative arts collectors, who often identified historic objects by their stylistic traits as opposed to their local origins. Applying the name "Shute" to the Massachusetts Bay House transformed it from the house of the "average" American colonist to the home of an actual family bound by specific class and racial distinctions. Just as antique dealers had abandoned associations as a way to increase the marketability of their wares, Watkins's denial of the specific histories of his antiques allowed him to expand their significance.

Watkins's ability to universalize collections is clearly evident in a display he dubbed the 1893 Child's Bedroom. He constructed this small period room in the 1950s and filled it with toys and bedroom furnishings to represent the nineteenth century's conceptions of childhood and domestic life. Visitors who viewed the exhibit saw an anonymous room representing a middle-class childhood. But what they did not know was that the room had a very specific history—it had belonged to Watkins's own mother. How did a professional curator who worked to transcend family histories come to enshrine his own personal past in the nation's capital? According to correspondence, Watkins and his mother conceived the child's bedroom display as a response to the problem of accuracy. From his arrival at the Smithsonian, Watkins took great pains to make sure each of his period rooms was furnished with objects appropriate to its time and region. But he recognized that he would never be able recreate a real room, one that was both completely accurate and fully authentic. He could represent the past, but he could not recreate it. The advantage of recreating his mother's bedroom was that accuracy was more fully obtainable. Lura Watkins possessed both the necessary furnishings and the knowledge to assemble them correctly. An earlier generation of collectors would have celebrated such a construction as a personal shrine, but Watkins reveled in it as an "infallible document" of the year 1893.[141] He believed the room so successful that he repeated the technique a few years later, when he created the Brooklyn Dining Room. Filled with machine-made, mass-marketed, Sears and Roebuck furnishings, the display demonstrated how far Watkins had gone in rejecting decorative arts interpretations of antiques that valued only handmade, artisanal goods. This room too had a family history. It had belonged to his wife's uncle.[142]

The Legacy of Everyday Life History

By collecting domestic interiors, kitchen utensils, ethnic crafts, and pre-industrial tools, Watkins anticipated the practice of social history in the 1970s in its attention to such mundane realities of life as domestic labor, jobs, education, and the attainment of material possessions. In this way, the Smithsonian differed from Colonial Williamsburg, with its elegantly furnished interiors and refined homes. But for social historians, Watkins's preference for typicality over historical specificity made using his collections difficult at best. A poignant example is the recent reinterpretation of the Ipswich House. Watkins helped obtain the Ipswich House in 1963, when Mrs. Daniel Lunt, wife of the president of the Ipswich, Massachusetts, Historical Society, alerted him to a historic house about to be torn down for parking lot construction.[143] For Watkins, the timing could not have been better. Anthony Garvan had just discovered framing problems in Greenwood's Massachusetts Bay House, which disqualified it as an example of early American building practices. Unlike the Massachusetts Bay House, which was subject to an invasive restoration, the Ipswich House was unrestored, the only modifications stemming from its 250-year history of continuous occupation. The building boasted two main structures: a small seventeenth-century rear ell and a larger Greek Revival main house constructed in the eighteenth century. In adapting the building to his exhibit plans, Garvan acquired both the seventeenth-century ell and three bays of the eighteenth-century house, stripped the building down to its frame, and installed it on the second floor of the National Museum of American History. Exhibited with mannequins demonstrating woodworking techniques of the period 1650–1750, the house exemplified the transfer of building technology from England to America.[144]

The Ipswich House was displayed in the "Growth of the U.S." exhibit until it closed in 1973. Three years later, Watkins reopened the house as an extension of the Hall of Everyday Life in the American Past, installing soon after a nineteenth-century balloon-framed home for comparison.[145] When HELAP closed in 1982, the Ipswich House was too difficult to move, so curators built a wall barricading it from public view. Since that time, there have been several unsuccessful attempts to reinterpret the house. In 1981, the Smithsonian hired the American History Workshop, a for-profit consultant group that produces public exhibitions and interpretive presentations, to design a multimedia display incorporating the Ipswich House. Titled "The Time Machine," the exhibit was designed to take visitors back through time, introducing them to the house's inhabitants through the use of projected images, sound, and film. Several less elaborate proposals followed. The historian Steven Mintz tried to use the Ipswich House to illustrate changes in the American family, while the 1993 "Welcome Home" and 1996 "Open House" proposals attempted to place the Ipswich House in a larger context of residential life in America. Lack of funding preventing any of these exhibits from being built, but all of the proposals embraced a long span of time and attempted to return specificity to the historic structure by examining the lives of the individuals who inhabited it.[146]

Money was not the only problem. The house's existing form also made it difficult to interpret its 250-year history. When Garvan stripped the house to reveal its structural members, he discarded evidence of the building's nineteenth- and twentieth-century history, its inhabitants' lives, and the modifications they made. What Garvan left was the one thing that remained unaltered during the house's long and varied past—its frame. Attempts to illustrate changes in family life were further undermined by the absence of both interior decor and two bays of the main house. Instead of a recognizable home, visitors encountered a bizarre structure, flanked on one end by an exposed fireplace and lacking domestic furnishings and decor. Information assembled during the collecting process provided little assistance in counteracting the effect of these missing elements. The Smithsonian hired Abbott Lowell Cummings in the 1960s to complete a structural analysis, but his inquiry focused on the question of how the seventeenth-century frame was incorporated in the later eighteenth-century structure. Likewise, the archeological survey, rushed because of the parking lot construction, turned up only a nineteenth-century coin and a few pieces of hardware. With such constraints, it is no wonder that the authors of the "Time Machine" proposal planned to fill in the gaps with a multimedia extravaganza.

Beginning in the late 1990s, curators interpreted the Ipswich House once again to include its 250-year history. But instead of relying on high-tech gadgetry, they returned to the structure itself to look for clues, such as paint chips and nail holes, that would provide evidence of the building's adaptation and change. Curators also tapped documentary sources in an effort to understand more about the actual inhabitants and the world in which they lived. The resulting exhibit, titled "Within These Walls. . . ," represented the first time social history methodology was successfully applied to the Ipswich House. Still, Watkins's influence remains.[147] Not only did he promote an everyday-life interpretation of history that advanced the contributions of middle-class Americans over those of the elite, but by building collections focused on the history of domestic life, preindustrial craft, and ethnic traditions, he created an institutional precedent for the study of women's history, work, race, and ethnicity. But Watkins cannot take sole credit for his accomplishments. His work was shaped by New England antiquarians who donated artifacts, provided models of interpretation, and established a tradition of valuing everyday objects. By exhibiting their collections at the Smithsonian and applying their interpretive methods, Watkins ensured that New Englanders would not only have a place in the nation's story, but that they would influence the presentation of other regions' histories as well.

Epilogue
The End of the Antique?

O n January 31, 2002, the antique firm of Israel Sack, Inc., closed its doors. After Israel Sack died in May 1959, his sons, Harold, Albert, and Robert, had continued the family tradition, joined by Albert's son Donald in 1968. Certainly the decision to close the firm was influenced by the brothers' advancing age. (The oldest brother, Harold, had died in 2000; Albert was in his eighties and Robert in his seventies.)[1] But the demise of Israel Sack, Inc., a firm that had been a leader in the collecting community for most of the twentieth century, also raises larger questions about the practice of antiquing today. How robust is the market for early American household furnishings, and what meanings do today's collectors attach to old things? If antiquing was an invention of the twentieth century, will it continue to thrive in the twenty-first?

On television, antiquing is alive and well, represented by the popular PBS program *Antiques Roadshow*, the art and antique appraisal show in which experts estimate the value of historic objects owned by average

Americans. Based on the BBC production of the same title, *Roadshow* has graced U.S. television sets since 1997, making it one of PBS's most long-lived hits. Expectant viewers who want to have their treasures evaluated register by lottery and endure long waits as *Roadshow* experts, who number between seventy and eighty for each event, appraise several thousand objects a day. The show's wide appeal has catapulted some of its appraisers to fame, most notably the twin brothers Leigh and Leslie Keno, experts in early American decorative arts who documented their own collecting adventures in *Hidden Treasures: Searching for Masterpieces of American Furniture.*[2] Blond and blue-eyed, the two have become the poster boys for twenty-first-century antiquing, reinforcing the hobby's elite image of years past with their tasteful suits and WASPish air.

Antiques Roadshow trades in a much more expanded notion of antiques than this study, demonstrating that the collecting canon constructed by early twentieth-century connoisseurs (including the beliefs that true antiques had to be made before 1830 and that an antique's primary value is aesthetic) has not prohibited American collectors from constructing their own ideas of what constitutes an "antique." Early American household furnishings and decorative objects are a staple on the program and bring some of the highest estimates, but *Roadshow* also includes a wide variety of other collectibles, from Native American textiles to baseball cards, 1970s lunch boxes to Renaissance statues, all drawing their cultural significance from a host of associations, emotions, and cultural values. *Roadshow* appraisers chat excitedly about a collection of movie posters evoking the glamour of the 1940s. They praise Civil War photographs for their ability to document an earlier time, reminisce about the simple humor of Charles Schultz when presented with a collection of his drawings, and applaud early twentieth-century art glass for its beauty. Indeed, watching *Antiques Roadshow* demonstrates that even though midcentury collectors dismissed historical associations as a source of value, the allure of the storied object has not gone away. Documented histories regularly increase an object's estimated price. When appraiser Don Ellis valued a Navajo blanket, woven between 1840 to 1860 for a Ute chief, at $350,000 to $500,000 (the show's highest on-air estimate until 2009), he added that he had not taken into consideration the owner's story that Kit Carson had given the blanket to his family. If that provenance could be proven, Ellis said, the blanket could be worth even more.[3]

Sentiment also plays an important role in the *Roadshow* drama. Regular viewers know the moment when one of the show's expert appraisers shocks the antique owner by announcing that an object that had been in his or her family for generations is worth thousands of dollars. Central to the drama of this moment is our knowledge of the owner's choice: sell the heirloom for financial gain or keep it and maintain family history. If the piece is sold and removed from its family context, its associational meaning is compromised; if it remains within the family, its monetary value cannot be realized. On the air, owners often maintain the importance of the object's sentimental value and deny that they will ever sell, but one wonders what decisions they will make when the cameras are gone.

By focusing on objects' monetary value, *Roadshow* reinforces the function of antiques as commodities, an idea central to the twentieth-century conception of the antique and one that remains powerful today. Just as George and Jessie Gardner paid careful attention to their collection's market value, *Antiques Roadshow* translates every object it features into dollars and cents. *Roadshow* appraisers frequently begin by asking how much the owner paid for the object. Viewers understand that this question sets the stage for a judgment of the owner's capability as a shopper. The show's regular trope is to dazzle viewers with estimates of economic gain. Frequently, participants will bring objects found at yard sales or junk shops and be rewarded with estimates far exceeding their original investment. The 2008 season included a special episode called "Trash to Treasures."[4]

Demonstrations of successful shopping celebrate the idea of antiquing as a test of knowledge, the savvy antiquer being the one who can distinguish trash from treasure. Occasionally *Roadshow* provides the more cautionary tale of an individual who overpaid or was duped by a forgery. In this sense, little has changed in the last hundred years of collecting. Just as early twentieth-century collectors looked to subvert the market by collecting door-to-door, so too do modern collectors scrounge tag sales and church bazaars. Similarly, as yesterday's antiquers worried about spurious antiques, contemporary junk snuppers fear forgeries and fakes. In all that has changed in the last hundred years, one thing remains constant: collecting remains grounded in the consumer experience.

The influence of technology is also an important theme in the history of collecting. While early twentieth-century collectors relied on the automobile to facilitate their searches, today's antiquers embrace the new technology of the Internet, particularly the online auction house eBay.[5] Founded as a trading site for Pez candy dispensers, eBay is hardly limited to the sale of antiques. Its shoppers purchase everything from electronic goods to real estate, and while antiques and collectibles make up a significant percentage of eBay sales, sales of early American household furnishings are relatively few.[6] Indeed, like *Antiques Roadshow*, eBay embraces a variety of collectibles and demonstrates that today's collectors find a dizzying variety of objects meaningful. In eBay's "Antique" category, one can find Chippendale chairs grouped with cast iron garden statues, twentieth-century art pottery, sewing machines, and model ships. The "Collectibles" category is even broader and includes everything from comic books to beer cans, lunch boxes to coins. While aesthetic considerations provide value to many eBay goods, nostalgia is also an important driver. In her *100 Best Things I've Sold on eBay* series, Lynn A. Dralle, the self-proclaimed Queen of Auctions, tells many stories in which everyday objects from the 1960s and 1970s find eager purchasers because of their ability to evoke personal memories.[7] Typical is the story of a gentleman who enthusiastically purchased a simple glass "sun tea" jar because it reminded him of his childhood. In this sense, aesthetics remains important for many collectors, but in today's market sentiment has value in and of itself.[8]

While the objects Dralle sells are very different from those offered by early twentieth-century dealers, her stories of yard-sale finds and hefty earnings underscore another constant: the profitability of antiques. People have always been attracted to the antique trade because of its accessibility. Pickers could enter the business with little more than determination, hard work, and enough charm to make a deal. Even so, pickers were constrained by the dealers they supplied. Lacking a storefront and a way to reach the customer, pickers had to accept what dealers offered for their finds, knowing full well that a sizable mark-up would be added. In many ways, eBay has liberated pickers. No longer in need of a physical store to reach customers, pickers sell directly to the public and increase their profits. A trip to the "Collectibles" section of the bookstore brings a multitude of how-to-books promising easy riches from antiques. Titles such as *Antiquing for Dummies, How to Sell Antiques and Collectibles on eBay . . . And Make a Fortune!* and *How to Make $20,000 a Year in Antiques and Collectibles without Leaving Your Job* demonstrate the popularity of antiquing as a commercial enterprise.[9] My own experience corroborates the idea that antiques make good business. During the formative years of this project, I lived next door to an antique dealer. He did not operate out of a storefront, but traveled around the country selling his finds at historical reenactments and flea markets. That was until eBay arrived. Suddenly, what had been a discreet little business boomed. My neighbor was out on the front lawn taking digital pictures of his merchandise, and his house became so cluttered with antiques and collectibles that shelves of merchandise blocked the windows and new employees crowded our shared driveway. Just as they had for the early twentieth-century Jewish dealers I described in chapter 2, antiques offered my neighbor an opportunity for financial independence.

The high-end market for early American furniture has also soared.[10] When I arrived at Brown University in the mid-1990s, people were still talking about a $12.1 million desk. Most likely crafted by John Goddard, a master Rhode Island cabinetmaker of the pre-Revolutionary period, and originally owned by Nicholas Brown, the desk had passed down in the Brown family. In 1989, the Browns decided to sell the desk and use the profits to restore the family's eighteenth-century home and endow it as a center for scholars working at Brown University.[11] (This book began in an office in that house and with a stipend from that endowment.) No piece of American-made furniture has toppled the desk's standing as bringing the highest price ever paid at auction for an object other than a painting, but the sale set off a wave of high-stakes buying. In 2005, another piece of furniture owned by Nicholas Brown and attributed to John Goddard brought an astounding price. This time it was a Chippendale mahogany scalloped-top tea table that sold for $8.4 million.[12] Both the desk and the tea table were purchased by members of the Sack family.

Such sales speak to the continued vitality of antiques in American culture, but dealers are telling another story about the antique market, one that suggests that antiques have lost their meaning for many Americans. According to many dealers, the "middle market" has gone soft. Pieces blessed with rarity, quality, and original condition bring impressive prices, while, thanks to the popularity of the shabby-chic decorating style, which features recycled old furniture and fabrics, inexpensive, heavily worn, or rustic furniture sells too. But middle-market objects, what *Maine Antiques Digest*, a periodical aimed at experienced collectors and dealers, has described as early American furnishings of "passable quality but otherwise undistinguished by . . . provenance, creator, or condition," have found few buyers. As proof, the magazine's writers offer the fact that Sotheby's auction house raised its minimum lot value to $5,000 and discontinued its second-tier auctions.[13]

No statistical evidence exists to document middle-market sales, but *Maine Antiques Digest* writer David Vazdauskas chronicles an era of economic uncertainty.[14] For many, the demise of the middle market is linked to another troubling trend, the lack of young collectors. In the rapidly graying antique market, "young" is defined as under forty-five years old. Clear in the understanding that their customer base is shrinking, many industry insiders are encouraging the cultivation of this younger buyer. *Maine Antiques Digest* now runs a regular column titled "The Young Collector," and offers advice to those seeking such business. Use the Internet, they urge. Take young collectors under your wing and educate them about collecting; create more attractive displays, provide more attentive sales people.[15] The advice is plentiful, if not a panacea.

Implicit in many of these suggestions is the recognition that buying antiques is a difficult consumer challenge, one that requires in-depth understanding of an object's rarity, quality, condition, and age. *Maine Antiques Digest* columnists suggest that dealers make education an implicit part of their services, just as Israel Sack did in the early twentieth century.[16] But the idea that buying antiques is difficult for those who are not trained experts remains. Certainly *Antiques Roadshow* does little to assuage such fears with its penchant for shocking viewers. If the objects featured by *Roadshow* function as commodities, they do so within a market impenetrable to the uninitiated consumer. Indeed, the show's premise is that ordinary people do not know how much their possessions are worth and that only trained "experts" can discern monetary value. During a recent pledge drive on a PBS member station, the announcer emphasized the appraisers' ability to navigate what he portrayed as a market turned upside down, in which objects assumed to be valuable rarities are found worthless while trinkets bring thousands of dollars. In this reading, regular viewing is offered as a kind of consumer education, providing viewers with insurance against their own lack of knowledge. Participants who bring their treasures for appraisal are eager for the chance to receive expert advice, but at the same time viewers assimilate the experts' teachings in the hope that they will be able to make their own finds. Parodies of the program are abundant on the online video site YouTube, and they often draw on the unequal power relationship between appraiser and owner for their humor. In one skit, the appraiser uses his authority to scam owners and purchase antiques at greatly devalued prices.[17] The piece plays on the general public's insecurity and its distrust of the antique market. One wonders to what degree such fears have undermined the middle market. Those who buy shabby-chic chests assume little risk, since the appeal of such items stems as much from their low prices as their aesthetics. Similarly, those buying at the market's high end can be confident in their decision, their new possessions having passed the scrutiny of connoisseurship. Middle-market antiques can be more problematic, as their mid-range price is tied to their lack of perfection; those who buy at such levels often find their purchases stigmatized as "undistinguished" or "mediocre."[18]

The middle-market problem also suggests a much larger dissatisfaction with antiques. Younger Americans might not be educated antique consumers, but do they even want to be? For collectors in the first half of the twentieth century, antiques provided evidence of an American artistic spirit and of the success of the capitalist order. Antiques were culturally significant; Jessie Gardner, for example, believed her antique collection would not only corroborate her class status, but also better her community. Contemporary articles in *Maine Antiques Digest* suggest that the meanings associated with antiques, whether patriotic, hegemonic, or status driven, have been lost. One article praises organizers of the Forty-fourth Delaware Antiques Show for making antiques more hip by serving Asian food and sake at the opening reception, a menu that suggests that antiques have lost their relevance as symbols of a distinctly American culture.[19] Other articles tie antiques to environmental concerns. "Antiques are green," declared David Vazdauskas in 2005.[20] While early American household furnishings are recycled, so too are Goodwill store purchases. Similarly, the promise that a two-hundred-year-old chest of drawers will not produce outgassing only reeks of desperation (figure 31). With such marketing schemes, it is of little surprise that some experts have suggested that the way to encourage new collectors is to abandon traditional antiques categories and encourage collecting in eras with high nostalgia appeal, particularly games and toys.[21]

The appeal of aesthetically defined antiques has lessened somewhat with scholars as well. Those studying the decorative arts in museums and universities might seem far removed from uncertainties of the antique

Figure 31. The magazine *Antiques and Fine Art* offered this window sticker to its readers in 2008 to promote the idea of antique collecting as an environmentally friendly practice. Image courtesy of *Antiques and Fine Art*.

market, but historically the concerns of decorative arts scholars have closely connected them to antique collectors. Indeed, decorative arts scholars often study questions of attribution, authenticity, and quality—precisely those attributes that bring value in the market.[22] By asserting the value of historic objects as anthropological evidence of cultural practices, Malcolm Watkins's work at the Smithsonian represented a challenge to traditional decorative arts scholarship. For Watkins, authenticity and identification mattered, but only as a starting point to allow the historian to use material objects as primary source texts in the exploration of the past. By the 1970s, the approach Watkins was taking would have its own name: material culture studies. Based on the idea that historic objects function as, in the words of Jules Prown, a reflection of "mind in matter," material culture studies dismissed decorative arts scholars as antiquarian, charging that they failed to place objects in historical context and instead fetishized the object.[23] Like Watkins, material culture scholars expanded the notion of what kinds of objects to study, maintaining that every man-made item reflects the culture of its maker and its user. As a result, many museums, particularly history museums, turned away from displaying high-style furniture and embraced more ordinary objects, while others, such as Colonial Williamsburg, reinterpreted their elite furnishings and buildings using the tools of social history.[24] In Connecticut, where I live, the Connecticut Historical Society now regularly presents everyday objects in its exhibits as material evidence of past practices. A comic book suggests boyhood fantasies, boxes of laundry detergent tell us about domestic labor, and typewriters illustrate the daily tasks of office workers. This penchant for ordinary objects is relatively new for the society. When Christopher Bickford wrote his history of the Connecticut Historical Society in 1975, he identified the society's commitment to collecting and documenting the state's contributions to the decorative and fine arts, a directive that began with collector George Dudley Seymour's gift of early American furniture, portraits, glass, and ceramics in 1945, as an enduring centerpiece of the museum's mission.[25] Today, visitors to the historical society's flagship building will find few examples of early American decorative arts on display.

All this makes one wonder if the fascination with aesthetically defined antiques is coming to an end. Are young, financially successful American couples, those who in years past entered the collecting community and supplied the antique market with new blood, too dedicated to a culture of carefully crafted eccentricity and personal expression to choose tradition-bound antiques as their furnishings? Has the construction of a more inclusive definition of what constitutes value in old things, both in the academic community and in the collectibles market, made fine early American furnishings obsolete? One thing remains certain. Americans' belief that the household furnishings of early American elites represents a distinctly American art is rooted in the history of the early twentieth century. Our understanding and appreciation for antiques, like every aspect of American culture, will have to adapt to the changing times.

Notes

INTRODUCTION

1. Betty C. Monkman, *The White House: Its Historic Furnishings and First Families* (New York: Abbeville Press, 2000), 186–91, 204–6. See also "Americanizing the White House," *New York Times*, 3 July 1925; H. I. Brock, "White House Arouses an Art Debate," *New York Times*, 12 July 1925; H. I. Brock, "The Hunt for the Old Widens," *New York Times*, 20 September 1925.

2. Monkman, *White House*, 206–8.

3. On Eleanor Roosevelt's interest in Lincoln's bed see Monkman, *White House*, 187.

4. "Americanizing the White House."

5. "Art of the American Home in New Wing of Museum," *New York Times*, 3 August 1924. See also "Open American Wing at Museum of Art," *New York Times*, 11 November 1924; "Mrs. Coolidge Shops for Ideas on Art," *New York Times*, 20 November 1925.

6. "A Household of Continuance" *New York Times*, 10 November 1924.

7. Luke Vincent Lockwood, *The Pendleton Collection* (Providence: Rhode Island School of Design, 1904).

8. One of the best sources for charting the history of antique collecting, and a valued precedent for this study, is Elizabeth Stillinger's pioneering work *The Antiquers* (New York: Random House, 1980); for the history of these early museum displays, see chaps. 10, 19, and 23. See also Michael Kammen, *Mystic Chords of Memory: The Transformation of Tradition in American Culture* (New York: Knopf, 1991), 343–50.

9. Carol Duncan, "Art Museums and the Ritual of Citizenship," in *Exhibiting Cultures: The Poetics and Politics of Museum Display*, ed. Ivan Karp and Steven D. Lavine (Washington, D.C.: Smithsonian Institution Press, 1991), 95.

10. I borrow the concept of "invention" from Eric Hobsbawm and Terence Ranger, eds., *The Invention of Tradition*, rev. ed. (Cambridge: Cambridge University Press, 1992). Other works important to my understanding of the production of collective memory include Maurice Halbwachs, *The Collective Memory* (New York: Harper and Row, 1980); Michel-Rolph Trouillot, *Silencing the Past: Power and the Production of History* (Boston: Beacon Press, 1995); Pierre Nora, *Realms of Memory: Rethinking the French Past*, 3 vols. (New York: Columbia University Press, 1996); David Lowenthal, *The Past Is a Foreign Country* (Cambridge: Cambridge University Press, 1986); Kammen, *Mystic Chords of Memory*; David Glassberg, "Public History and the Study of Memory," *Public Historian* 18, no. 2 (Spring 1996): 7–23; David Thelen, ed., *Memory and Collective Remembering* (Bloomington: Indiana University Press, 1990); George Lipsitz, *Time Passages: Collective Memory and American Popular Culture* (Minneapolis: University of Minnesota Press, 1990); John R. Gillis, ed., *Commemorations: The Politics of National Identity* (Princeton: Princeton University Press, 1994); John Bodnar, *Remaking America: Public Memory, Commemoration, and Patriotism in the Twentieth Century* (Princeton: Princeton University Press, 1992); James M. Lindgren, *Preserving Historic New England: Preservation, Progressivism, and the Remaking of Memory* (New York: Oxford University Press, 1995); David Thelen and Roy Rosenzweig, *The Presence of the Past: Popular Uses of History in American Life* (New York: Columbia University Press, 1998); Benedict Anderson, *Imagined Communities: Reflections on the Origin and Spread of Nationalism*, rev. ed. (London: Verso, 1991).

11. Stephen J. Summerhill and John Alexander Williams, *Sinking Columbus: Contested History, Cultural Politics, and Mythmaking during the Quincentenary* (Gainesville: University Press of Florida, 2000); Claudia L. Bushman, *America Discovers Columbus: How an Italian Explorer Became an American Hero* (Hanover, N.H.: University Press of New England, 1992).

12. On Americans' ignorance of their nation's history, see Sam Wineburg, *Historical Thinking and Other Unnatural Acts: Charting the Future of Teaching the Past* (Philadelphia: Temple University Press, 2001), vii–viii.

13. Kammen, *Mystic Chords of Memory*, chap. 1. For additional scholarship on the Colonial Revival, see Alan Axelrod, ed., *The Colonial Revival* (New York: W. W. Norton for the Henry Francis du Pont Winterthur Museum, 1985); Geoffrey L. Rossano, ed., *Creating a Dignified Past: Museums in the Colonial Revival* (Savage, Md.: Rowman and Littlefield in association with Historic Cherry Hill, 1991); Sarah L. Giffen and Kevin D. Murphy, eds., *A Noble and Dignified Stream* (York, Maine: Old York Historical Society, 1992); Lindgren, *Preserving Historic New England*; Marla R. Miller and Anne Digan Lanning, "'Common Parlors': Women and the Recreation of Community Identity in Deerfield, Massachusetts, 1870–1920," *Gender and History* 6, no. 3 (1994): 435–55; William H. Truettner and

Roger Stein, eds., *Picturing Old New England: Image and Memory* (New Haven: Yale University Press for the National Museum of American Art, Smithsonian Institution, 1999); Christopher P. Monkhouse and Thomas S. Michie, *American Furniture in Pendleton House* (Providence: Museum of Art, Rhode Island School of Design, 1986); Christopher Monkhouse, "The Spinning Wheel as Artifact, Symbol, and Source of Design," in *Victorian Furniture: Essays from a Victorian Society Autumn Symposium*, ed. Kenneth Ames (Philadelphia: Victorian Society in America, 1983), 155–71; Rodris Roth, "The Colonial Revival and 'Centennial Furniture,'" *Art Quarterly* 27, no. 1 (1964): 57–81; William Rhoads, *Colonial Revival* (New York: Garland Press, 1977); Thomas Denenberg, *Wallace Nutting and the Invention of Old America* (New Haven: Yale University Press, 2003); Karal Ann Marling, *George Washington Slept Here* (Cambridge: Harvard University Press, 1988); Richard Guy Wilson, Shaun Eyring, and Kenny Marotta, eds., *Re-creating the American Past: Essays on the Colonial Revival* (Charlottesville: University of Virginia Press, 2006).

14. I use the phrase "aesthetic antique" to refer to historic household furnishings valued for their artistic qualities, rather than assigning such objects to the "decorative arts." The "decorative arts" label is widely used by museum scholars to refer to ornamental and functional works in ceramic, wood, glass, metal, or textile, and was intended to distinguish such works from the traditional fine arts of painting, sculpture, drawing, and photography. The term is problematic for this study, however, because it is tied to the field of art history, a discipline more concerned with aesthetic judgments and explorations than with the contextual nature of historical inquiry. As Kenneth Ames has argued, much of the scholarship that has come out of the decorative arts field is itself oriented toward the questions and concerns of collectors. My choice of terms is therefore a deliberate decision to distance this study from that field and place it within the context of historical scholarship. On the development of the decorative arts as a scholarly field, see Kenneth L. Ames, "American Decorative Arts / Household Furnishings," *American Quarterly* 35, no. 3 (1983): 280–303; Michael J. Ettema, "History, Nostalgia, and American Furniture," *Winterthur Portfolio* 17, no. 1 (1982): 135–44.

15. On the need for an American culture to match the nation's increasing military and political power, see Emily S. Rosenberg, *Spreading the American Dream: American Economic and Cultural Expansion, 1890–1945* (New York: Hill and Wang, 1982).

16. In thinking about collectibles as consumer goods, I am indebted to Russell Belk, *Collecting in a Consumer Society* (London: Routledge, 1995); Arjun Appadurai, *The Social Life of Things: Commodities in Cultural Perspective* (Cambridge: Cambridge University Press, 1986); Grant McCracken, *Culture and Consumption: New Approaches to the Symbolic Character of Consumer Goods and Activities* (Bloomington: Indiana University Press, 1988).

17. William Leach, *Land of Desire* (New York: Pantheon, 1993), 13. My understanding of the history of consumption in the early twentieth century is also influenced by Jackson Lears, *Fables of Abundance* (New York: Basic Books, 1994); Roland

Marchand, *Advertising the American Dream* (Berkeley: University of California Press, 1985); Susan Strasser, *Satisfaction Guaranteed* (New York: Pantheon, 1989); Charles McGovern, *Sold America* (Chapel Hill: University of North Carolina Press, 2006); James D. Norris, *Advertising and the Transformation of American Society* (New York: Greenwood Press, 1990); Simon J. Bronner, ed., *Consuming Visions: Accumulation and Display of Goods in America, 1880–1920* (New York: W. W. Norton for the Henry Francis du Pont Winterthur Museum, 1989).

18. T. J. Jackson Lears, *No Place of Grace: Antimodernism and the Transformation of American Culture, 1880–1920* (New York: Pantheon, 1981), 14.

19. Stow quoted in *Antiques Dealer* 4, no. 1 (January 1952): 5. For a similar condemnation of post-1825 furniture, see Wallace Nutting, "Poverty of Invention in Design," in *Furniture Treasury* (New York: Macmillan, 1948–1949).

20. Marchand, *Advertising the American Dream*, 217–28.

21. In the mid-1920s, Jordan Marsh regularly advertised its "Little Colonial House" in the magazine *Antiques*. For examples of these advertisements, see "Through This Door to Yesterday," *Antiques*, April 1926, inside back cover; "In the Pine Room of Our Little Colonial House," *Antiques*, February 1925, inside back cover. On Altman's, see Louise Shepard, "Half an Acre of Early American in B. Altman's Country Shop," *Antiques Dealer*, June 1951, 21 and 36. For an example of a Lord and Taylor advertisement, see "Opening the New Floor of Antiques, Reproductions, Decoration," *Antiques*, November 1926, 335. On the link between museums and department stores, see Leach, *Land of Desire*, 164–73; Neil Harris, *Cultural Excursion: Marketing Appetites and Cultural Tastes in Modern America* (Chicago: Chicago University Press, 1990), 56–81.

22. Leslie Gross, *Housewives' Guide to Antiques* (New York: Exposition Press, 1959), 15.

23. Robert Lacey recounts the history of New York's elite auction houses, including the growth of American Art Association and Anderson Galleries (which merged in 1929), the dominance of the Parke-Bernet auction house in the 1930s, and Parke-Bernet's fall to London's Sotheby's in the 1960s. See Robert Lacey, *Sotheby's: Bidding for Class* (Boston: Little, Brown, 1998), 125–43.

24. Peter G. Buckley, "The Old Curiosity Shop and the New Antique Store: A Note on the Vanishing Curio in New York City," *Common-place* 4, no. 2 (January 2004), www.common-place.org/vol-04/no-02/buckley/ (accessed 5 January 2009).

25. Richard Henry Saunders, "American Decorative Arts Collecting in New England, 1840–1920" (master's thesis, University of Delaware, 1973), 25. A version of Saunders's thesis has been published as "Collecting American Decorative Arts in New England, 1793–1876" part 1, *The Magazine Antiques*, May 1976, 996–1003; part 2, October 1976, 754–63.

26. The Association of Antique Dealers was formed in Boston in 1922. See "An Association of Antique Dealers," *Antiques*, June 1922, 249. In 1951 *Antiques Dealer*, a magazine aimed at the antique retail trade, reported that 20.6% of its surveyed readers belonged to a dealer association. See "Practices and Policies of Dealers in Antiques," *Antiques Dealer*, December 1951, 8.

27. Stillinger, *Antiquers*, chaps. 2, 3, and 4.

28. Steven M. Gelber, *Hobbies: Leisure and Culture of Work in America* (New York: Columbia University Press, 1999).

29. Henry Wood Erving to Harry Watson, 18 July 1919, and unsigned letter to Francis H. Bigelow, 30 January 1911, both in the Joseph Downs Collection, Winterthur Library, Henry Francis du Pont Winterthur Museum, Winterthur, Del. (hereafter cited as Downs Collection, Winterthur).

30. Nina Fletcher Little, *Little by Little* (New York: Dutton, 1991), 26, 29–30. Many of these groups continue to operate and can be found on the web: the Pewter Club, members.aol.com/pewterpcca/; the Early American Industries Association, www .eaiainfo.org/; the Rushlight Club, www.rushlight.org/; the National Early American Glass Club (now the National American Glass Club), www.glassclub.org/.

31. Edward L. Ayres et al., *All Over the Map: Rethinking American Regions* (Baltimore: Johns Hopkins University Press, 1996); Dona Brown, *Inventing New England: Regional Tourism in the Nineteenth Century* (Washington, D.C.: Smithsonian Institution Press, 1995); Dona Brown, *A Tourist's New England: Travel Fiction, 1820–1920* (Hanover, N.H.: University Press of New England, 1999); Patricia Nelson Limerick, *The Legacy of Conquest: The Unbroken Past of the American West* (New York: W. W. Norton, 1988); Patricia Nelson Limerick, *Desert Passages: Encounters with the American Desert* (Niwot: University Press of Colorado, 1989); Joseph Conforti, *Imagining New England: Explorations of Regional Identity from the Pilgrims to the Mid-Twentieth Century* (Chapel Hill: University of North Carolina Press, 2001).

32. For an overview, see David H. Watters, introduction to the section "Images and Ideas" in *The New Encyclopedia of New England*, ed. Burt Feintuch & David H. Watters (New Haven: Yale University Press, 2005) 724–25.

33. Examples of studies that examine the construction of New England identity largely from an internal perspective include Conforti, *Imagining New England*; Truettner and Stein, *Picturing Old New England*; Lindgren, *Preserving Historic New England*. Works that examine how New England's history and landscape have been bought and sold do more to consider how New England's identity has been disseminated. See, for example, Denenberg, *Wallace Nutting*; Brown, *Inventing New England*.

1. PRICELESS AND PRICE

1. O. C. Hill, "Inventory," 1 February 1902, and "Antique Furniture on Hand," June 22, 1909, both in O. C. Hill Collection, Downs Collection, Winterthur.

2. Hill, "Antique Furniture on Hand."

3. While accounts of the Centennial attribute the cradle to Peregrine White, images of the New England Kitchen published in *Frank Leslie's Illustrated*, 10 June 1876, and Philip Sandhurst et al., *The Great Centennial Exhibition* (Philadelphia: P. W. Zeigler, 1876), 542, cast doubt on this attribution. The cradle depicted in both *Frank Leslie's Illustrated* and *The Great Centennial Exhibition* bears no resemblance to the Peregrine White cradle that is currently housed in the collections of the

Pilgrim Hall Museum in Plymouth, Massachusetts. It is made of wicker, while the one depicted in the two publications is clearly constructed of solid boards. In his *Illustrated History of the Centennial Exhibition* (Cincinnati: Jones Brothers, 1876), James McCabe refers to the cradle as the "Fuller cradle, in which rocked little Peregrine White" (723), and the cradle pictured in both *Frank Leslie's Illustrated* and *The Great Centennial Exhibition* does more closely resemble a cradle that descended in the family of Samuel Fuller that is also today in the collections of Pilgrim Hall Museum. Such discrepancies suggest that while the organizers of the New England Kitchen valued historic associations, they might not have always gotten them right.

4. Contemporary descriptions of the New England Kitchen include McCabe, *Illustrated History of the Centennial Exhibition*, 722–23; J. S. Ingram, *The Centennial Exposition Described and Illustrated* (Philadelphia: Hubbard Brothers, 1876), 706–8; Sandhurst et al., *The Great Centennial Exhibition*, 542; Frank Leslie, *Frank Leslie's Historical Register of the United States Centennial Exposition* (New York: Frank Leslie's Publishing House, 1877), 87. On the Colonial Revival at the Philadelphia Centennial, see Rodris Roth, "The New England, or 'Olde Tyme,' Kitchen Exhibit at Nineteenth-Century Fairs," in *The Colonial Revival*, ed. Alan Axelrod (New York: W. W. Norton for the Henry Francis du Pont Winterthur Museum, 1985), 159–83. My understanding of the use of antiques at the Centennial's kitchen exhibit is also influenced by Laurel Thatcher Ulrich, "Fiction in the Kitchen, 1876" (paper presented at the symposium "Reckoning with Wallace Nutting," Wadsworth Atheneum, Hartford, Conn., 14 June 2003).

5. Robert Emlen, "Colonial Relics, Nativism, and the DAR Loan Exhibition of 1892," in *New England Collectors and Collections* (Annual Proceedings of the Dublin Seminar for New England Folklife), ed. Peter Benes (Boston: Boston University, 2004), 171, 176–82, quote on 182.

6. Fred Bishop Tuck, *Antiqueman's Diary: The Memoirs of Fred Bishop*, ed. Dean A. Fales Jr. (Gardiner, Maine: Tilbury House, 2000), v, viii.

7. Ibid., 36, 33–34, 16–17. Donation parties were an annual ritual in which a congregation supplemented its minister's income by providing him and his family with gifts of farm produce, wood, and other household goods.

8. Ibid., 58, 39.

9. Ibid., 122.

10. Norman Isham to Henry Kent, 2 December 1934, Walpole Society Collection, Downs Collection, Winterthur.

11. Elizabeth Stillinger's *The Antiquers* contains biographies of important collectors; for a discussion of Bigelow's activities as a silver dealer, see 144–46.

12. William Hosley, "Hartford's Role in the Origins of Antiques Collecting in America," in Benes, *New England Collectors and Collections*, 113–14.

13. Stillinger, *Antiquers*, 113–21. Also useful for its description of some of the earlier and lesser-known collectors of American antiques is Saunders, "American Decorative Arts Collecting."

14. On the history of the Walpole Society see *A Collection of Collectors: Celebrating Seventy-five Years of the Walpole Society* (Lunenburg, Vt.: Meriden-Stinehour Press, 1985).

15. Irving Whitall Lyon, *The Colonial Furniture of New England: A Study of the Domestic Furniture in Use in the Seventeenth and Eighteenth Centuries* (Boston: Houghton, Mifflin, 1891).

16. Irving Whitall Lyon, *The Colonial Furniture of New England: A Study of the Domestic Furniture in Use in the Seventeenth and Eighteenth Centuries* (1924 ed.), with an introduction by Dean A. Fales Jr. (New York: Dutton, 1977), xxiv.

17. Luke Vincent Lockwood, *Colonial Furniture in America* (New York: Charles Scribner's Sons, 1901), 24, 37.

18. Luke Vincent Lockwood, *Colonial Furniture in America*, rev. ed. (New York: Charles Scribner's Sons, 1913), 41–42.

19. Dean A. Fales Jr. points out Lyon's misspelling and lack of regard for Hepplewhite furniture in his introduction to Lyon, *Colonial Furniture of New England*, xviii.

20. Israel Sack, "The Reminiscences of Mr. Israel Sack," interview by Owen Bombard, 11 February 1953, transcript, Oral History Collection, Henry Ford Museum, Dearborn, Mich., 30.

21. Isabel Erskine Brewster, *Recollections* (Concord, N.H.: Rumford Press, 1934), 260.

22. Maurice C. Rider, "Why We Buy and Love Antiques," *Antiquarian*, October 1926, 26.

23. "Carolyn Coleman Duke Collection," *Antiquarian*, December 1923, 6.

24. See du Pont's day books for 5 January 1929 (for the bottle) and 3 May 1926 (for the plate); the day books are available at the Winterthur Archives, Winterthur Library.

25. Israel Sack, "Pie Crust Saga," *Antiques Dealer*, February 1951.

26. Advertisement, "Turkey Hills Antique Shop," *Antiques*, July 1925, 25.

27. Huldah Wellington Spaulding, *Intimate Incidents of an Antique Shop* (n.p.: Published by the Author, 1932), 29–33.

28. Bondome [Homer Eaton Keyes], "Shop Talk," *The Magazine Antiques*, August 1930; and "Shop Talk," February 1930.

29. George Thomas Kurian, ed., *Datapedia of the United States* (Lanham, Md.: Bernan Press, 2004), 121.

30. Bondome [Keyes], "Shop Talk," August 1930.

31. Whitlock's Book Store, Inc., inventory lists, 10 October 1929, and 24 February 1930, Edgar Mead Collection, Downs Collection, Winterthur.

32. Beginning in January 1928 the title on the cover changed to *The Magazine Antiques*; it changed back to *Antiques* from August 1952 to February 1971, after which it again became *The Magazine Antiques*. Throughout the text I generally refer to it as *Antiques*, but because the two titles often have separate catalog entries and some libraries shelve them apart, in the notes I give the title as it appeared at the time of the cited article.

33. Bondome [Keyes], "Shop Talk," February 1930.

34. Richard Huntley, "An Antiques Primer," *American Collector*, April 1939, 13.

35. Wallace Nutting, "That an Antique Is Valuable Merely Because of Its Age," undated manuscript, Local History Collection, Framingham Public Library, Framingham, Mass.

36. Bondome [Keyes], "Shop Talk," February 1930.

37. Sack, "Reminiscences," 29–30.

38. Bondome [Homer Eaton Keyes], "Shop Talk," *The Magazine Antiques*, December 1929.

39. Bondome [Keyes], "Shop Talk," February 1930.

40. For examples of exploratory research on early American furniture makers, see Walter A. Dyer, "John Goddard and His Block-Fronts," *Antiques*, May 1922; Bondome [Homer Eaton Keyes], "The Home Market," *Antiques*, February 1923.

41. Louis Guerineau Myers, "Duncan Phyfe," in *Girl Scouts of America Loan Exhibition of Eighteenth and Early Nineteenth Century Furniture and Glass* (New York: Printed by Lent and Graff Co., 1929), unpaged.

42. Ginsburg & Levy, Inc., Sales Books 1911–1919. Ginsburg & Levy, Inc., Collection, Downs Collection, Winterthur.

43. Bondome [Homer Eaton Keyes], "Shop Talk," *The Magazine Antiques*, November 1928.

44. *Addresses on the Occasion of the Opening of the American Wing* (New York: Metropolitan Museum of Art, 1925), 3.

45. Royal Cortissoz, "The Field of Art," *Scribner's Magazine*, January 1925.

46. Carol Duncan, "Art Museums and the Ritual of Citizenship," in *Exhibiting Cultures: The Poetics and Politics of Museum Display*, ed. Ivan Karp and Steven D. Lavine (Washington: Smithsonian Institution Press, 1990), 97–99.

47. "The Antiquarian Meanders," *Antiquarian*, June 1926, 16.

48. Kenneth L. Roberts, *Antiquamania* (Garden City: Doubleday, Doran, 1928), 51–52.

49. Homer Eaton Keyes, "Questions of Price," *Antiques*, March 1922, 104.

50. Phoebe Phillips Prime Scrapbooks and Card File, 1917–1960, Downs Collection, Winterthur.

51. Charles Over Cornelius, "The Museum and the Collector," *Antiques*, January 1922, 35–36.

52. Wilton Lackaye, "How Not to Buy Your Antiques," *American Collector*, January 1937, 1.

53. Advertisement, "Twenty-Five Years Ago . . . ," *Antiques*, June 1927, inside front cover.

54. Harold Sack and Max Wilk, *American Treasure Hunt* (New York: Ballantine, 1986), 23.

55. Walter Dyer, *The Lure of the Antique* (New York: Century, 1910), 483.

56. Ibid., 5.

57. Caroline Woolsey Ferriday, "A Self-guided Tour of the Bellamy-Ferriday House," Bellamy-Ferriday Collection, Archives of Connecticut Landmarks, Hartford.

58. Dyer, *Lure of the Antique*, 13.

59. Alice Van Leer Carrick, *Collector's Luck* (Boston: Atlantic Monthly Press, 1919), 158–59.

60. Albert Sack, interview by author, 15 April 2004, Philadelphia.

61. C. R. Clifford, *The Junk Snupper* (New York: Macmillan, 1927), 89; Spaulding, *Intimate Incidents*, 120–21.

62. Spaulding, *Intimate Incidents*, 118.

63. "Fake Lowestoft," *Time*, 3 November 1930, 63–64.

64. Dyer, *Lure of the Antique*, 474–75; Sack, "Reminiscences," 17.

65. Dyer, *Lure of the Antique*, 476–80.

66. Clifford, *Junk Snupper*, 101.

67. Sack and Wilk, *American Treasure Hunt*, 29; Dyer, *Lure of the Antique*, 480.

68. Felice Davis, "Chats with Dealers," *Antiquarian*, February 1926, 19.

69. Nutting, "That an Antique Is Valuable."

70. Henry Wood Erving to Norman Isham, 10 August 1934, Walpole Society Papers, Downs Collection, Winterthur; on Hosmer's collecting habits, see also Henry Wood Erving to Harry Watson, 13 November 1918, in the same collection; William Hosley, "Hartford's Role in the Origins of Antiques Collecting in America," in Benes, *New England Collectors and Collections*, 113.

71. Record book for 1915 of Ernest C. Molinder, Edgar Mead Papers, Downs Collection, Winterthur.

72. Roth, "Colonial Revival and 'Centennial Furniture'"; Monkhouse, "Spinning Wheel as Artifact."

73. Tuck, *Antiqueman's Diary*, 82.

74. Sack, "Reminiscences," 37; Henry Francis du Pont to Israel Sack, 15 August 1954, du Pont Papers, Antique Dealer Correspondence, Winterthur Archives, Winterthur Library (hereafter cited as du Pont Papers, Antique Dealer Correspondence).

75. Sack, "Reminiscences," 38.

76. Grant McCracken discusses the importance of patina in seventeenth-century Europe in affirming status and acknowledges that twentieth-century American antique markets transformed patina's status symbolism by making it available for purchase. See McCracken, *Culture and Consumption*, 31–43.

77. Denenberg, *Wallace Nutting*, 133.

78. Harold Margolis, the son of antique dealer and reproduction furniture craftsman Nathan Margolis, experienced this problem when he tried to mass-market reproduction furniture. See Harold D. Margolis to J. Mason Read, 28 July 1966, and [Harold D. Margolis] to Pat, 27 February [no year], both in the Harold D. Margolis Collection, Downs Collection, Winterthur.

79. Denenberg, *Wallace Nutting*, 127, 139.

80. "Reproductions Should Reproduce," *Antiques*, April 1926, 219–20.

81. Tuck, *Antiqueman's Diary*, 43.

82. "A Rare Southern Table," *Antiques*, July 1925, 12.

83. On the history of historic preservation in Charleston, see Robert R. Weyeneth,

Historic Preservation for a Living City (Columbia: University of South Carolina Press, 2000). On Charleston's antique industry, see Jonathan Daniels, *A Southern Discovers the South* (New York: Macmillan, 1938), 327–28.

84. W. Fitzhugh Brundage, *The Southern Past: A Clash of Race and Memory* (Cambridge: Belknap Press of Harvard University Press, 2005), 203–5.

85. Joseph Downs's comments are related by Frank Horton in Penelope Niven, "Frank L. Horton and the Roads to Mesda," *Journal of Early Southern Decorative Arts* 27, no. 1 (Summer 2001): 59.

86. Ibid.

87. On the history of *Antiques*, see Wendell Garrett and Allison Eckardt Ledes, "Seventy-five Years of *Antiques*, 1922–1997," *The Magazine Antiques*, January 1997, 178–83.

88. "A Criticism Foreseen and Accepted," *Antiques*, January 1922, 9.

89. Advertisement, "Throughout the Country Those Who Buy Antiques Read *Antiques*," *Antiques*, August 1926, 91.

90. Sack's changing address and changing advertising methods can be traced in the following advertisements: "A Block Front Chest of Drawers . . . ," *Antiques*, January 1926, inside front cover; "Philadelphia Chippendale Chair . . . ," *The Magazine Antiques*, January 1928, inside front cover.

91. Untitled editorial column, *Antiques Dealer*, June 1951, 5.

92. Kammen, *Mystic Chords of Memory*, 347.

93. Paula Deitz, "Uncertain Future for 1754 Mansion," *New York Times*, 2 September 1982; Rita Reif, "Treasures of Lindens," *New York Times*, 14 January 1983; Jeanne Schinto, "Israel Sack and the Lost Traders of Lowell Street," *Maine Antiques Digest*, April 2007, C33, maineantiquedigest.com/articles_archive/articles/apr07/sack0407.htm; Albert M. Sack, "Letter to the Editor," *Maine Antiques Digest*, May 2007, A4 (not available online).

94. These are the categories Albert Sack made famous in his *Fine Points of Furniture: Early American* (New York: Crown Publishers, 1950).

2. THE JEWISH DEALER

1. Sack, "Reminiscences," 1–7.

2. *Boston Directory Supplement and Business Directory* (Boston: Sampson & Murdock, 1904); *Boston Business Directory* (Boston: Sampson & Murdock, 1918); *Boston Business Directory* (Boston: Sampson & Murdock, 1924).

3. *Boston Business Directory*, 1918 and 1924; Bureau of the Census, *Fourteenth Census of the United States, 1920* (Washington, D.C.: National Archives and Records Administration, 1920); Bureau of the Census, *Fifteenth Census of the United States, 1930* (Washington, D.C.: National Archives and Records Administration, 1930); Sack and Wilk, *American Treasure Hunt*, 40–42.

4. R. P. Way, *Antique Dealer* (New York: Macmillan, 1956), 86; Dyer, *Lure of the Antique*, 483; obituary, "Benjamin Ginsburg, 89, Dealer in Antique American Furniture," *New York Times*, 2 February 1994.

5. Frank Lawton, "The Day of the Dealer," *Antiquarian*, May 1926, 24.

6. Roger Daniels, *Coming to America* (New York: Harper Perennial, 1991), 225.

7. Ronald Takaki, *A Different Mirror: A History of Multicultural America* (Boston: Little, Brown, 1993), 298–300.

8. Andrew Heinze, *Adapting to Abundance* (New York: Columbia University Press, 1990), 196–98.

9. "Antique Dealers Only Seem Crazy," *American Collector*, October 1936, 6.

10. On the Jewish "back to the land" movement in Connecticut, see Janice P. Cunningham and David F. Ransom, *Back to the Land: Jewish Farms and Resorts in Connecticut, 1890–1945* (Hartford: Connecticut Historical Commission / Jewish Historical Society of Greater Hartford, 1998); Richard Moss, "Jewish Farmers, Ethnic Identity, and Institutional Americanization in Turn-of-the-Century Connecticut," *Connecticut History* 45, no. 1 (Spring 2006): 31–55.

11. Obituary, "Nathan Liverant Dies at Age 83," *Hartford Courant*, 12 April 1973; C. H. Bailey, "Colchester Jews . . . Notes on Interview with Zeke Liverant," 10 February 1986, Oral History Collection, Jewish Historical Society of Greater Hartford; Arthur Liverant, interview by author, 15 August 2007, Colchester, Conn.

12. Arthur Liverant, interview by author.

13. Advertisement, "Auction," *Hartford Courant*, 29 April 1930. See also "Auction . . . Oct. 16, 1930," broadside, private collection of Arthur Liverant, Colchester, Conn.

14. Liverant, interview by author.

15. Jessie Barker Gardner, "Experiences in Lowboys," and "Bungling in Chippendale Mahogany Armchairs," Barker-Gardner Family Papers, University Archives, Brown University Library.

16. Dyer, *Lure of the Antique*, 14.

17. The problem of dealers in the Walpole Society came to a head in 1919 when one of the group's founding members started selling antiques. See, for example, Henry Wood Erving to Harry Watson, 18 July 1919, Walpole Society Papers, Downs Collection, Winterthur. On dealers' exclusion from other clubs, see "Ye Notice Board . . . ," *American Collector*, 9 January 1934, 2.

18. Jeanne Schinto has found that in the 1903 city directory Stephenson's address was listed as 73A Brimmer Street, also near Beacon Hill. It is not clear if Sack ever worked in the Brimmer Street location, since he arrived, according to his oral history, in October 1903, and Stephenson's listing in the 1904 City Directory shows that he was by then established on Charles Street.

19. Sack, "Reminiscences," 17.

20. For tracking Sack's earliest business locations, and for her willingness to share her research, I am indebted to Jeanne Schinto. Her research is published in "Israel Sack and the Lost Traders of Lowell Street."

21. Jonathan D. Sarna and Ellen Smith, eds., *The Jews of Boston: Essays on the Occasion of the Centenary of the Combined Jewish Philanthropies of Greater Boston* (Boston: Combined Jewish Philanthropies of Greater Boston, 1995), 5–8.

22. Sack, "Reminiscences," 15.

23. Bureau of the Census, *Thirteenth Census of the United States, 1910* (Washington, D.C.: National Archives and Records Administration, 1910).

24. Sack, "Reminiscences," 23.

25. See, for example, Albert Sack, *Fine Points of Furniture: Early American*, with a foreword by Israel Sack (New York: Crown Publishers, 1950), vii.

26. See text by Albert Sack, *Israel Sack: A Record of Service, 1903–1953* (New York: Israel Sack, Inc., 1953), 23. This pamphlet is available in the Winterthur Museum Rare Book Collection.

27. Israel Sack to Henry Francis du Pont, 4 January 1950, du Pont Papers, Antique Dealer Correspondence.

28. Stanley Stone to Albert Sack, 17 August 1953, reproduced in Albert Sack, *Israel Sack: A Record of Service*.

29. Albert Sack, interview by author.

30. Henry Francis du Pont to Israel Sack, 15 January 1929, du Pont Papers, Antique Dealer Correspondence.

31. "List of objects sold to Mr. H. F. du Pont by Israel Sack," 4 January 1928, du Pont Papers, Antique Dealer Correspondence.

32. *American Collector*, 20 February 1934, 8; Denenberg, *Wallace Nutting*, 114.

33. Sack and Wilk, *American Treasure Hunt*, 63.

34. Obituary, "Geo. S. Palmer Dies at 78 in Florida Home," *Hartford Courant*, 25 January 1934.

35. Stillinger, *Antiquers*, 184.

36. Henry Wood Erving to Harry Watson, 13 November 1918, Walpole Collection, Downs Collection, Winterthur; Malcolm Vaughan, "Adventures of George Palmer, Connecticut Antique Pioneer," *Hartford Courant*, 21 October 1928.

37. "Connecticut Pioneer Found Many Fine Museum Pieces," *Hartford Courant*, 14 October 1928.

38. Vaughan, "Adventures of George Palmer."

39. "New Wing of Boston Museum Will Be Opened This Month," *Hartford Courant*, 11 November 1928.

40. Edward Crowninshield to Harry Francis du Pont, 5 May 1928, du Pont Papers, Antique Dealer Correspondence.

41. Albert Sack, interview by author; Sack and Wilk, *American Treasure Hunt*, 84–85.

42. Advertisement, *Antiques*, July 1925, inside front cover.

43. Sack and Wilk, *American Treasure Hunt*, 22–23.

44. Marchand, *Advertising the American Dream*, 6.

45. Undated brochure published by the editors of *Antiques*, *New Thoughts on Advertising Old Things*, available in the Edgar Mead Collection, Downs Collection, Winterthur.

46. Sack's son Albert believed his father was at least largely responsible for authoring the advertisement's content; Albert Sack, interview by author. Susan Strasser discusses the transition from text-based to pictorial advertisements in *Satisfaction Guaranteed*.

47. Untitled advertisements printed in *Antiques*, April 1923, December 1922, and August 1922, all inside front cover.

48. Advertisement, "Safeguarding Your Investment in Antiques," *Antiques*, June 1922, inside front cover.

49. Untitled advertisement, *Antiques*, February 1925, inside front cover.

50. Advertisement, "Buy From Your Ancestors: Sell to Prosperity," *Antiques*, December 1922, inside front cover.

51. Untitled advertisement, *The Magazine Antiques*, January 1928, inside front cover.

52. Editors of *Antiques*, *New Thoughts on Advertising Old Things*.

53. Bondome [Homer Eaton Keyes], "Shop Talk," *The Magazine Antiques*, November 1928, 554.

54. Sack and Wilk, *American Treasure Hunt*, 90.

55. Israel Sack to Henry Francis du Pont, 24 December 1929, du Pont Papers, Antique Dealer Correspondence.

56. Sack and Wilk, *American Treasure Hunt*, 77–78.

57. Harold recounts this chapter in the family's history in Sack and Wilk, *American Treasure Hunt*, chaps. 6–7.

58. "A Collector's Portrait," *American Collector*, 25 July 1935, 5, 13.

59. Lawton, "Day of the Dealer," 24.

60. Nutting, "That an Antique Is Valuable."

61. Sack and Wilk, *American Treasure Hunt*, 53.

62. "Funeral of Eli Jacobs, an Auto Victim, Today," *Boston Daily Globe*, 3 June 1919; "Alpert and Rosenthal Were Brothers-in-Law," *Boston Daily Globe*, 2 June 1923.

63. Robert Wallace, "Zeke the Seeker," *Life*, 27 July 1953, 94.

64. Liverant, interview by author. Zeke Liverant purchased both the chair and the account book from Miss Haley. He sold the journal to Albert Sack, who then sold it to the Winterthur Museum. The chair was sold to a private collector, but today is in the collection of Zeke's son, Arthur Liverant, who has offered to sell it to the Winterthur Museum. The account book is currently located in the John Gaines Papers, Downs Collection, Winterthur.

65. Sack and Wilk, *American Treasure Hunt*, 44–45.

66. *Boston Business Directory*, 1924.

67. Albert Sack, interview by author; Liverant, interview by author.

68. Clifford, *Junk Snupper*, 151; Thomas Rohan, *Confessions of a Dealer* (New York: Frederick A. Stokes, 1925), 34–36.

69. Wallace, "Zeke the Seeker," 102.

70. Edwin Valentine Mitchell, *The Romance of New England Antiques* (New York: Current Books, 1950), 33–34.

71. Mary D. Brine, *Grandma's Attic Treasures: A Story of Old-time Memories*, 2nd ed. (New York: Dutton, 1886).

72. Dyer, *Lure of the Antique*, 13.

73. Wallace, "Zeke the Seeker," 94.

74. "Traveling About," *American Collector*, September 1938, 11. "Yankee" dealer J. A.

Lloyd Hyde also pursued American antiques, Chinese export porcelain, and antique chandeliers abroad, traveling to such places as Barbados, China, Hong Kong, India, Egypt, Turkey, South Africa, Portugal, and England. In the mid-1970s, Hyde was working on a book about his antiquing adventures, to be titled "After the Antique: An Autobiographical Essay on Collecting." The manuscript is available in the J. A. Lloyd Hyde Papers, Downs Collection, Winterthur.

75. "Remarks Made by Mr. Israel Sack, Aug. 14th 1941," Antique Dealer Correspondence, Winterthur Archives, Winterthur Library. On the history of the construction of individual period rooms in the Winterthur Museums see John A. H. Sweeney, "The Evolution of Winterthur Rooms," *Winterthur Portfolio* 1, no. 1 (1964): 106–20.

76. Sack to du Pont, 24 December 1929.

77. Mechanization in the American furniture industry was a slow and uneven process that spanned the adoption of water-, steam-, and later electric-powered machinery and mass production techniques. While the producers of inexpensive furniture began employing powered machinery and mass production techniques as early as the 1850s, handcraft work persisted in the high-end market, as it does today. See Michael J. Ettema, "Technological Innovation and Design Economics in Furniture Manufacture," *Winterthur Portfolio* 16, no. 2/3 (1981): 197–223.

78. Jewish immigrant woodworkers were also important contributors to the carousel industry, carving elaborate horses and exotic animals. See Murray Zimiles, *Gilded Lions and Jeweled Horses: The Synagogue to the Carousel* (Hanover, N.H.: University Press of New England, 2007).

79. Sack, "Reminiscences," 21.

80. Schinto, "Israel Sack and the Lost Traders of Lowell Street." See also Albert Sack's comments on Schinto's research, Sack, "Letter to the Editor."

81. Morris Silverman, *Hartford Jews, 1659–1970* (Hartford: Connecticut Historical Society, 1970), 289.

82. Harold D. Margolis, interview by John Rockmore, 13 December 1978, transcript, and Harold D. Margolis, "Lecture at Reading, PA Museum, 11-15-78," both in Margolis Collection, Jewish Historical Society of Greater Hartford.

83. "Desks and Highboys Are Favored at Sale," *New York Times*, 11 April 1926.

84. Advertisement, "Exhibition Open To-Day . . . ," *New York Times*, 15 April 1923.

85. Margolis, interview by Rockmore, 10.

86. Stillinger, *Antiquers*, 236.

87. "The Status of Reproductions," *Antiques*, April 1926, 219.

88. On the history of Colonial Revival furniture, see Monkhouse, "Spinning Wheel as Artifact"; Roth, "Colonial Revival and 'Centennial Furniture'"; Rhoads, *Colonial Revival*; Denenberg, *Wallace Nutting*; Marling, *George Washington Slept Here*. On adapting historic furniture patterns for modern use, see H. P. Hodgman to Philip Walker, 15 February 1967; Harold D. Margolis to Colin C. Carpi, 20 September 1969; David J. Brunn to Harold D. Margolis, 4 August 1966; all Harold D. Margolis Collection, Downs Collection, Winterthur. On Wallace Nutting's furniture line, see Kammen, *Mystic Chords of Memory*, 343.

89. Denenberg, *Wallace Nutting*, chap. 5.

90. "Living with Antiques" became a regular feature in *The Magazine Antiques* in 1943.

91. Eileen S. Pollack, "Furnishing Community: The Role of Margolis Furniture in the Lives of Hartford's Gentile and Jewish Families, 1920–1970" (master's thesis, History of the Decorative Arts, Cooper-Hewitt National Design Museum and Parsons School of Design, 2004). On the history of the Margolis reproduction firm, see also Helen M. Psarakis, "'Antiques of the Future:' The Nathan Margolis Shop, 1925–1953" (master's thesis, Cooperstown Graduate Program, State University of New York College at Oneonta, 1995). Additional sources on Margolis furniture can be found in the Joseph Downs Collection, Winterthur Library, which holds Margolis furniture patterns, and in the collections of the Connecticut Historical Society, which owns several Margolis pieces. My own knowledge of the Margolis reproductions was greatly enhanced by Nickolas Kotula, a Hartford antique conservator and former Margolis apprentice, and Mike Margolis, a descendant and contemporary dealer in Margolis reproductions, which have become collectibles in their own right. Along with Eileen Pollack, Kotula and Margolis participated in a panel discussion with me on the history of Margolis furniture sponsored by the Connecticut Historical Society and the Jewish Historical Society of Greater Hartford, 2 December 2007.

92. Psarakis, "Antiques of the Future," 15.

93. Obituary, "Nationally Known Cabinetmaker Dead," *Hartford Courant*, 9 February 1925.

94. "Margolis Found Guilty and Fined," *Hartford Courant*, 6 August 1915.

95 Margolis, interview by Rockmore, 11–12.

96. Silverman, *Hartford Jews*, 158.

97. I am indebted to Nickolas Kotula for information on the labeling of Fineberg furniture.

98. Advertisement, "Nathan Margolis," *Hartford Courant*, 6 December 1898.

3. JESSIE BARKER GARDNER AND GEORGE GARDNER

1. Leah Dilworth, ed., *Acts of Possession* (New Brunswick, N.J.: Rutgers University Press, 2003), 4.

2. Jessie Barker Gardner to Walter Prichard Eaton, 7 March 1937, Barker-Gardner Family Papers, University Archives, Brown University Library (hereafter cited as Barker-Gardner Papers).

3. Jessie Barker Gardner to Advisory and Executive Committees, Brown University, 9 May 1932, Barker-Gardner Papers.

4. Ibid.

5. Jessie Barker Gardner to A. D. Mead, 15 November 1931, Barker-Gardner Papers.

6. Jessie Barker Gardner's journals, titled "Story of Gardner House," are part of the Barker-Gardner Papers.

7. Jessie Barker Gardner, "Changes in Furniture Again Urged by George Warren Gardner a Few Hours Before His Death," Barker-Gardner Papers.

8. Jessie Barker Gardner to Harold C. Field, 24 January 1937, and Jessie Barker Gardner to Dr. Wriston, 1 December 1941, Barker-Gardner Papers.

9. Gardner to Field, 24 January 1937.

10. Gardner to Wriston, 1 December 1941.

11. The material in this paragraph is taken from Jessie Barker Gardner, "Attitudes toward Antiques," Barker-Gardner Papers.

12. Jessie Barker Gardner, "Furniture and Furnishings Bought and Repaired," Barker-Gardner Papers; Gardner to Wriston, 1 December 1941.

13. Gardner, "Experiences in Lowboys," Barker-Gardner Papers.

14. Gardner, "Bungling in Chippendale Mahogany Armchairs," Barker-Gardner Papers.

15. Gardner, "Experiences in Lowboys"; Jessie Barker Gardner to James Collins, 5 February 1938, Barker-Gardner Papers.

16. Jessie Barker Gardner, "Reconstruction of 106 George Street from June 1933 to July 1, 1934," October and November 1937, Barker-Gardner Papers.

17. Gardner to Mead, 15 November 1931.

18. Jessie Barker Gardner to Dr. Bumpus, 2 August 1933, Barker-Gardner Papers; quotes in this paragraph are taken from the same letter. On the construction of Colonial Williamsburg as a historic site, see Anders Greenspan, *Creating Colonial Williamsburg* (Washington: Smithsonian Institution Press, 2002).

19. George W. Gardner, "Chairs from Scotland," and Jessie Barker Gardner, "Changes in Furniture November 1936 through 1939," both in Barker-Gardner Papers.

20. George W. Gardner, "Buying at the Source," Barker-Gardner Papers.

21. Quotes in the remainder of this paragraph are from Jessie Barker Gardner, "An Answer to an Add [sic]," Barker-Gardner Papers.

22. George Gardner, "Buying at the Source."

23. Ibid.

24. Ibid.

25. George W. Gardner, "Aaron Willard Shelf Clock and Horn of Plenty Mirror," Barker-Gardner Papers.

26. Clarence Cook, *The House Beautiful* (New York: Charles Scribner's Sons, 1881).

27. All quotes are from Mrs. Charles Norman, "Heirlooms and Degeneracy," *American Cookery*, March 1921, 655, 657, 657, 656.

28. Jessie Barker Gardner and George Warren Gardner to the Advisory and Executive Committee, 9 May 1932, Barker-Gardner Papers.

29. Gardner to Mead, 15 November 1931.

30. Gene Wise, "'Paradigm Dramas' in American Studies: A Cultural and Institutional History of the Movement," *American Quarterly* 31, no. 3 (1979): 293–337.

31. On Garvan's collecting career, see Catherine Whalen, "The Alchemy of Collecting: Material Narratives of Early America, 1890–1940" (PhD diss., Yale University, 2007).

32. Gardner and Gardner to the Advisory and Executive Committee, 9 May 1932.

33. The Carnegie grant resulted in the publication of a book on the history of Rhode Island building traditions by the architectural historian Antoinette Downing. Antoinette Downing, interview by George Goodwin, 27 October 1992, Graphics Department, Rhode Island Historical Society, Providence.

34. Mead, Brown's vice president, assumed this role while the president, Clarence Augustus Barbour, was on a nine-month trip to study missions in Japan, China, Burma, and India. Martha Mitchell, ed., *Encyclopedia Brunoniana* (Providence: Brown University Library, 1993), s.v. "Albert D. Mead."

35. Jessie Barker Gardner, "Where Ignorance is Bliss," Barker-Gardner Papers.

36. Ibid.

37. Jessie Barker Gardner to Edwin A. Burlingame, 17 August 1933, Barker-Gardner Papers.

38. Jessie Barker Gardner to Dr. Bumpus, 18 October 1932, Barker-Gardner Papers.

39. Jessie Barker Gardner to Dr. Mead, 19 November 1932, Barker-Gardner Papers.

40. Jessie Barker Gardner to Henry Wriston, 18 February 1938, Barker-Gardner Papers.

41. Gardner to Burlingame, 17 August 1933.

42. Jessie Barker Gardner to Advisory and Executive Committee Brown University, 25 May 1932, Barker-Gardner Papers.

43. Wallis Howe to Jessie Barker Gardner, 21 July 1932, Barker-Gardner Papers.

44. Jessie Barker Gardner to Edwin A. Burlingame, 20 August 1933, Barker-Gardner Papers; Gardner, "Reconstruction of 106 George Street."

45. Jessie Barker Gardner to Dr. Bumpus, 31 August 1933, Barker-Gardner Papers.

46. Jessie Barker Gardner to Dr. Mead, 24 November 1932, Barker-Gardner Papers.

47. Jessie Barker Gardner to Dr. Bumpus, 13 August 1933, and Jessie Barker Gardner to Dr. Bumpus, 25 August 1933, Barker-Gardner Papers.

48. Gardner, "Reconstruction of 106 George Street."

49. Ibid.

50. Jessie Barker Gardner, "At Last a Free Woman," Barker-Gardner Papers.

51. Ibid.

52. Gardner, "Reconstruction of 106 George Street"; Jessie Barker Gardner, "Vicissitudes of the Henry Ames Barker Room, Part I," and Wallis Howe to Jessie Barker Gardner, 14 February 1933, both in Barker-Gardner Papers.

53. Jessie Barker Gardner to Mr. Leeming, 8 July 1933, Barker-Gardner Papers.

54. Jessie Barker Gardner to Dr. Bumpus, 6 August 1933, Barker-Gardner Papers; Gardner to Bumpus, 25 August 1933; Gardner to Burlingame, 17 August 1933.

55. Gardner to Burlingame, 20 August 1933.

56. Gardner to Bumpus, 25 August 1933.

57. Jessie Barker Gardner to Dr. and Mrs. John N. Force, 9 September 1934, Barker-Gardner Papers.

58. Gardner, "Vicissitudes of the Henry Ames Barker Room, Part I."

59. "Dr. G. W. Gardner Is Dead in Maine," *Providence Evening Bulletin*, 14 November 1936.

60. Jessie Barker Gardner, "Changes in Furniture Again Urged by George Warren Gardner."

61. Jessie Barker Gardner to Dr. Bumpus, 15 April 1939, Barker-Gardner Papers.

62. Gardner, "Changes in Furniture Again Urged by George Warren Gardner."

63. Gardner, "Changes in Furniture November 1936 through 1939."

64. Gardner, "Attitudes toward Antiques."

65. Gardner to Dr. and Mrs. Force, 9 September 1934.

66. Kevin D. Murphy, "The Politics of Preservation," in Giffen and Murphy, *A Noble and Dignified Stream*, 193.

67. Isham's philosophic differences with women's groups came to a head during his 1920s restoration of the 1743 home of Stephen Hopkins, a former Rhode Island governor and signer of the Declaration of Independence. In keeping with his scholarly approach to preservation, Isham based his interior furnishing plan on a probate inventory taken at the time of Hopkins's death. Innocuous as this plan may seem, it angered the Rhode Island Women's Temperance Union because several cut-glass liquor bottles were included in the inventory. Isham claimed that he never intended to display the bottles, but the dispute illustrates the conflict between traditional female-led forms of preservation, which saw historic structures as repositories of community values, and the more scientific approach espoused by the new preservation architects. "W.C.T.U. Protest against 'Bottles' May Be Withheld," "Stephen Hopkins House Opens for Public Inspection," "Perhaps They Talked Intemperately on the Rights of Man!" "Bottles Worry Dries, but Not Architect," all undated newspaper clippings, Norman Morrison Isham Papers, RIHS.

68. Gardner to Dr. and Mrs. Force, 9 September 1934.

69. Jessie Barker Gardner to Mr. Isham, 31 October 1932, Barker-Gardner Papers. The fact that Gardner questioned Isham about appropriate flooring is particularly interesting because the house still had its original floors when Gardner began the restoration. Apparently, Gardner wished to improve on the reality that she encountered. For this insight I am indebted to Brown University curator Robert Emlen.

70. Gardner to Dr. and Mrs. Force, 9 September 1934.

71. Gardner to Isham, 31 October 1932.

72. Jessie Barker Gardner, "Notes from 'Colonial Architecture of Salem' by Cousins and Riley and Their Application to 106 George Street, Gardner House," Barker-Gardner Papers.

73. Gardner to Dr. and Mrs. Force, 9 September 1934.

74. Gardner, "Vicissitudes of the Henry Ames Barker Room, Part I"; Gardner, "Where Ignorance is Bliss"; Jessie Barker Gardner, "Then Came Damberg," Barker-Gardner Papers; Gardner to Dr. and Mrs. Force, 9 September 1934.

75. Jessie Barker Gardner, "Brownstone Porch and Steps," Barker-Gardner Papers.

76. Jessie Barker Gardner, "Salem the Inspiration for Doing Over," Barker-Gardner Papers.

77. Gardner, "Notes from 'Colonial Architecture of Salem.'"
78. Ibid.
79. Gardner, "Vicissitudes of the Henry Ames Barker Room, Part I."
80. Ibid.
81. Gardner, "Notes from 'Colonial Architecture of Salem.'"
82. Gardner, "Then Came Damberg."
83. Gardner to Isham, 31 October 1932.
84. Gardner, "Vicissitudes of the Henry Ames Barker Room, Part I."
85. Gardner, "Where Ignorance is Bliss."
86. Gardner, "Vicissitudes of the Henry Ames Barker Room, Part I."
87. Gardner to Collins, 5 February 1938.
88. R. T. H. Halsey and Charles O. Cornelius, *A Handbook of the American Wing*, 7th ed., rev. by Joseph Downs (New York: Metropolitan Museum of Art, 1942), vi.
89. On debates over the propriety of removing interior woodwork from standing houses to create museum rooms, see Charles B. Hosmer Jr., *Presence of the Past: A History of the Preservation Movement in the United States Before Williamsburg* (New York: Putnam, 1965), 218–31.
90. Quotes in this paragraph are from Jessie Barker Gardner, "Henry A. Barker Fund," Barker-Gardner Papers.
91. Jessie Barker Gardner, "Notes Prepared by Jessie Barker Gardner and Read to Dr. Bumpus in the Winter or Early Spring of 1932," Barker-Gardner Papers.
92. Jessie Barker Gardner to Dr. and Mrs. Mead, 3 June 1936, Barker-Gardner Papers.
93. Gardner to Mead, 15 November 1931.
94. Gardner to Collins, 5 February 1938.
95. Jessie Barker Gardner, "Changes in Furniture as Visioned by George Warren Gardner to Make the Collection Ideal. May 31 and June 1, 1936," Barker-Gardner Papers.
96 Gardner to Mead, 3 June 1936.
97. Jessie Barker Gardner to James, January 1937, Barker-Gardner Papers.
98. Gardner to Collins, 5 February 1938.
99. Jessie Barker Gardner, "Chinese Chippendale Table and King Charles Chairs," Barker-Gardner Papers.
100. Conforti, *Imagining New England*; Thomas Andrew Denenberg, "Consumed by the Past: Ideology and Craft in 'Old' New England" (paper presented at the annual meeting of the American Studies Association, Washington, D.C., October 1997). On the larger historic house movement see Patricia West, *Domesticating History: The Political Origins of American's House Museums* (Washington, D.C.: Smithsonian Institution Press, 1999).
101. Miller and Lanning, "Common Parlors," 437.
102. Information on the number of historic house museums in America is taken from the museum directory in Laurence Vail Coleman, *Historic House Museums* (Washington, D.C.: American Association of Museums, 1933), 113–59.

103. Jessie Barker Gardner, "From Historic House Museums," Barker-Gardner Papers, reproducing passages from Coleman, *Historic House Museums*, 35.

104. Gardner to Mead, 15 November 1931.

105. Jessie Barker Gardner to James C. Collins, 7 September 1941, Barker-Gardner Papers.

106. Lizabeth Cohen discusses working-class women's desire for ornate home decor in "Embellishing a Life of Labor: An Interpretation of the Material Culture of American Working-class Homes, 1885–1915," *Journal of American Culture* 3 (Winter 1980): 752–75, reprinted in *Material Culture Studies in America*, ed. Thomas Schlereth (Nashville: American Association for State and Local History, 1982), 289–305.

107. Gardner, "From Historic House Museums," quoting Coleman, *Historic House Museums*, 65 (the capitalization is Gardner's).

108. "Henry A. Barker, Civic Leader for Many Years, Dead," *Providence Evening Bulletin*, 27 February 1929.

109. Henry A. Barker, "An American Shortcoming," n.d., Barker-Gardner Papers.

110. On the City Beautiful movement see Alison Isenberg, *Downtown America: The History of the Place and the People Who Made It* (Chicago: University of Chicago Press, 2004), chap. 1; Jon A. Peterson, *The Birth of City Planning in the United States, 1840–1917* (Baltimore: Johns Hopkins University Press, 2003); William H. Wilson, *The City Beautiful Movement* (Baltimore: Johns Hopkins University Press, 1989).

111. Jessie Barker Gardner to Mrs. Mead, 17 May 1935, Barker-Gardner Papers.

112. Gardner, "Attitudes toward Antiques."

113. Gardner to Collins, 7 September 1941.

114. Dr. Bumpus to the Advisory and Executive Committee of Brown University, 11 June 1932, Barker-Gardner Papers.

115. Jessie Barker Gardner, "Note added August 1934," Barker-Gardner Papers.

116. Ibid.

117. Jessie Barker Gardner, "The dedication of the Henry Ames Barker Room . . . ," Barker-Gardner Papers.

118. Jessie Barker Gardner to Dr. Mead, 17 April 1935, Barker-Gardner Papers.

119. Jessie Barker Gardner, "Letter to Mr. Collins," 4 June 1935, Barker-Gardner Papers.

120. Jessie Barker Gardner, "Termite Report, 1934," Barker-Gardner Papers.

121. Gardner, "Letter to Mr. Collins."

122. Undated clipping pasted on the index to "Story of Gardner House," Barker-Gardner Papers.

4. HIGHBOYS AND HIGH CULTURE

1. Henry Flynt to Ben Hibbs, 6 August 1959, Flynt Papers, Henry N. Flynt Memorial Library of Historic Deerfield, Deerfield, Massachusetts (hereafter cited as Flynt Papers, Historic Deerfield).

2. Miller and Lanning, "Common Parlors," 437. On the 1704 attack, see John Demos, *The Unredeemed Captive: A Family Story from Early America* (New York: Alfred A. Knopf, 1994), and Evan Haefeli and Kevin Sweeney, "Revisiting 'The Redeemed Captive': New Perspectives on the 1704 Attack on Deerfield," *William and Mary Quarterly* 52, no. 1 (1995): 3–46.

3. Much has been written about the history of historic preservation and antique collecting in Old Deerfield. This chapter builds on Elizabeth Stillinger, *Historic Deerfield: A Portrait of Early America* (New York: Dutton Studio Books, 1992). Stillinger's beautifully illustrated book includes both anecdotes about Henry Flynt's collecting and commentary on the authenticity of his preservation and exhibition methods. Stillinger also consulted records available only in private collections and interviewed many who knew and worked with the Flynts. Michael C. Batinski's more recent study, *Pastkeepers in a Small Place: Five Centuries in Deerfield, Massachusetts* (Amherst: University of Massachusetts Press, 2004), has also been helpful for comparing Flynt's work to earlier generations who preserved Deerfield's past. For groundbreaking research on Flynt's tenure at Deerfield I am also indebted to David Christopher Bryan, "The Past as a Place to Visit: Reinventing the Colonial in Deerfield, Massachusetts" (honors thesis, Amherst College, 1989). Finally, interviews conducted 24–25 March 1998, with Donald Friary, then the executive director of Historic Deerfield, Amelia Miller, Deerfield historian and one of Flynt's researchers, and Peter Spang, the Flynts' first curator, were essential in helping me recognize the Flynts' evolving connoisseurship and collecting practices.

4. Cornelius Vanderbilt Jr., *The Living Past of America: Pictorial Treasury of Our Historic Houses and Villages That Have Been Preserved and Restored* (New York: Crown Publishers, 1955), 14, quoted in Bryan, "The Past as a Place to Visit," 140.

5. Abbott Lowell Cummings, "Origins of Historic Preservation in Massachusetts," *Proceedings of the Massachusetts Historical Society* 87 (1975): 3–13; J. M. Arms Sheldon, "The 'Old Indian House' at Deerfield, Massachusetts, and the Effort Made in 1847 to Save It from Destruction," *Old-Time New England*, January 1922, 99–108. Hosmer, *Presence of the Past*, 33–35.

6. *Greenfield Gazette and Courier*, 23 November 1847, quoted in Hosmer, *Presence of the Past*, 33.

7. Hosmer, *Presence of the Past*, 33–34.

8. Suzanne L. Flynt, Susan McGowan, and Amelia F. Miller, *Gathered and Preserved* (Deerfield: Pocumtuck Valley Memorial Society, 1991), 44.

9. Hosmer, *Presence of the Past*, 34. Michael C. Batinski also discusses the return of the door in *Pastkeepers*, 127–28.

10. Emma Lewis Coleman, *A Historic and Present Day Guide to Old Deerfield* (Norwood, Mass.: Plimpton Press, 1907), 31; McGowan and Miller, *Gathered and Preserved*, 5; Jennie Marie Sheldon, "Deerfield Memorial Stones," *History and Proceedings of the Pocumtuck Valley Memorial Society* 4 (1905): 242–50.

11. For the history of the PVMA, see Flynt, McGowan, and Miller, *Gathered and Preserved*.

12. Ibid., 10; Anne Farnam, "George Francis Dow: A Career of Bringing the 'Picturesque Traditions of Sleeping Generations' to Life in the Early Twentieth Century," *Essex Institute Historical Collections* 121, no. 2 (1985): 77–90; David R. Proper, "The Fireplace at Memorial Hall, Deerfield, Massachusetts: 'Picturesque Arrangements; Tender Associations,'" in *Foodways in the Northeast* (Annual Proceedings of the Dublin Seminar for New England Folklife), ed. Peter Benes (Boston: Boston University, 1982), 114–29. While Sheldon's period rooms pre-dated Dow's by twenty-seven years, Dow's rooms in Salem's Essex Institute are frequently cited as the first. See Kammen, *Mystic Chords of Memory*, 160; Dianne H. Pilgrim, "Inherited From the Past: The American Period Room," *American Art Journal* 10, no. 1 (1978): 5–23.

13. George Sheldon, quoted in Stillinger, *Historic Deerfield*, 3.

14. Timothy C. Newman, prefatory note to Flynt, McGowan, and Miller, *Gathered and Preserved*, 3.

15. Flynt, McGowan, and Miller, *Gathered and Preserved*, 10–11.

16. Batinski, *Pastkeepers*, 136–37, Sheldon quote on 137.

17. *Catalogue of the Relics and Curiosities in Memorial Hall, Deerfield, Mass.* (Deerfield, Mass.: Pocumtuck Valley Memorial Association, 1886), 1, 25, 23, 33.

18. Much of this discussion of the Deerfield arts and crafts movement is drawn from Miller and Lanning's insightful article, "Common Parlors"; on women as economic developers, see 438–39.

19. Ellen Boris, *Art and Labor: Ruskin, Morris, and the Craftsman Ideal in America* (Philadelphia: Temple University Press, 1985); on the New England arts and crafts movement, see also Axelrod, *Colonial Revival in America*; Giffen and Murphy, *Noble and Dignified Stream*; Truettner and Stein, *Picturing Old New England*, chap. 3.

20. Coleman, *Historic and Present Day Guide*, 99.

21. Miller and Lanning, "Common Parlors," 446; Truettner and Stein, *Picturing Old New England*, 85–87.

22. Coleman, *Historic and Present Day Guide*, 98–102. On men's contributions, see Denenberg, "Consumed by the Past"; Ellen M. Snyder-Grenier, "Cornelius Kelly of Deerfield, Massachusetts: The Impact of Change on a Rural Blacksmith," in *The Substance of Style: Perspectives on the American Arts and Crafts Movement*, ed. Bert Denker (Winterthur, Del.: Henry Francis du Pont Winterthur Museum, 1996), 263–79.

23. For discussion of the social function of "common parlors," see Miller and Lanning, "Common Parlors."

24. Susan McGowan and Amelia F. Miller, *Family and Landscape: Deerfield Homelots from 1671* (Deerfield, Mass.: Pocumtuck Valley Memorial Association, 1996), 59–60, 159.

25. Henry Flynt, "Old Deerfield: Where Time Was Asked to Stand," reprinted in the *Berkshire Eagle*, 14 August 1970.

26. Bart McDowell, "Deerfield Keeps a Truce with Time," *National Geographic*, June 1969, 780, 789, 808.

27. Frank Boyden to J. Sheldon, 12 March 1923, Deerfield Academy Archives, quoted in Brian Cooke, *Frank Boyden of Deerfield: The Vision and Politics of an Educational Idealist* (Lanham, Md.: Madison Books, 1994), 95.

28. Frank Boyden to Frederick Cooley, 28 March 1923, Deerfield Academy Archives, quoted in Cooke, *Boyden of Deerfield*, 96.

29. John McPhee, *The Headmaster: Frank L. Boyden of Deerfield* (New York: Farrar, Straus and Giroux, 1966), 60–62.

30. Frank Boyden to William Sumner Appleton, 22 April 1924, Deerfield Academy Archives, quoted in Cooke, *Boyden of Deerfield*, 97.

31. Henry and Helen Flynt, interview by Charles B. Hosmer, 1 August 1969, transcript, Henry N. Flynt Memorial Library, 5.

32. Stillinger, *Historic Deerfield*, 15.

33. Henry and Helen Flynt, interview by Hosmer, 4.

34. Stillinger, *Historic Deerfield*, 12–13.

35. Ibid., 35, 81–82; "A Statement of Facts and a Proposal for the Board of Trustees, Deerfield Academy Archives," n.d., Flynt Papers, Deerfield Academy Archives, Deerfield, Mass. (hereafter cited as Flynt Papers, Deerfield Academy).

36. McGowan and Miller, *Family and Landscape*, 171.

37. Stillinger, *Historic Deerfield*, 82.

38. Henry and Helen Flynt, interview by Hosmer, 27.

39. "West Side / East Side" tables, 1945, Flynt Papers, Deerfield Academy.

40. *Heritage Foundation Quarterly*, August 1962, 5, Henry N. Flynt Memorial Library.

41. Stillinger, *Historic Deerfield*, 41.

42. Henry Flynt, "From Tomahawks and Arrows to Atomic Bombs," *Delaware Antiques Show Catalog* (Wilmington: Delaware Antiques Show, December 1969): 89.

43. Henry Flynt, "Deerfield, Massachusetts: Its Meaning," *Ellis Memorial Antiques Show Catalog* (Boston: Ellis Memorial and Eldridge House, 1963), 35.

44. Roger Bowen, "The Light Falls Where the Light Fell," *Yankee*, September 1967, 132.

45. Flynt, "From Tomahawks," 87.

46. Samuel Chamberlain to Henry Flynt, 11 December 1951, Flynt Papers, Historic Deerfield.

47. Henry Flynt to Samuel Chamberlain, 9 January 1952, Flynt Papers, Historic Deerfield.

48. Samuel Chamberlain and Henry N. Flynt, *Frontier of Freedom: The Soul and Substance of America, Portrayed in One Extraordinary Village, Old Deerfield, Massachusetts* (New York: Hastings House, 1952), 1.

49. Kammen, *Mystic Chords of Memory*, 573–79, 581–87.

50. Henry Flynt to Samuel Chamberlain, 28 September 1951, 1 November 1951, and 26 November 1951, Flynt Papers, Historic Deerfield.

51. Advertisement, "Geo. C. Flynt, Munson, Mass.," *Antiques*, March 1922, 143.

52. Henry and Helen Flynt, interview by Hosmer, 1.

53. Summaries and quotes in this paragraph are from ibid., 1–4.

54. Stillinger, *Historic Deerfield*, 32–33.

55. Ibid., 44–46.

56. Henry and Helen Flynt, interview by Hosmer, 12.

57. Receipt from John Kenneth Byard to Mrs. Henry N. Flynt, 9 May 1958, John Kenneth Byard Collection, Downs Collection, Winterthur (hereafter cited as Byard Collection).

58. Receipt from John Kenneth Byard to Mr. Henry N. Flynt, 3 May 1958; see also receipts dated 10 September 1953 and 10 April 1958, all in the Byard Collection.

59. See, for example, receipts from John Kenneth Byard to Mr. Henry N. Flynt dated 22 May 1958, 29 December 1958, and 27 May 1959, Byard Collection.

60. Receipts from John Kenneth Byard to Mr. Henry N. Flynt dated 10 May 1958, 13 May 1952, 21 May 1959, and 10 April 1958, Byard Collection.

61. Henry and Helen Flynt, interview by Hosmer, 23.

62. Ibid., passim.

63. Kammen, *Mystic Chords of Memory*, 566.

64. On Henry Francis du Pont's collecting habits, see Ruth Lord, *Henry du Pont and Winterthur: A Daughter's Portrait* (New Haven: Yale University Press, 1999); Pauline K. Eversmann, *Discover the Winterthur Estate* (Winterthur, Del.: Henry Francis du Pont Winterthur Museum, 1998).

65. Israel Sack to Henry Francis du Pont, 22 August 1933, Henry Francis du Pont to [Harry] Arons, 18 September 1937, and Henry Francis du Pont to Harry Arons, 9 August 1944, all in du Pont Papers, Antique Dealer Correspondence.

66. Henry Francis du Pont to Isabella Barclay, 19 November 1928, du Pont Papers, Antique Dealer Correspondence.

67. Henry Flynt to Henry Francis du Pont, 1 November 1946, Flynt Papers, Historic Deerfield. For Henry Francis du Pont's influence, see also Henry and Helen Flynt, interview by Hosmer, 14.

68. Stillinger, *Historic Deerfield*, 76–77.

69. Henry Flynt to Mrs. Frank Thomas and Mrs. Metcalf, 1958, Flynt Papers, Historic Deerfield.

70. Henry Flynt to Elizabeth Boyden, 31 January 1952; see also Henry Flynt to Alice Winchester, 23 May 1956; both in Flynt Papers, Historic Deerfield.

71. Stillinger, *Historic Deerfield*, 175–77.

72. Henry and Helen Flynt, interview by Hosmer, 20.

73. Henry Flynt, "How's Your Wardrobe, or Have the Sheldon-Hawks Sempstresses Kept You au Courant?" (1960), Flynt Papers, Historic Deerfield.

74. Stillinger, *Historic Deerfield*, 26–31, quote on 30.

75. Jennie Maria Arms Sheldon to William Sumner Appleton, 4 December 1933, quoted in ibid., 26.

76. Henry and Helen Flynt, interview by Hosmer, 17.

77. Stillinger, *Historic Deerfield*, 26–29.

78. Henry Flynt to William Gass, 14 May 1947, Flynt Papers, Historic Deerfield.

79. Henry and Helen Flynt, interview by Hosmer, 18.

80. J. T. Wiggin, "Report to the Heritage Foundation," 1956, Flynt papers, Henry N. Flynt Memorial Library.

81. "Deerfield Revisited," *Antiques*, May 1959, 464–67.

82. Joseph Peter Spang III, "The Parker and Russell Silver Shop in Old Deerfield," *Antiques*, June 1962.

83. *The Dwight-Barnard House, Deerfield, Massachusetts*, booklet published for Henry and Helen Flynt, n.d., Henry N. Flynt Memorial Library, 12.

84. "'New' Dwight House Door," *Greenfield Recorder-Gazette*, 23 June 1954.

85. *Dwight-Barnard House*, 15.

86. Peter Spang (former Heritage Foundation curator), interview by author, 24 March 1998, Deerfield, Mass.

87. Stillinger, *Historic Deerfield*, 129.

88. Spang, interview by author.

89. Elizabeth Baker's will quoted in Stillinger, *Historic Deerfield*, 111.

90. Henry and Helen Flynt, interview by Hosmer, 13.

91. "List of Items Presented to Pocumtuck Valley Historical Society for Furnishing Room in Frary House," 21 June 1955, Byard Collection.

92. Stillinger, *Historic Deerfield*, 43–44, Flynt quoted on 43.

93. Henry Flynt to Mrs. Arthur Savage, 27 May 1954, Flynt Papers, Historic Deerfield. See also Flynt, "From Tomahawks," 89; Henry Flynt, "Old Deerfield: A Living Community," *Art in America*, May 1955, 41.

94. Henry Flynt to Irving S. Olds, 1953, Flynt Papers, Historic Deerfield.

95. Henry and Helen Flynt, interview by Hosmer, 15.

96. Kammen, *Mystic Chords of Memory*, 551.

97. On Flynt's respect for places like Williamsburg, see Bowen, "The Light Falls," 132; Henry and Helen Flynt, interview by Hosmer, 25–26; Henry Flynt to Miss Elizabeth Fuller, 19 October 1945, Flynt Papers, Historic Deerfield.

98. Henry Flynt to Mr. and Mrs. Dudley F. Underhill, 22 November 1961, Flynt Papers, Historic Deerfield.

99. On Flynt's anti-tourism, see Henry Flynt to Mr. Morrison Heckscher, 13 November 1963, Henry Flynt to Mr. John G. Lewis, 3 November 1959, and Flynt to Underhill, 22 November 1961, all in Flynt Papers, Historic Deerfield.

100. Henry Flynt to Ms. Elizabeth Shoemaker, 1947; see also Henry Flynt to Mr. Herbert Brean, 2 June 1947 (both in Flynt Papers, Historic Deerfield); Flynt to Winchester, 23 May 1956.

101. Flynt to Brean, 2 June 1947.

102. Henry Flynt to Elizabeth Shoemaker, 10 August 1947, Flynt Papers, Historic Deerfield.

103. Henry Flynt to Samuel Chamberlain, 18 December 1950, Flynt Papers, Historic Deerfield.

104. Bowen, "The Light Falls," 65; Henry Flynt to Frank Boyden, 3 April 1957, Flynt Papers, Deerfield Academy.

105. Bowen, "The Light Falls," 64–65.

106. Ibid.; Helen Comstock, "American Silver at Deerfield," *Antiques*, December 1958, 528–31; "Deerfield Revisited."

107. Henry Needham Flynt, "Old Deerfield," *Connecticut Antiquarian*, June 1953, 19–28; Flynt, "Old Deerfield, A Living Community." For pointing out these articles I am indebted to Bryan, "The Past as a Place to Visit," 129.

108. Henry Flynt to *Christian Science Monitor*, 27 August 1963, Flynt Papers, Historic Deerfield.

109. Henry Flynt to Mitchell Goodman, 30 June 1955, Flynt Papers, Historic Deerfield.

110. Henry Flynt to *Antiques*, 28 August 1956, and Henry Flynt to Helen Ashley, 2 June 1958, both in Flynt Papers, Historic Deerfield.

111. Henry Flynt to Marshall B. Davidson, 15 August 1966, Flynt Papers, Historic Deerfield. Similarly, Flynt warned *Ladies Home Journal* that their photographer should have "an understanding about just what he is to take." See Henry Flynt to Richard Pratt, 1 February 1954, Flynt Papers, Historic Deerfield.

112. H. E. Page to Henry Flynt, 21 April 1953 and 6 May 1953, Henry Flynt to H. E. Page, 22 March 1953, and accompanying advertisement titled "Deerfield for Living Room, Dining Room and Bedroom," all in Flynt Papers, Historic Deerfield.

113. "Deerfield for Living Room, Dining Room and Bedroom."

114. Henry Flynt to B. Altman and Company, 14 May 1962, G. William Moore to Mr. Murray Stein, 17 May 1962, Henry Flynt to William Moore, 14 June 1962, and accompanying advertisement, "Something Wonderful Happens to Your Bedroom," all in Flynt Papers, Historic Deerfield.

115. Benton and Bowles, Inc., to Henry Flynt, 3 January 1961 and 14 February 1961, with accompanying television commercial script, "Proctor and Gamble, Ivory Snow," Flynt Papers, Historic Deerfield.

116. Henry Flynt to H. E. Page, 6 May 1953, Flynt Papers, Historic Deerfield.

117. Robert W. Carrick to Henry Flynt, 27 December 1957, and Henry Flynt to Robert W. Carrick, 3 January 1958, both in Flynt Papers, Historic Deerfield.

118. Walentyna S. Pomasko, "Museum Reproduces Antiques," *Sunday Republican* (Springfield, Mass.), 25 November 1979.

119. Richard Hatch to Henry Flynt, 14 November 1952, Flynt Papers, Historic Deerfield.

120. Henry Flynt to Mrs. Frank Boyden, 25 April 1951, Flynt Papers, Historic Deerfield.

121. Flynt, "Old Deerfield: A Living Community," 41–47, 73–75.

5. EXHIBITING THE ORDINARY

1. Sanka Knox, "For Home: Caution on 'Early American' Furniture," *New York Times*, 21 July 1951.

2. C. Malcolm Watkins to Peter Marcio, "Thoughts on Cultural History," n.d., Watkins Papers, Record Unit 7322, Smithsonian Institution Archives (hereafter cited as Watkins Papers, SIA).

3. Curators' Annual Reports, Department of Anthropology, Division of Ethnology, 1951–1952, Record Unit 158, SIA.

4. On the history of collecting at the Smithsonian and the institution's relationships with donors, see Steven Lubar and Kathleen M. Kendrick, *Legacies: Collecting America's History at the Smithsonian* (Washington D.C.: Smithsonian Institution Press, 2001). On Malcolm Watkins's career and its relationship to folklife studies at the Smithsonian, see William Walker, "A Living Exhibition: The Smithsonian, Folklife, and the Making of the Modern Museum" (PhD diss., Brandeis University, 2007).

5. C. Malcolm Watkins, interview by Pamela Henson, 26 February 1992, SIA.

6. Watkins maintained his interest in lighting devices at the Smithsonian. He curated the Hall of Heating and Lighting in the Natural History Building and wrote several articles on lighting devices as well as the pamphlet *Artificial Lighting in America, 1830–1860,* Publication 4080 (Washington: Smithsonian Institution, 1952).

7. Lura Watkins also published several short plays. *Buried Treasure* (Boston: Charles Baker, 1933) is the story of a widow forced to sell her family antiques, and *Last of the Joneses* (Boston: Charles Baker, 1928) depicts love at the genealogical society.

8. On the history of glass collecting, see Alice Winchester, "Perspective," *The Magazine Antiques*, January 1972; Little, *Little by Little*, 26–29.

9. Lura Woodside Watkins, *Cambridge Glass: The Story of the New England Glass Company* (New York: Bramhall House, 1930).

10. Henry Francis du Pont, daybook, 8 November 1928 and 9 November 1928, both in the Winterthur Archives, Winterthur Library.

11. Dudley Brown to Samuel Laidacker, 25 October 1945, Samuel Laidacker Collection, Downs Collection, Winterthur.

12. This information is taken from a small 1983 exhibit at the National Museum of American History titled "Lura Woodside Watkins: Cultural Historian, 1887–1982," curated by Regina Lee Blaszcyk and the staff of the Division of Ceramics and Glass. Records of the exhibit can be found in the files of Ceramics and Glass, Division of Domestic Life, National Museum of American History (the files of the Division of Domestic Life are hereafter cited as DDL, NMAH). See also C. Malcolm Watkins, "Historical Archaeology," interview by M. Cohen, n.d., transcript, Watkins Papers, SIA.

13. Lura Watkins, *Early New England Potters and Their Wares* (Cambridge: Harvard University Press, 1950). Later works by Lura Watkins include *Early New England Pottery* (Sturbridge, Mass.: Old Sturbridge Village, 1966) and *Middleton, Massachusetts: A Cultural History* (Salem, Mass.: Essex Institute, 1970).

14. Little, *Little by Little*, 5; Winchester, "Perspective"; Watkins, *Early New England Potters*.

15. Laura E. Abing, "Old Sturbridge Village: An Institutional History of a Cultural Artifact" (PhD diss., Marquette University, 1997), 2–8.

16. C. Malcolm Watkins, quoted in Abing, "Old Sturbridge Village," 8.

17. Abing, "Old Sturbridge Village," 15.

18. Watkins to Marcio, "Thoughts on Cultural History."

19. Charles B. Hosmer Jr., *Preservation Comes of Age: From Williamsburg to the National Trust, 1926–1949*, 2 vols. (Charlottesville: University of Virginia Press for the Preservation Press, National Trust for Historic Preservation in the United States, 1981), 109–21.

20. C. Malcolm Watkins, interview by Susan Myers, 14 May 1995, transcript, SIA, 13, 28–29.

21. John Brenton Copp to Secretary, Smithsonian Institute, 19 January 1937, Copp Collection Files, no. 28810, Office of the Registrar, National Museum of American History (hereafter cited as Copp Files, NMAH).

22. On the Copp collection, see Gary Kulik, "Designing the Past: History-Museum Exhibitions from Peale to the Present," in *History Museums in the United States: A Critical Assessment*, ed. Warren Leon and Roy Rosenzweig (Urbana: University of Illinois Press, 1989), 7–12; Lubar and Kendrick, *Legacies*, 176; Grace Rogers Cooper, *The Copp Family Textiles* (Washington D.C.: National Museum of American History, 1971); Smithsonian Institution, *Annual Report*, 1881, 86, and Smithsonian Institution, *Annual Report*, 1895, 90, SIA.

23. Some state exhibits were displayed in the Government Building and Women's Building rather than the state's own pavilion. See Susan Prendergast Schoelwer, "Curious Relics and Quaint Scenes: The Colonial Revival at Chicago's World's Fair," in Axelrod, *Colonial Revival*, 184–216.

24. Ibid.

25. John Brenton Copp to the Secretary of the Smithsonian, 20 March 1896, Copp Files, NMAH. Copp's request that his donation be displayed in its entirety and in no more than four cases does not appear to have been legally binding; it was later housed in eight cases, and Smithsonian curators have selectively employed objects from the collection in a variety of exhibits. As early as 1904 Copp wrote to museum officials to complain that some items had been relegated to storage. While staff apparently acceded to his request and again placed the entire collection on display, Copp wrote about the same issue again in 1937. See John Brenton Copp to the Secretary of the Smithsonian, 19 January 1937, Copp Files, NMAH.

26. Kulik, "Designing the Past," 9.

27. Ibid., 8–9, quote on 8.

28. Copp to the Secretary of the Smithsonian Institution, 19 January 1937.

29. Ibid.

30. Assistant Secretary to Mr. Belote, 14 December 1927, Gertrude Ritter Webster Files, no. 71679, Office of the Registrar, National Museum of American History (hereafter cited as Webster Files, NMAH). Steven Lubar and Kathleen M. Kendrick also discuss the history of the Ritter room in *Legacies*, 178–80.

31. Gertrude Ritter to Dr. Walcott, 18 April 1924, Webster Files, NMAH; C. Malcolm Watkins, interview by Susan Myers, 12 May 1995, transcript, SIA, 6.

32. Administrative Assistant to the Secretary to Mr. Belote, 28 December 1923, and Charles Lyon to Gertrude Ritter, 17 April 1924, both in Webster Files, NMAH.

33. Lyon to Ritter, 17 April 1924. Curators at the Smithsonian Institution are now not certain who lived in the house that contained the paneling Ritter donated. In the 1980s, Edward F. Zimmer ruled out the possibility of Reuben Bliss. According to Barbara Clark Smith (*After the Revolution: The Smithsonian History of Everyday Life in the Eighteenth Century* [New York: Pantheon Books for the National Museum of American History, 1985], ix) the best candidate is the merchant Samuel Colten, who built a house in Longmeadow, Massachusetts, between 1753 and 1755.

34. C. Malcolm Watkins to Dr. Remington Kellogg, 5 August 1949, Webster Files, NMAH.

35. On the symbolism of the spinning wheel, see Monkhouse, "Spinning Wheel as Artifact."

36. Mrs. Ritter to Mr. Goldsmith, 16 May 1924, Webster Files, NMAH.

37. Theodore Belote to Mr. Ravenel, 23 May 1924, Webster Files, NMAH.

38. Beals and Nicholson to Secretary, Smithsonian Institution, 28 August 1939, Webster Files, NMAH.

39. Ritter to Goldsmith, 16 May 1924.

40. Ritter to Walcott, 18 April 1924; Administrative Assistant to Mr. Belote, 28 December 1923.

41. Beals and Nicholson to Secretary, Smithsonian Institution, 28 August 1939.

42. Watkins, interview by Myers, 12 May 1995, 3.

43. Theodore Belote to Mr. Ravenel, 4 November 1930, and W. de C. Ravenel to Gertrude Webster, 26 December 1930, both in Webster Files, NMAH; Watkins, interview by Myers, 12 May 1995, 4–5.

44. Beals and Nicholson to Secretary, Smithsonian Institution, 28 August 1939, Secretary to Beals and Nicholson, September 1939, and Beals and Nicholson to C. D. Abbott, 10 October 1939, all in Webster Files, NMAH.

45. Watkins to Marcio, "Thoughts on Cultural History"; Curators' Annual Reports, 1951–1952; Assistant Secretary to Belote, 14 December 1927; Watkins, interview by Myers, 12 May 1995, 6.

46. Watkins to Marcio, "Thoughts on Cultural History."

47. One of the best sources of on the life of Edna Greenwood is her diary, which remains under family control. Her son, Edward Little of Claremont, California, has compiled and annotated selected entries, which I have consulted. On Greenwood's collecting, see also Ted Ashby, "Her 1702 Farmhouse an Americana Museum," *Boston Daily Globe*, 29 July 1958; Henry Harlow, "Edna Greenwood and Her Collections," 1972. Harlow's essay is reproduced in the Greenwood diary and is also available in William Sumner Appleton's Correspondence, Marlboro, Massachusetts Files, Historic New England, Boston.

48. Edward Little, annotation to Greenwood diary. After the death of Edna Greenwood's father around 1900, she and her mother were supported by her uncle Edward Albert Filene, head of the Filene's department store chain and one of the

nation's most successful and wealthiest merchants. Committed to the idea that mass-production systems must be matched with equally developed distribution systems, Filene was on the front lines of the advancement of twentieth-century consumer culture, both in America and in Europe. A progressive employer, an active philanthropist known for his role in establishing credit unions in the United States, and a committed internationalist, Filene was also a Jew, the child of German Jewish parents. While he never denied his Jewish heritage, Filene was not religious. He did not speak Yiddish and he distanced himself from the Jewish community. What impact, if any, the family's Jewish heritage had on Edna Greenwood is impossible to say. It is interesting to speculate, however, on whether Greenwood in any way shared Israel Sack's propensity to use early American antiques as a way to shape his cultural identity. On Edward Filene's place within the American Jewish community, see Saul Engelbourg, "Edward A. Filene: Merchant, Civic Leader, Jew," *American Jewish Historical Quarterly* 66, no. 1 (1979): 106–22. On Filene's contributions to the spread of United States retail culture, see Victoria de Grazia, *Irresistible Empire: America's Advance through Twentieth-Century Europe* (Cambridge: Belknap Press of Harvard University Press, 2005), 130–83.

49. Greenwood diary, 6 August 1912, 3 September 1912.
50. Ibid., 9 August 1928, 30 July 1928, 23 July 1928.
51. Ibid., 5 July 1928.
52. Ibid., 17 July 1928, 28 July 1928, 19 July 1928.
53. Ibid., 24 January 1928.
54. Ibid., 23 July 1928.
55. Edward Little's comments in the Greenwood diary.
56. Harlow, "Edna Greenwood."
57. Greenwood diary, 11 May 1925, 8 June 1925, 9 July 1925.
58. Harlow, "Edna Greenwood"; Anne A. Grady, Lucinda A. Brockway, and Chris L. Eaton, "The Goodale Farm, Hudson, Massachusetts: Historic Structure Report," August 1990, available in the library of Historic New England, Boston.
59. William Sumner Appleton to Edna Little, 7 May 1925, William Sumner Appleton Correspondence, Historic New England.
60. Grady, Brockway, and Eaton, "The Goodale Farm," 80–82.
61. Ibid., 76.
62. Greenwood diary, 17 July 1928.
63. Alice Winchester, "Living with Antiques: Time Stone Farm in Marlboro, Massachusetts," *The Magazine Antiques*, June 1951, 460; Harlow, "Edna Greenwood."
64. Wall, "Time Stone Farm," 12.
65. Greenwood diary, letter to Amos Little, 18 August 1928.
66. Edward Little's comments in the Greenwood diary.
67. Little, *Little by Little*, dedication page.
68. Edward Little's comments in the Greenwood diary.
69. Ibid. See also 9 May 1926, 12 May 1928; Edna Little to Amos Little, 14 August

1928, Amos Little to Edna Little, 15 August 1928, and Edna Little to Amos Little, 18 August 1928, all reproduced in the Greenwood diary.

70. Edward Little's comments in the Greenwood diary; Greenwood diary, 30 June 1928.

71. Greenwood diary, letter from Amos Little to Edna Little, 15 August 1928.

72. Greenwood diary, letter to Amos Little, 18 August 1928.

73. Greenwood diary, 1 June 1934.

74. Watkins, interview by Myers, 12 May 1995, 3.

75. In an interview, Greenwood raised the figure to 3,000. Ashby, "Her 1702 Farmhouse."

76. C. Malcolm Watkins, "The Greenwood Gift to the Smithsonian Institution," *Chronicle of Early American Industries* 4, no. 1 (January 1951): 1.

77. Ibid., 1–2.

78. Edna Greenwood to Mr. Taylor, 15 June 1949, Greenwood Accession Records, no. 182022, Office of the Registrar, National Museum of American History (hereafter cited as Greenwood Records, NMAH).

79. This estimated value was made by the Parke-Bernet Galleries and reported to the Smithsonian Institution by Edna Greenwood. See C. Malcolm Watkins to F. M. Setzler, 16 February 1949, Greenwood Records, NMAH. On Greenwood's finances, see Edward Little's comments in the Greenwood diary.

80. C. Malcolm Watkins to Mr. F. M. Setzler, 18 April 1949, Greenwood Records, NMAH.

81. C. Malcolm Watkins to Dr. Carmichael, 29 November 1954, and undated, unaddressed response, DDL, NMAH.

82. On the Greenwood Gift and Watkins's exhibition program, see Lubar and Kendrick, *Legacies*, 180–82.

83. On the history of the period room, see Pilgrim, "Inherited from the Past." On sanitary fair exhibits as predecessors to the period room, see Roth, "The New England, or 'Olde Tyme,' Kitchen Exhibit."

84. "News Release," 23 January 1957, DDL, NMAH; "Exhibit Depicts Early America," *Washington Post*, 20 January 1957; "National Museum Opens Early American Hall," *Museum News*, 1 February 1957.

85. Watkins to Marcio, "Thoughts on Cultural History."

86. Watkins to Kellogg, 5 August 1949.

87. On the significance and function of relics, see Lubar and Kendrick, *Legacies*, 36–41; Brooke Hindle, "How Much Is a Piece of the True Cross Worth?" in *Material Culture and the Study of American Life*, ed. Ian M. G. Quimby (New York: Published for the Henry Francis du Pont Winterthur Museum, Winterthur, Del., by W. W. Norton, 1978), 5–20; Rachel P. Maines and James J. Glenn, "Numinous Objects," *Public Historian* 15 (Winter 1993): 9–25.

88. Peter Novick, *That Noble Dream: The "Objectivity Question" and the American Historical Profession* (Cambridge: Cambridge University Press, 1988), chaps. 1 and 2.

89. Murphy, "The Politics of Preservation," 193; Gail Lee Dubrow, "Restoring a Female Presence: New Goals in Historic Preservation," in *Architecture: A Place for Women*, ed. Ellen Perry Berkeley (Washington: Smithsonian Institution Press, 1989), 163–64.

90. Watkins to Setzler, 18 April 1949.

91. William Sumner Appleton to Edna Little, 12 May 1928, 23 July 1929, 11 November 1929, and 9 October 1933, all in Appleton Correspondence, Historic New England.

92. Greenwood diary, June 1928; July 1928.

93. Ibid., June 1928.

94. On Dow's life and work in Salem, see Hosmer, *Presence of the Past*, 213–16; Charles B. Hosmer, "George Francis Dow," in *Keepers of the Past*, ed. Clifford L. Lord (Chapel Hill: University of North Carolina Press, 1965), 157–66; Farnam, "George Francis Dow," 77–90.

95. J. Frederick Kelly, "Time Stone Farm," *Walpole Society Notebook*, 1946, 41, quoted in Hosmer, "George Francis Dow."

96. Hosmer, "George Francis Dow," 159.

97. George Francis Dow, *Everyday Life in Massachusetts Bay Colony* (Boston: Society for the Preservation of New England Antiquities, 1935).

98. Board of Park Commissioners, City of Salem, Massachusetts, *Guide to Salem, 1630: Manual for the Participants and Spectators at the Pageant of the Arrival of Governor Winthrop* (n.p.: Berkeley Press, 1930); Board of Park Commissioners, City of Salem, Massachusetts, *A Reference Guide to Salem, 1630*, rev. ed. (Portland, Maine: Southworth-Anthoensen Press, 1935). Both are in the collections of the Salem Public Library.

99. Ogden Codman to George Francis Dow, 21 May 1918, Dow Collection, Massachusetts Historical Society.

100. Albert R. Rogers, *The Historic Voyage of the Arbella, 1630: Official Souvenir of the Arbella on Exhibition Charles River Basin, Boston 1930* (n.p.: published under the auspices of the Massachusetts Bay Tercentenary, 1930), 15–16.

101. Handwritten note on a copy of Winchester, "Living with Antiques: Time Stone Farm," contained in the Greenwood Records, NMAH.

102. C. Malcolm Watkins to Kenneth M. Wilson, 1 February 1960, Watkins Papers, SIA.

103. C. Malcolm Watkins, "The Greenwood Gift," *The Magazine Antiques*, February 1950, 121.

104. Watkins to Setzler, 18 April 1949.

105. Ironically, Morris donated her Virginia room after she had already brought New England to Washington by moving The Lindens, a Georgian mansion, from Danvers, Massachusetts, to Kalorama Road in the Northwest Quadrant of Washington, D.C., where it became both her home and a setting for her antiques (see chapter 1). On the history of The Lindens, see "The Renaissance of the 'Lindens,'" *The Magazine Antiques*, February 1938, 67–68; "Living with

Antiques: The Washington Home of Mrs. George Maurice Morris," *Antiques*, January 1956, 60–61; "Living with Antiques: The Lindens, Washington, D.C.," *The Magazine Antiques*, April 1979, 744–49.

106. Untitled, undated list of reasons to accept the Greenwood Gift, Greenwood Records, NMAH. On Watkins's desire to make his collections more nationally inclusive, see also Curators' Annual Reports, 1963, Division of Cultural History, Record Unit 158, SIA; Watkins to Marcio, "Thoughts on Cultural History."

107. C. Malcolm Watkins to Alice Winchester, 18 July 1962, Watkins Papers, SIA.

108. Untitled, undated proposal for a series of publications designated "Smithsonian Contributions to Cultural History," Division of Cultural History, National Museum of History and Technology (NMHT), Record Unit 258, SIA, 2.

109. "Hall of Everyday Life in American Past," undated list of exhibit cases, Photograph File, Director and Deputy Director, NMHT, 1920s–1970s, Record Unit 285, SIA.

110. C. Malcolm Watkins, sabbatical application, "The Origins and Development of American Traditional Ceramics," n.d., Watkins Papers, SIA.

111. "Accessions, Fiscal Year 1957," Curators' Annual Reports, United States National Museum, Record Unit 158, SIA.

112. Lindgren, *Preserving Historic New England*, 41, 50–51.

113. C. Malcolm Watkins to Mr. and Mrs. George Watson, 23 April 1954, DDL, NMAH; C. Malcolm Watkins to Charles F. Montgomery, 6 November 1957, and C. Malcolm Watkins to Dr. Kellogg, 17 December 1957, both in Story House Files, no. 219013, Office of the Registrar, National Museum of American History.

114. John C. Ewers to Mr. F. A. Taylor, 8 June 1956, DDL, NMAH; Watkins, interview by Henson, 24–28. The son of antique collector Francis P. Garvan, Anthony Garvan is best known as the first chairman of the historic preservation department at the University of Pennsylvania.

115. Peter C. Welch to Mr. Taylor, 9 January 1964, DDL, NMAH.

116. C. Malcolm Watkins to Chairman, Subcommittee on Exhibits, 10 May 1954, DDL, NMAH.

117. C. Malcolm Watkins to Mr. Anthony Wilding, 29 July 1954, DDL, NMAH.

118. Untitled, chronological account of Watkins's efforts to secure the Richard Tavern from Jorge Epstein, DDL, NMAH.

119. A. W. Wilding to Jorge Epstein, 20 October 1954, DDL, NMAH.

120. Watkins, interview by Myers, 12 May 1995.

121. C. Malcolm Watkins to Dr. Kellogg, 5 December 1957, Story House Files, no. 219013, Office of the Registrar, National Museum of American History. Henry Francis du Pont installed the Story House kitchen at Winterthur, but it is no longer on display.

122. For examples of Watkins's archeological work, see C. Malcolm Watkins, *North Devon Pottery and Its Export to America in the Seventeenth Century*, Contributions from the Museum of History and Technology, U.S. National Museum Bulletin

no. 225 (Washington, D.C.: Smithsonian Institution, 1960), 17–59; Ivor Noel Hume and C. Malcolm Watkins, *The 'Poor Potter' of Yorktown*, Contributions from the Museum of History and Technology Bulletin no. 249 (Washington, D.C.: Smithsonian Institution, 1968); C. Malcolm Watkins, *The Cultural History of Marlborough, Virginia*, U.S. National Museum Bulletin no. 253 (Washington, D.C.: Smithsonian Institution, 1968).

123. "Gold Rush Kitchen Is on Display in East," newspaper clipping, and C. Malcolm Watkins to Brklacy [*sic*], "News Release on California Room Exhibit," 20 April 1965, both in Watkins Papers, SIA.

124. "Gold Rush Kitchen Is on Display in East."

125. C. Malcolm Watkins to Mr. James M. Brown III, 28 August 1967, Watkins Papers, SIA.

126. Watkins to Brklacy [*sic*], 20 April 1965.

127. On the history of colonial kitchen exhibits, see Roth, "The New England, or 'Olde Tyme,' Kitchen Exhibit."

128. Untitled, undated exhibit map for Hall 26, Watkins Papers, SIA; "Hall of Everyday Life in American Past."

129. "Accessions," Annual Report, 1959, Division of Cultural History, NMHT, 1952–1967, Record Unit 258, SIA; "Conceptual Script for Revision of Hall of Everyday Life in the American Past," Department of Cultural History, Record Unit 831, SIA; "Everyday Life in Early America," Exhibit synopsis, DDL, NMAH.

130. HELAP exhibit binder, DDL, NMAH.

131. "Data for Annual Report: 1965," Division of Cultural History, NMHT, 1952–1967, Record Unit 258, SIA.

132. C. Malcolm Watkins to Mrs. Adele Earnest, 21 January 1969, Watkins Papers, SIA. For a history of the Smithsonian's exhibition of black culture, see Michele Gates Moresi, "Exhibiting Race, Creating Nation: Representations of Black History and Culture at the Smithsonian Institution, 1895–1976" (PhD diss., George Washington University, 2002).

133. Exhibit tour script titled "Manuscript Prepared by Mr. C. Malcolm Watkins of the Smithsonian Museum Staff," Record Unit 261, Division of Domestic Life, SIA; Watkins, interview by Myers, 14 May 1995, 17–19.

134. "Conceptual Script for Revision of Hall of Everyday Life in the American Past." For pointing out this quote I am indebted to Smith, *After the Revolution*, xv.

135. Smith, *After the Revolution*, xvi–xvii.

136. "300-Yr.-Old Marlboro House Starts New Life," newspaper clipping, Record Unit 258, Division of Cultural History, NMHT, 1952–1967, SIA.

137. While the log house was later placed on display in the National Museum of American History's "After the Revolution" exhibit, contemporary curators removed the paneling. On Watkins's acquisition of the Delaware Log House, see C. Malcolm Watkins, interview by Susan Myers, 8 May 1995, transcript, SIA, 40–46; Watkins, interview by Henson, 29–32.

138. For an example of how Watkins researched his period rooms, see "Dearest

Mal," letter from Lura Watkins to C. Malcolm Watkins, 5 January 1956, DDL, NMAH.

139. Hall 26 Exhibit Binder, DDL, NMAH.

140. C. Malcolm Watkins to Mr. Mendel Peterson, 17 April 1957, DDL, NMAH.

141. Lura Woodside Watkins to Remington Kellogg, 10 January 1953, Lura Watkins Childhood Room Files, no. 197232, Office of the Registrar, National Museum of American History; Watkins, interview by Myers, 14 May 1995, 19.

142. Watkins, interview by Myers, 14 May 1995, 14–17.

143. Concerning the Ipswich House's collection, see Watkins, interview by Henson, 24–28; Margo Edwards, "Chronology of the Ipswich House and the Smithsonian: 1962 to Present," 23 March 1998, DDL, NMAH; C. Malcolm Watkins to Mr. Taylor, "Gift of Seventeenth Century House," 22 August 1963, Ipswich House Files, no. 252318, Office of the Registrar, National Museum of American History; William Rice, "Ancient House Heads for Smithsonian," *Washington Post*, 26 September 1963.

144. Edwards, "Chronology of the Ipswich House."

145. Richard Ahlborn to Dr. Brooke Hindle, "An Exhibition Proposal: An Introduction to the Hall of Everyday Life in the American Past," 20 February 1975, Watkins Papers, SIA. On the balloon-framed house, see Rodris Roth to Mr. James Lyons, 1 April 1976, and Rodris Roth to Dr. Brooke Hindle, "Travel to Chicago and Vicinity Re: Balloon Frame Project 29 July," 4 August 1976, both in Record Unit 831, Files of the Department of Cultural History, SIA.

146. For documentation of the "Time Machine" proposal, see Record Unit 551, Department of Exhibits, National Museum of American History 1957–92, SIA. "Welcome Home," "Open House," and the Mintz proposal remain in the active files of the Division of Domestic Life, NMAH.

147. On the reinterpretation of the Ipswich House, see Briann Greenfield, "A House in the Nation's Attic," *American Quarterly* 56, no. 1 (2004): 151–62.

EPILOGUE

1. Sack Heritage Group, www.sackheritagegroup.com/history.php (accessed 5 January 2009).

2. Leigh Keno and Leslie Keno with Joan Barzilay Freund, *Hidden Treasures: Searching for Masterpieces of American Furniture* (New York: Warner Books, 2000).

3. "First Place in the Antiques Roadshow Top Ten Items," YouTube, www.youtube.com/watch?v=wlkYn39i4Fw (accessed 5 January 2009).

4. PBS, "On Your TV," www.pbs.org/wgbh/roadshow/cities/ (accessed 5 January 2009).

5. The most extensive corporate biography of eBay is Adam Cohen, *The Perfect Store: Inside eBay* (Boston: Little, Brown, 2002).

6. Pamela Wiggins, "So What's Hot on eBay," About.com, antiques.about.com/od/onlinepriceguides/a/bleBayMay04.htm (accessed 17 May 2008).

7. See Lynn Dralle's *The 100 Best Things I've Sold on eBay: My Story* (Palm Desert, Calif.: All Aboard, 2003), *More 100 Best Things I've Sold on eBay—Money Making Madness—My Story Continues* (Palm Desert, Calif.: All Aboard, 2006), and *The 3rd 100 Best Things I've Sold on eBay . . . Ka-Ching! My Story Continues* (Palm Desert, Calif.: All Aboard, 2007).

8. Dralle, *3rd 100 Best Things*.

9. Ron Zoglin and Deborah Shouse, *Antiquing for Dummies* (Foster City, Calif.: IDG Books, 1999); Dennis L. Prince and Lynn Dralle, *How to Sell Antiques and Collectibles on eBay . . . And Make a Fortune!* (New York: McGraw-Hill, 2005); Bruce E. Johnson, *How to Make $20,000 a Year in Antiques and Collectibles without Leaving Your Job* (New York: Ballantine, 1986).

10. For a behind-the-scenes look at the antique market of the 1980s and 1990s, see Thatcher Freund, *Objects of Desire: The Lives of Antiques and Those Who Pursue Them* (New York: Penguin, 1993).

11. Rita Reif, "A Newport Desk's Towering Style," *New York Times*, 26 February 1989; Rita Reif, "Rare Desk from 1760's on the Block," *New York Times*, 15 February 1989; Rita Reif, "18th-Century Desk Sold for Record $12.1 Million," *New York Times*, 4 June 1989.

12. Rita Reif, "Ripples Awaited from Auction Splash," *New York Times*, 11 June 1989; Wendy Moonan, "A Potter's Dream: American Porcelain," *New York Times*, 28 January 2005.

13. Andrew Richmond and Hollie Davis, "The Young Collector: The Stigma of the Middle Market," *Maine Antiques Digest*, www.maineantiquedigest.com/stories/index.html?id=428 (accessed 5 January 2009).

14. See, for example, David Vazdauskas, "No Laughing Matter, But We Can Still Hope," *Maine Antiques Digest*, www.maineantiquedigest.com/stories/index.html?id=154 (accessed 5 January 2009); David Vazdauskas, "The New Lure of the Antiques Trade," *Maine Antiques Digest*, www.maineantiquedigest.com/stories/index.html?id=169 (accessed 17 May 2008).

15. David Vazdauskas, "If the Young Only Knew," *Maine Antiques Digest*, www.maineantiquedigest.com/stories/index.html?id=157 (accessed 5 January 2009); Andrew Richmond and Hollie Davis, "The Young Collector: Connecting with the Young eCollector," *Maine Antiques Digest*, www.maineantiquedigest.com/stories/index.html?id=362 (accessed 5 January 2009); Andrew Richmond and Hollie Davis, "The Young Collector: Who Is the Young Collector?" *Maine Antiques Digest*, www.maineantiquedigest.com/stories/index.html?id=315 (accessed 5 January 2009).

16. Vazdauskas, "If the Young Only Knew"; Richmond and Davis, "Connecting with the Young eCollector."

17. "Antique Roadshow Scams!" YouTube, www.youtube.com/watch?v=TAsIBTn0YdU (accessed 5 January 2009). There are more parodies of *Antiques Roadshow* available on YouTube: "The Antiques Roadshow," www.youtube.com/watch?v=ja51Dye5Uhg; "Antiques Roadshow: Arkham, MA," www.youtube.com/watch?v=VFWHteD4EsU; "Bunifa on the Antiques Roadshow," www.youtube.com/watch?v=iwSyQUSh_ZA; (all accessed 5 January 2009).

18. *Maine Antiques Digest* writers Andrew Richmond and Hollie Davis recognize that middle-market goods are often belittled as "undistinguished" or "mediocre" by high-end collectors; see "The Young Collector: The Stigma of the Middle Market."

19. Lita Solis-Cohen, "The 44th Annual Delaware Antiques Show," *Maine Antiques Digest*, www.maineantiquedigest.com/stories/index.html?id=428 (accessed 5 January 2009).

20. David Vazdauskas, "Going . . . Going . . . Green!" *Maine Antiques Digest*, www.maineantiquedigest.com/stories/index.html?id=151 (accessed 5 January 2009).

21. David Vazdauskas, "Marketing to Younger Buyers: A Vintage Appeal?" *Maine Antiques Digest*, maineantiquedigest.com/articles_archive/articles/jan03/mark0103.htm (accessed 5 January 2009).

22. Kenneth L. Ames makes the argument that decorative arts scholarship has traditionally been oriented to the concerns and questions of collectors in "American Decorative Arts / Household Furnishings."

23. Jules Prown, "Mind in Matter: An Introduction to Material Culture Theory and Method," *Winterthur Portfolio* 17, no. 1 (Spring 1982): 1–19. While the literature of material culture is too large to catalog here, key texts establishing the approach include John Kouwenhoven, *Made in America: The Arts of Modern Civilization* (Garden City, N.Y.: Doubleday, 1948); Alan Gowans, *Images of American Living: Four Centuries of Architecture and Furniture as Cultural Expression* (Philadelphia: Lippincott, 1964); James Deetz, *In Small Things Forgotten: The Archeology of Early American Life* (Garden City, N.Y.: Anchor Press / Doubleday, 1977); Quimby, *Material Culture and the Study of American Life*; Schlereth, *Material Culture Studies in America*; Robert Blair St. George, ed., *Material Life in America, 1600–1860* (Boston: Northeastern University Press, 1988); Dell Upton and John M. Vlach, eds., *Common Places: Readings in American Vernacular Architecture* (Athens: University of Georgia Press, 1986); Katherine C. Grier, *Culture and Comfort: People, Parlors, and Upholstery, 1850–1930* (Amherst: Published for the Strong Museum, Rochester, N.Y., by the University of Massachusetts Press, 1988); John Michael Vlach, *The Afro-American Tradition in the Decorative Arts* (Athens: University of Georgia Press, 1990); Kenneth L. Ames, *Death in the Dining Room and Other Tales of Victorian Culture* (Philadelphia: Temple University Press, 1992); Richard Bushman, *The Refinement of America: Persons, Houses, Cities* (New York: Knopf, 1992); Henry Glassie, *Material Culture* (Bloomington: Indiana University Press, 1999); Laurel Thatcher Ulrich, *The Age of Homespun: Objects and Stories in the Creation of an American Myth* (New York: Knopf, 2001); Bronner, *Consuming Visions*.

24. For a study of how high-style furnishings and architecture have been reinterpreted using the tools of social history, see Richard Handler and Eric Gable, *New History in an Old Museum: Creating the Past at Colonial Williamsburg* (Durham, N.C.: Duke University Press, 1997).

25. Christopher Bickford, *The Connecticut Historical Society, 1825–1975: A Brief Illustrated History* (Hartford: Connecticut Historical Society, 1975), 78–83, 85.

Index

Page numbers in italics refer to illustrations.

African-American history, 199
Allen, Margaret Harris, 153
Allen House (Deerfield, Mass.), 145,
    150, 156, 157, 159, 163
Alpert, William, 77
American Art Association, 8, 29, 75,
    218n23
American Collector, 31, 38, 60, 68, 171
American Heritage, 163–64
American History Workshop, 203
American Studies, 105
American Wing (of the Metropolitan
    Museum of Art), 2, 34, 50,
    53–54, 91, 114
  influence of, on American views of
    antiques, 34
  period rooms in, 2, 3, 8, 50, 177,
    187
Ames, Kenneth, 217n14
Anderson Galleries, 8, 29, 39, 70, 84,
    218n23
  Israel Sack and, 73–75
Andrus, Vincent D., 146
Antiquarian magazine, 26–27, 35, 63,
    71, 76, 91
antique dealers. *See* dealers
antique manuals. *See* manuals
antiquers. *See* collectors
antique shops, 8–9, 58. *See also*
    dealers
Antiques magazine, 63, 86, 91, 163,
    171, *183,* 191
  advertising in, 39, 71–73, *74*
  and aesthetic standards, 30, 132
  dealers and, 63
  on geographical considerations,
    50, 52
  and growth of national market, 52
  on market value of antiques, 30, 32
  move of, to New York City, 52
  name changes of, 221n32
  on reproduction furniture, 49, 84

see also Winchester, Alice
Antiques and Fine Art magazine, *212*
Antiques Dealer, 53
Antiques Roadshow, 7, 205–7, 210–11
anti-Semitism, 63–64, 75, 97, 100
Appleton, William Sumner, 53–54,
    113, 118–19, 143, 189
Arbaugh, George Washington, 198
Aronovsky, Abraham, 87
art history, 3–4, 31, 34, 217n14
Art Institute of Chicago, 53, 68
art museums, 3, 13, 34, 53, 68
  period rooms in, 2, 3, 8, 50, 70,
    118–19, 177, 187
  see also specific museums
Arts and Crafts, 25, 49, 102, 140–42,
    143, 160
Ashley House (Deerfield, Mass.), 132,
    145, 146, *147,* 157, 158, 164
associational meanings, 4, 10, 20–22,
    30, 175, 178
  C. Malcolm Watkins and, 169,
    188, 201
  eclipse of, 3, 10–11, 18, 25–26, 55,
    172
  George Sheldon and, 139–40, 166,
    201
  persistence of, 30–37, 171, 206–7
  and selling price, 31–32
  and sentiment, 26–27, 32, 35–36,
    79–80, 207, 208
auction houses, 8, 39, 210, 218n23.
    See also American Art
    Association; Anderson
    Galleries
auctions, 32, 58, *62,* 73–75, 94, 210
  high prices in some, 28–29, 70,
    84, 209
  see also eBay
authenticity, 84, 158, 188–89,
    212–13
  architectural, 118

and City Beautiful movement, 125
as collectors, 22–23
and craftwork, 140–41
and historic preservation, 112–13,
        141, 189–90, 199, 232n67

Yale University, 3, 84, 105
Yankee magazine, 162

Zea, Philip, 156

BRIANN G. GREENFIELD is an associate professor of history at Central Connecticut State University, where she administers the Public History Program. She received her PhD in American Civilization from Brown University and a master's degree in Museum Studies/American Civilization, also from Brown. She has worked for several museums and historical societies, including the Slater Mill Historic Site and Historic New England, and currently serves as a board member for the Connecticut Humanities Council. Originally from Gilmanton, New Hampshire, she now lives in New Britain, Connecticut, with her husband, Morgan Hanna.